D0149388

RUN TO WIN

RUN TO WIN

Lessons in Leadership for
Women Changing
the World

STEPHANIE SCHRIOCK

with Christina Reynolds

DUTTON

DUTTON

An imprint of Penguin Random House LLC
penguinrandomhouse.com

Copyright © 2021 by Stephanie Schriock
Foreword © 2021 by Kamala Harris
Penguin supports copyright. Copyright fuels creativity, encourages diverse voices,
promotes free speech, and creates a vibrant culture. Thank you for buying an
authorized edition of this book and for complying with copyright laws by not
reproducing, scanning, or distributing any part of it in any form without
permission. You are supporting writers and allowing Penguin to continue
to publish books for every reader.

DUTTON and the D colophon are registered trademarks
of Penguin Random House LLC.

LIBRARY OF CONGRESS CATALOGING-IN-PUBLICATION DATA
has been applied for.

ISBN 9781524746803 (hardcover)
ISBN 9781524746827 (ebook)

Printed in the United States of America
1   3   5   7   9   10   8   6   4   2

BOOK DESIGN BY KATY RIEGEL

While the author has made every effort to provide accurate telephone numbers,
internet addresses, and other contact information at the time of publication,
neither the publisher nor the author assumes any responsibility for errors or for
changes that occur after publication. Further, the publisher does not have any
control over and does not assume any responsibility for author or third-party
websites or their content.

33614082157719

This book is dedicated to every woman who is working to change the world for the better.

Contents

Contents

Foreword

Kamala Harris

WE ARE AT an inflection point in the history of our nation. At the time of this writing, our country is in the midst of the coronavirus pandemic, thrusting families into a public health and economic crisis unlike any other we've seen in our lifetime. As businesses shutter across the country, millions of Americans who were already living paycheck to paycheck are now wondering how they are going to afford basic items like groceries. We are also grappling with the deaths of Breonna Taylor, George Floyd, and countless others who have compelled us to protest and highlight the deep and systemic inequities that Black communities have faced in this country for far too long. Hate crimes against the Asian American community are on the rise as elected officials deliberately fan the flames of racism and use words meant to sow hate and division. And we are now in the middle of election season, where we are witnessing officials in certain states use this unprecedented crisis as a further excuse to suppress the right to vote. The American Dream—and our American democracy—is on the line like never before.

That is why we all have a responsibility and a role in fighting for a nation with equal treatment, collective purpose, and justice for all. We need economic justice, environmental justice, health care justice, and, yes, justice for women. And, frankly, we know that when we lift up women, we lift up our children, we lift up our families, and we lift up our economy. All of society benefits. Unfortunately, today, there are not enough women, particularly women of color, seated at the decision-making table to make that change happen.

I'm glad that you picked up this book, which contains such authentic and inspiring advice to create your own path to improve the world. The advice you are about to read is the same kind of advice that helped me succeed in my calling to build a career focused on fighting for the people. In fact, my mother used to say, "Don't sit around and complain about things; do something." And by picking up this book, you are on the path to doing just that.

Running for office is one of the most powerful steps you can take to speak your truth and influence the world around you. When I decided to run for district attorney of San Francisco over fifteen years ago, it was because I saw so many problems that could be fixed and I believed that I could make the system work better for everyone, not just some. No one like me had served in the role before, but I was up for the challenge.

Running for office isn't glamorous work. I used to go to grocery stores using my ironing board as a standing desk while asking for people's vote. As people would carry their groceries to their car, I would listen to them. I learned what mattered to them, what kept them up at night, and what kind of America they envisioned. And I didn't stop there; I met and spoke with anyone and everyone that I could, and a team of volunteers who became more like family helped me knock on doors and make calls around the clock. On Election Day, I won.

To be sure, a lot of people—including some friends—doubted I could win. I had people tell me that the odds were against me, that I didn't fit into the typical mold of a DA, and that I couldn't beat an established incumbent. I'm not the first woman to hear that from the so-called experts. In fact, women across all fields hear the same doubts and questions about their qualifications and ability to lead. Those are the comments that make us consider what we know and the questions that make us wonder whether there will be support for our ideas. But here's the thing: I didn't listen.

If I had listened to what people told me was not possible, I wouldn't be where I am today. I wouldn't have had the opportunity to show little girls everywhere that someone like me could win, not only to become district attorney of a major city but to go on to become the first woman attorney general of California and only the second Black woman in history to serve as a US senator and, as of this writing, the first Black and Indian American woman to be on a major party ticket. If the congresswomen who won in 2018 had listened to the naysayers, the power in the United States House of Representatives wouldn't have switched hands. If legends like Shirley Chisholm, Geraldine Ferraro, and Hillary Clinton had listened to the negativity, they wouldn't have followed the call to unapologetically crack the glass ceiling of putting a woman in the White House. It's time for you, reader, to turn inward and realize the strength that is already within you to change the world for the better.

As I wrote this foreword, I couldn't help but think of the 2017 Women's March. As I stood onstage and saw that inspiring sea of women, I marveled at our power. At what we can do when we come together to answer the question "Who are we?" with our values and our strength.

Many women decided to answer that call by running for office. In fact, in the first three or so years after Donald Trump's election, more than fifty thousand women reached out to EMILY's List for the first time, looking to run for office. You'll read more about that in this book—those women include members of Congress, state legislators, women still planning their first run. These women are changing the country, and as more of them get elected, they are changing their communities and the face of power in this country. But this book is not just about running for office; it's about using our strength in many ways to improve the world around us.

Becoming an elected official and advocating and raising awareness for issues important to you are some of the most difficult but rewarding challenges you can take on in life. And we all have a role—both little and big—that works toward the collective goal of changing our world for the better. Making change happen is not easy, but the book you are about to read gives you a blueprint to start.

After dedicating years in politics and the last decade to fighting the challenges women face every day, Stephanie Schriock is an expert in this area. I know you'll enjoy the stories in this book, and I urge you to use the lessons. No matter your field, your passion, or your concern, you will find valuable insight on how to conquer common fears and obstacles that have held many back.

Learn these lessons and use them to help you find your own path. Take your own best practices from them. Do the work and prove the naysayers wrong. Because when they tell us we can't win or we shouldn't win, we know better.

As I always say, see and fight for what can be, unburdened by what has been. Run to win.

Introduction

SO YOU'VE DECIDED to change the world.

Maybe you've been an activist for years, fighting to make things better. Maybe the 2016 election and everything that came after it woke something up within you. Maybe you're inspired by the women who have taken matters into their own hands and decided to make their own change, by running for office or demanding more from their leaders. Maybe you just know you need to change your own world by making changes in your own life.

I've had all of those same thoughts.

No doubt we are living in a stressful time. Every day is full of anxiety. I hear it from friends and family, particularly women. I see it on the news. I wake up feeling that way, too, and wonder what is happening. White nationalism, sexism, xenophobia, racism, anti-Semitism, bigotry, misogyny: They are all coming at us, all at once.

Then we were hit by COVID-19, with no true leadership from our president or his administration. We were already dealing with enough anxiety; now this? As a country, we socially distanced to help our communities stay safe and healthy. We supported those on the front lines, from health care professionals to grocery store workers to first responders. We worried about the impact on our kids, with no school, and our economy, as millions were pushed into unemployment and businesses across the country closed. We mourned the loss of so many lives, and many of those who survived still faced challenges healing or getting through their loss without the ability to grieve in traditional ways.

Then, following George Floyd's and Breonna Taylor's deaths at the hands of police, we saw protests and rapid change in public sentiment and understanding of issues like systemic racism and police reform, and we reckoned with how best to make the changes we knew were desperately needed. And the whole time, we wished for better leadership from the White House, instead of grandstanding and lies.

The way I see it, we have two choices. We can hide in our beds with the covers over our heads. *Or,* we can take power into our own hands. So, let's push away those covers, stop listening to the doubters (even when *you* are one of the doubters), and ignore anyone who tells you that you can't do it. Because I'm here to tell you that you can.

You can change the world. You can save the world. The time is now.

You have power that you haven't tapped into. And if you're

willing to learn, deal with some tough circumstances, feel uncomfortable once in a while, and above all, work hard, you can do it. You have the ability to make that change because changing the world starts small. By taking action in your community or being elected to office, you can rise up in your workplace or community as a force for good.

I know a lot of you are already doing much of this work for others without having the decision-making power to drive the agenda. You are executing someone else's plan. That work is important, but if women are going to lead the conversation and ignite change, it has to start somewhere. Why not with you? That's right: It's time for you to lead. And I am here to help you do it.

No matter what your goal is—elected office, becoming a leader in your community, getting a promotion or a raise at work—this change won't be easy. I am not going to sugarcoat it. If you were expecting a quick fix or an easy path, this is not the book for you.

They often call me "Coach Stephanie" in my office because I'm full of good pep talks, but I'm also going to make you train to reach your goals. I'll make you run the laps, lift the weights; I'll also cheer you on every step of the way. This—whatever your "this" is—will take your heart, your brains, and your determination. To use an old adage, anything worth having is worth working hard for. Well, I am a believer in hard, smart work.

With the right direction, some good lessons, and the willingness to put in the effort, I know you can get anything done. I've seen it happen. Still, I understand how daunting this might all feel at the beginning. So imagine putting a puzzle together. When you first drop all those pieces on the table, it's a huge mess. But then you find the corner pieces, then the edges, and pretty soon the picture starts coming into view. I am here to help you understand what all those pieces are and then sort the pieces, to find the corners and the edges. The structure for your big picture is a set of skills to be learned, some tips on how to master those skills, and information on how to put it all together to run and win.

How do I know?

Because I've spent the last decade at EMILY's List getting pro-choice Democratic women elected to office at every level of government across the country, breaking records and shattering glass ceilings all over the place. I've watched women just like you bust out of their comfort zone, take big risks, run for office, and yes, change the world.

And I know because I've done it myself.

All my life, I've had to choose whether to hide in bed or take the plunge. And I keep choosing to bet on myself for one simple reason: Social change matters to me. It's the thing that wakes me up in the morning.

Growing up in Butte, Montana, I found my passion for politics early. Before I go further, you need to know a little bit about Butte, Montana. My hometown is known for being a tough place full of folks who might be quicker to fight than have a conversation. It is also full of passion for organizing and standing up for what is right. We sit atop the "richest hill on earth," named so for the copper that was pulled out of the ground by brave miners for decades. It has long been an epi-center of union fights and standing up against corporate corruption. This strongly Irish-Catholic, Democratic-leaning, union-strong working-class town instilled in me early, fierce passion to fight for what is right.

In Butte, I learned that passion doesn't always translate to victories. I lost my first few class elections, but I also learned not to let a loss stop me. In school, I kept right on running my own student government campaigns (by the way, I am a *huge* fan of student government). Now, as an adult, I've made a ca-reer of it. I've been in the middle of campaigns for the presi-dency of the United States of America; I've worked for an antiwar upstart presidential candidate from Vermont; I've successfully managed two tough red-to-blue pickup Senate races. I've been the scrappy junior staffer, and I've been the one in charge. Though my name hasn't been on the ballot since my days in student government, I have sure been there with many candidates awaiting their fate on election night, some ending in cheers and others in tears.

After all of those jobs, I chose to take one more big risk to lead me to where I am now. In 2010, the EMILY's List board was looking for a new leader—only the second president ever, following twenty-five years under the founder, Ellen Malcolm. They took a chance by offering the job to me, a former cam-paign staffer who had always been behind the scenes. I had doubts of my own, about my qualifications and readiness, de-spite everything I'd done to prepare for that moment.

It wasn't an easy decision, but I conquered my doubts—or

at least I ignored them long enough to say yes—and it's been the biggest blessing in my life. In the past ten years, I have led an organization with more than one hundred team members to help elect hundreds of pro-choice Democratic women, including the amazing women who took back the House majority for Democrats in 2018; expanded the EMILY's List mission and staff; and raised close to half a billion dollars.

I'm not the only one who struggles with self-doubt. I hear it from candidates, my friends, and many of my political peers. We question whether we're ready for a job even when we're undoubtedly prepared. We wonder if there's not someone who knows more or could do it better. That's not just candidates, who often buy into the argument that someone else would be more electable. It's all of us women, something we've been taught to do. That's why I've spent years thinking about how best to help women put those doubts in perspective and get right to doing the important work.

How we do that work is something I've thought about throughout my career. Over the last few decades, I've learned some valuable lessons from all of those campaigns. What might surprise people who don't work in politics is that while the candidates, the districts, and the political environments might be completely different from race to race, the fundamentals of winning campaigns don't ever really change.

But this book—and the lessons in it—isn't just for women considering running for office. It's for anyone looking to erase their doubts, take the risks, and make the big changes in any arena. So if for any number of reasons being on the ballot doesn't appeal to you, I urge you to stick around.

Women are changing the world in a wide variety of ways and from an even wider variety of backgrounds. They are lawyers, working to get children out of deportation centers. They are mothers, fighting to prevent gun violence. They are women of all ages, standing together to protect reproductive freedom. They are local activists, working to build a playground or get an extra stop sign. They are creating clubs to raise money for local and national causes. They are running the PTAs and the churches. They are organizing protests and marches. They are forming unions. They are knocking on doors and breaking glass ceilings. They are doing things I can't even imagine, and we owe them an enormous debt for their action and dedication.

Are you one of these women already? Are you trying to process what's going on in the world or figure out what you can do to help? I know it can be hard to recognize that there is good happening around us these days, when the news is so overwhelmingly bad, scary, depressing, rage-inducing—take your pick. Challenges like climate change, immigration, gun violence, a global pandemic, health care, racism, sexism, education, hunger, the opioid crisis, economic security, and the assault on reproductive rights are too big for any one person to consider. Who has the ability to help?

The answer, of course, is you.

Even taking on a little part of one of those issues and giving a bit of your time and talent can make a big difference. If we could all do that, even just a little, we would change the world for the better.

The next question is: How do you want to help? The answer to this one is completely personal and completely open-ended. If you're interested in the environment, work with others to clean up your local waterway. If you love animals, find a local shelter or rescue and offer your help. If you care about a specific issue or piece of legislation, you can create a group to push elected officials to pass it. There's always a need for help in neighborhood schools, or with a faith-based group, or with some other like-minded group of people. Before you know it, you might be running one of these organizations. That is my hope: to get women into positions of leadership at every level of society.

This is the cornerstone belief behind EMILY's List. If a lot of people put in a little bit, we can make big change together. We've been helping people support incredible candidates for office with small contributions that make an enormous difference for more than thirty-five years. And let me tell you, we're just getting started.

So if you're still reading, I assume you've decided you're ready to make change. Congratulations! That's a huge step, and perhaps the most important one. Now you just have to find a way to get it done. I believe that whether you have a detailed plan of action or just a vague idea, the lessons you're about to learn, honed during decades of campaigns and personal experience helping women transform into strong and savvy leaders, can offer guidance and actionable steps to your success.

The truth is, leadership is hard work. But the best things in life are hard fought and even harder won. And the toughest wins feel *really* great as a result.

There is another important truth to come to terms with, and I won't sugarcoat this, either. You are going to face discrimination and challenges because of your gender (and, for some of you, your race, your sexual orientation, your religion, your physical abilities). I'm incredibly proud of the work that my team does at EMILY's List and I believe that each of the women we've elected makes it a little bit better for the next woman to run or lead in general. The patriarchy won't topple itself! But we still have a lot of work to do. And while things have gotten better for many women over the last few decades, we are laughably far from gender equality in America, and especially in American politics.

For all of the successes in the 2018 cycle—the second so-called Year of the Woman—as of the writing of this book, less than one quarter of the voting members of the United States Congress are women. Things are better on the state legislative level, but barely. Nationwide, as of 2019, women are less than a third of legislators. After the 2018 elections, only nine women were governors, and women held less than 30 percent of executive offices.[1] There have been fewer women elected to the US House over the entire history of this country[2] than episodes of *Grey's Anatomy.*[*][3] Considering women have had the right to

---

*You can insert any number of shows here, from *NCIS* to *Law & Order,* and the statistic is just as depressing, but I figured why not point to the success of an amazing woman (and EMILY's List Creative Council member) like Shonda Rhimes?

vote for barely a century, this seemingly small fraction proves the forward march of progress, with every victory a significant step toward the distant goal of equal representation.

It's not just politics. In fact, we find this disparity in nearly every field. As of 2020, the percentage of Fortune 500 CEOs who were women was at an all-time high. Brace yourself— that high was just 7.4 percent. And women are less than a quarter (22.5 percent) of Fortune 500 board members.[4] As of 2016, only 30 percent of university and college presidents were women.[5]

Even though women are nearly half of all law associates, they are less than a quarter of the partners and only about 20 percent of equity partners.[6] Women have earned the majority of doctorates awarded over the last eight years, but only 32 percent of full professors are women.[7]

These numbers are even worse for women of color. According to statistics from 2018, women of color make up nearly 20 percent of the workforce but only 5 percent of senior-level officials and managers in the S&P 500.[8] And as of this writing, in 2020, only three women of color (and no Black women) are CEOs of Fortune 500 companies.

I know these numbers might feel depressing, so take a breath and let's look at the good news. There were nearly as many women running for president in the 2020 Democratic primary as had ever run from a major party in the history of the country. How great was it to look up onstage during those debates and see multiple women, raising the challenges women face and the ways they would tackle them?

The 2018 midterm election saw the election of more women than ever before, from the first majority-women legislature (way to go, Nevada!) to the first time more than one hundred women have been elected to the US House. They included the first Native American women, the first women under the age of thirty, the youngest African American woman, and the first two Latinas from Texas ever elected to the House, all contributing to the most diverse class ever. From Nancy Pelosi's becoming Speaker again (and second in line to the presidency) to women taking the chairs of six committees in the House as well as a joint committee and select committee,[9] women took control and stepped into leadership roles in a major way. Women also led the four major Democratic Party campaign committees for the first time, perhaps a nod to our success in recent years at winning elections.*

At EMILY's List, we watch with pride as the women we've helped elect work incredibly hard to get other women elected. And we got to watch as some of those women were literally in charge of those campaign committees, leading the efforts to elect even more women. It's a long way from the days when the so-called establishment used to dismiss women candidates out of hand.

And there are more on the horizon. I see hope in the

---

*I'm particularly proud to note that Nevada Senator Catherine Cortez Masto (Democratic Senatorial Campaign Committee), Rhode Island Governor Gina Raimondo (Democratic Governors Association), Illinois Representative Cheri Bustos (Democratic Congressional Campaign Committee), and New York Senate Majority Leader Andrea Stewart-Cousins (Democratic Legislative Campaign Committee) are all EMILY's List women, and DLCC President Jessica Post and DCCC Executive Director Lucinda Guinn are both EMILY's List alumnae. The Old Girls' Club just might be taking over.

millions of women in their pink hats, marching for our rights, and the ways in which those women keep fighting to make their communities better. I see hope in the #MeToo movement, showing the power of women standing up for each other and amplifying each other's voices. I see it in the tens of thousands of women running for office for the first time. In the champions of the US national women's soccer team, who broke records and stood up to their own employer, demanding equal pay.

And just as important, I see hope in you, reader, the woman who has decided to make change in her community and her life.

My wish is that this book helps you in that urgent and necessary work. You should know that this is not a how-to book. But it will provide you with some concrete advice and real stories from my experience of a lifetime in politics. These are the lessons we teach women at EMILY's List, lessons we've honed over the last thirty-five years and that have helped get hundreds of women elected. I am excited to share them with you now.

They are more than just good tips for setting up and winning a political campaign. After all, if you can learn how to ask someone for a donation, you can learn how and when to ask for a raise. If you can learn how to delegate work to a campaign staff, you can learn how to delegate work in your office. Building a campaign team is very similar to building your own support system in order to conquer the world (or just make things better in your hometown). And we all need to know how to bounce back from a loss or liberally celebrate a

success—whether those are electoral wins and losses or victories of some other kind.

I am grateful for the opportunity I've had to both teach and
learn from our EMILY's List candidates. Each one leads in a
different way, having learned from her own campaigns and
community, proving that there's no one way to do it. Every
woman looking to make change can be a leader. And every
woman leader can take valuable lessons from the women
around us, because the best leaders also know how to follow a
good example.

You may not be running for office (yet), but if you've picked
up this book, it's because you're ready to launch a campaign of
your own to change the world. And at EMILY's List, we're here
for all kinds of campaigns led by strong women like you.

Now let's get to it. The world won't change itself.

CHAPTER 1

Getting Started

*What You Need to Know Before You Start and What
You Can Learn on the Way*

IF A JOURNEY of one thousand miles starts with a single step, the journey to elected office starts with a single decision. That first step is deciding you are going to run for office. So, let's talk about how to make that decision.

How many of you have looked at a job description and thought, *I am not qualified because I don't have one hundred percent of the qualifications listed*? Come on, be honest. I am the president of the nation's largest resource for women in politics and even I did it with this job before I threw my hat in the ring. I saw what EMILY's List was looking for and I didn't have all the qualifications. I had been the staffer behind the powerful leader. I had been the finance director, the campaign manager, and the chief of staff, but I had never been the one out front. EMILY's List was looking for a strategist (check) who could raise money (check) and be the head spokesperson with the press and public (UGH—PRESS???). I was so afraid to talk to the press I almost didn't apply for the job.

But that would have been the wrong decision. Because whether you already have all of the qualifications is the wrong question. The right question is whether you are ready and willing to learn on the job. To make the decision to run and take that jump, the first step is to convince yourself that you can do it. You have so much to bring to the table, and you can learn the rest. More on that later. PS: I talk to the press quite a bit now and I am pretty good at it most of the time.

At EMILY's List, we spend a lot of time convincing women to run for office. Recruiting is one of my favorite parts of the job and something we do a lot of. My team and I have talked to thousands of women around the country in the last ten years. We've heard every concern and excuse a potential candidate might have for *not* running. Some of those concerns are very valid, and we will talk about those in the next chapter. But most excuses are just that—excuses, masking a lack of confidence.

I assumed for a long time that there was a magic gene that candidates had, one that gave them the underlying confidence to run for office. I figured most elected officials had been dreaming of running since they were kids. I thought that some people were just made to do it. There are, after all, people who are naturally gifted at public speaking, great debaters, policy wonks, people who are effortlessly charismatic, charming, and well connected. I assumed these people with the innate gifts became the candidates, because they knew how to do it, because they were somehow meant to run.

I suspect we've all been around people like this. They are typically men, and they carry themselves in a way that makes it easy to assume there is a secret playbook the rest of us don't have access to. You know who I'm talking about. The person in the meeting whose confident answer makes you believe yours must be wrong, despite the research you've done and the facts backing you up. The coworker who offers opinion as fact. The person who has been on the job far less time than you but gives off the vibe of having mastered the work years ago. Clearly, they know something we don't, right?

Wrong.

What I've learned in years of doing campaigns, and what I've tried to share with the women who doubt their abilities, is that there is no secret playbook or magic gene. There's no mystery to it. There's just a hunger to learn what you need to know and a willingness to do the hard work of building confidence in yourself. It can still feel impossible. And there's a good reason why.

For one, the Old Boys' Club is a very real thing. The smoke-filled back rooms are still around, albeit with less smoke and perhaps just a little more diversity than in days of old. In politics and campaigns, as in nearly everything, there's an "establishment" that the rest of us are up against. Those are the people who decide who gets the promotions, the best jobs and projects, the opportunities to chase bigger and better things. The establishment is exactly what we are challenging, thanks to decades of knocking down the door of that smoke-filled room and helping women carry in their own chairs when they are told there's no room at the table.

Today, I work with party leaders to recruit women and help more of them achieve victory every day. I'm proud to say it's a very different place from where we started.

EMILY's List was created thirty-five years ago to tear down the Democratic establishment's Old Boys' Club. As of 1984, no Democratic woman had ever been elected to the Senate in her own right. My friend and Minnesota Senator Tina Smith's favorite fun fact: In the history of the United States, there have been almost as many men named Charles elected to the Senate as there have been women.

EMILY's List founder, Ellen Malcolm, had watched as Harriett Woods ran a great race for a United States Senate seat in Missouri in 1982 despite being dismissed by the Democratic establishment as not being a viable candidate. They told her she would never be able to raise enough money to run a successful campaign. Of course, the fact that the party wouldn't support her further undercut her ability to raise money and meant she had to pull her ads off the air at a key moment. In the end, even with the deck stacked firmly against her, Woods lost by less than two points.

With that loss, Ellen had had enough. She pulled together a group of her women friends who were working across the political field and were equally frustrated by the lack of electoral success by women. Ellen knew that the core of the problem was that the party didn't believe women candidates could win elections. In Washington, the one thing above all that catches people's notice is money—so Ellen knew what women needed to be taken seriously: a funding source.

Of course, this was unheard of at the time. Women donors were few and far between. It was a time when the wealth held by women was significantly less than it is today—and the wealth gap between men and women is still significant. Women in office were also, sadly, few and far between, with only twenty-four women in Congress total, in both houses and from both parties.[1] But Ellen and her friends were determined to change things for women running for office.*

They didn't have all the answers or all the power, so they used what they did have access to—time, contacts, and a willingness to help—and they went to work. Armed with their Rolodexes,† they sat together in Ellen's basement and worked their own networks. They each wrote their friends, families, and like-minded contacts, asking them to give $100 to this movement to elect more women and $100 each to the first two candidates: Barbara Mikulski, for her 1986 Senate run in Maryland, and Harriett Woods, running for a second time in Missouri. Those friends of Ellen's friends sent checks that were then bundled together for both campaigns, boosting their finances and their chances. Though Woods lost, this effort ultimately helped Barbara Mikulski in Maryland become the first Democratic woman elected to the Senate in her own right. She became the longest-serving woman in the Senate.[2]

Ellen decided to name that effort EMILY's List because she knew that Early Money Is Like Yeast: It makes the dough rise.

---

*This story and many more are in Ellen's wonderful book *When Women Win*. It's an absolute must-read for more on the history of EMILY's List and women in politics.
†For our younger readers who might not have heard of a Rolodex, think of it as the contacts in your phone in paper form.

Yes, we are named after a baking joke. Our first logos were based on the Fleischmann yeast packet.

In the thirty-five years since that first success, we've helped elect hundreds of women and hopefully begun to neutralize the boys' club a bit. More and more often, the Democratic establishment sees the value in nominating and running women, often working hand in hand with EMILY's List. Though we don't always agree and there are many times we have to use our power to get women through the process, it's definitely progress. We know that every woman who runs makes it a bit easier for the next one—and we know that we get better government with more women involved. Challenges still remain, but every election cycle it gets better.

And yet, these are things we still hear all the time: It's hard for women to run. The establishment is against me. They tell me it's not my turn. I've never done it before. I just can't do it.

Time and again, our response is the same: Yes, you can.

The so-called establishment is not the be-all and end-all in this process. All you need to be a good candidate is integrity, passion, energy, commitment, and a true willingness to work hard, learn, and ask for help. If you have a passion for your community and want to make change, you should figure out which elected office has the authority to make that change and run for it. Your voice and your individual perspective are what we need in office. We have had nearly 250 years of white men, for the most part, running our government at all levels, but no more. If you know why you are running, and you are willing to work really hard, then you are the woman for the job.

I know what you're thinking: "But, Stephanie, I don't know how to get started. It's too much."

To that I say, one thing at a time. First, decide to run, and trust me that the rest you can learn. Much of becoming a candidate or starting that new career is about on-the-job training. It takes research, work, lots of questions, and probably some missteps. But you don't *need* to know how to do all of this before you decide to run.

This isn't rocket science. It's about learning the right pieces and how to put them together. Everything you need to know to build a successful campaign is teachable. Are you convinced yet? Stick around and let me prove it to you.

My team and I have had this conversation with more potential candidates than we can count. We've given them plans and training and materials, but too often, they're doubting the wrong thing. They're worried about whether they have it within themselves simply because they've never done it before. But what we know, proven through our work with literally thousands of success stories, is that anyone can become a great candidate.

So, don't decide not to take that next step because you don't know how you are going to do all aspects of the job. Decide to take on the job and let me help you figure out the rest.

Of course, I don't promise our candidates they will win every race or secure every nomination. There are so many variables that go into elections that are out of your control. And the sad truth is, the best candidate running the best campaign won't win every time. What we can promise is that if you do the work and you have the following traits, you can put yourself in the best position possible to make change in your community. That is true for candidates. That is true for applying for any promotion. That is just true for all of us. And the journey will change your life for the better.

So, let's talk in more detail about what candidates *do* need.

INTEGRITY

I like quoting the many women we've helped elect over the years, but I'll make an exception for this gem from Oprah Winfrey: "Real integrity is doing the right thing, knowing that nobody's going to know whether you did it or not."

Being a good leader means being honest and being driven by moral principles and values. It means being willing to stand up for what's right, even if it's difficult, even when no one's watching or giving you credit. *Especially* when no one's watching or giving you credit. It means everything from following the law to setting an example for the people around you. In a political system that is far from perfect, I suppose I need to note that these are things a leader *should* do. And I'm proud to say these traits are what our EMILY's List candidates and leaders of our organization have exemplified consistently over the years.

For us, that means we expect transparency and honesty from the women we work with, even when that's hard. We promise that same honesty in return. Sometimes that means making a tough call when we decide not to give a candidate the support she anticipated. Those calls are some of my least favorite parts of my job, but the only way I can do my job is to be transparent and do the right thing for our organization, even when it's hard.

I remember when I called Katie McGinty in 2013. Katie was running for governor in Pennsylvania in a multicandidate primary that included soon-to-be EMILY's List–endorsed Congresswoman Allyson Schwartz. I wanted Katie to hear from me that we were going to endorse the other woman in the race. It was not the news she wanted to hear. She had hoped we would stay out of a multiwoman primary, but when there were so few women governors, we knew we had to get involved.

On the call, Katie made her case, and I will be honest, I was impressed. I knew she didn't have a path to become governor that year, but I could tell she had something. So I told her at the end of the call that whether she won or lost this primary, I was going to be her first call, because I wanted to help with her next political steps if she was willing. As promised, I called her the night she lost that election—and I called her again the next year to recruit her for a 2016 United States Senate race. She ran another great campaign, this time with EMILY's List's support the whole way, and she barely lost to the incumbent by less than 2 points. And though she didn't win, Katie was surely an inspiration for the women who broke down barriers and flipped seats in Pennsylvania in 2018.

Throughout the course of campaigns, candidates are sometimes given the chance to take the easy path. I could have not called Katie to tell her we weren't endorsing her. But then we would have missed out on future opportunities. Or worse, in some cases, campaigns may even be asked or told to cut corners or skirt the law. But what's easy today can become much tougher down the road. Not only will voters often sniff out the lack of integrity, but cutting corners often comes back to haunt you in more concrete ways. In short, it's not worth it. At EMILY's List, we are careful to endorse women who know that a candidate should live her espoused values and that you can't ask people to vote for you if they can't believe in you. These women are competitive, and they want to win badly. But they know they have to win in a way they and their supporters can be proud of: with integrity.

Of course, the hard part about integrity is that it requires you to make the right choice, even when it's costly. Theresa Greenfield was a farm kid who grew up wanting to serve her community. She also happens to be a fellow graduate of Minnesota State University in Mankato, Minnesota. She had announced her campaign for Iowa's Third Congressional District and was building a campaign, meeting voters, and doing the hard work that comes with the territory of being a candidate. Unfortunately, right before the filing deadline, she learned of a major problem. Her campaign manager had been in charge of gathering the signatures needed to get her on the ballot, but he had cut corners and was short of the number of signatures that Theresa needed. He had gone as far as to forge some of them.

Theresa found out and was rightly mortified. Without knowing exactly how many signatures were forged, Theresa knew she had only one option. She had to tell the authorities what had happened and withdraw the petition. She made the difficult choice to start over on gathering signatures. The time frame was too short, and Theresa didn't make it.[3] She took responsibility, and ultimately it cost her getting on the ballot. The end result was a huge blow to Theresa, who had already devoted time and resources to her run.

Though Theresa wasn't aware of and hadn't caused the situation, as soon as she became aware, she took action, even to her own detriment. That is integrity. She did the right thing. She was disappointed, but she knew she had done the only possible thing she could. And sure enough, time proved her right. Less than two years later, Theresa ran again, this time for the US Senate. And instead of her previous campaign's being considered a vulnerability, it signaled to voters that she would do the right thing for the state of Iowa and stand up for the law.

Here's the lesson. If you run your campaign based on your values, you show the voters how you will serve them in office. That is the key here. You are not doing this just for yourself. You are doing this in service to your neighbors, your community, your friends. Running with integrity shows you will govern with integrity, and that is what people deserve from their leaders. They deserve to know that when the tough call needs to be made, you will make it based on strong moral principles, even when that decision is difficult or unpopular.

And integrity in office (or at work or in your community) means telling people what you truly believe, not what they may want to hear. It means doing the tough thing when it's the right thing. In fact, it means doing the right thing simply because it's the right thing, even if it might cost you something.

This brings up another point: You've got to have the facts. As a candidate, just like any leader, you have to actively seek all of the information to form a solid position. This kind of homework is tough and time-consuming, but it's necessary and it's worth it. You need to understand the consequences of your decisions. You will not always get it right, but you will know you have done your best. And sometimes you may get rewarded for the tough decision even when it feels like the public is not with you.

I've seen the aftereffects of those tough decisions up close as a staffer. I've advised many candidates and elected officials on key issues. In some cases, I've been asked by party and congressional leaders to convince candidates to do one thing or another. To fall in line and cast a specific vote—sometimes to pass a bill, sometimes to do the thing most supported by their voters, and so on. And over the years, I've realized something: Voters may not always agree with you and they may have a different opinion, but since it is impossible to please everyone, sticking to your core beliefs is always the best option. Selling something you don't believe can spell a quick death to a campaign, to a candidate, to a leader.

Voters are tired of what they see as politics as usual. They want authenticity, not leaders who will promise anything to get a vote. Employees want a manager who they know will do the right thing, even if it's not the easiest path. Having integrity is its own reward, to be sure, but sometimes it can help you reach your goals as well.

We should demand this kind of integrity from our elected officials. And we should commit to that same thing in our own lives. Just imagine the difference in our home, in our work, in the world, if we all committed to doing what's right. Think of what it would mean to our communities if we all lived up to the ideal of the people we want to be and tried to set a positive example for those around us. And though it's unlikely that *everyone* will suddenly learn to live with integrity, if you want to earn the respect of voters and be worthy of the office you seek, committing to integrity is an amazing place to start.

PASSION

Changing the world isn't easy. If you're thinking you've already heard that a lot from me, get used to it. Our communications team would call that "message discipline." I'd call it speaking the truth until it sinks in. And this is an important truth: The most successful campaigns and movements are built on the things that inspire the most passion in us.

It's that passion that drives our candidates to run. The vast majority of the women we work with run in order to bring about change, often a specific change, or deal with an issue that directly impacts their community and the people they love. They run to solve a problem. And I think they run better as a result.

That passion can come from any number of sources. For some, it's an issue or an incident that has hit them head-on. For many, particularly in recent years as Obamacare has been under threat, it's watching a loved one deal with a health issue while battling our insurance system. Passion comes from personal experience.

Illinois Representative Lauren Underwood was a child with a chronic heart condition who became a nurse and a health care policy expert. I remember so vividly the first time I met her. It was at a progressive conference in Chicago in the fall of 2017. EMILY's List had been in touch with Lauren, but we thought that the congressional district was too Republican to elect a Democrat. From the start of the election cycle, we just didn't think the district was winnable because Donald Trump had done well and the Republicans always won the district with a pretty wide margin. We were thrilled Lauren was running because we need women running everywhere. But even we were skeptical about the race despite the fact that we kept hearing about Lauren. Much of the so-called establishment didn't believe she could win, which hampered her ability to raise money. But when I met her in person, I saw that this smart and focused badass had a plan to win a six-way primary and then the general, and I knew she would win over voters even in this tough district. So EMILY's List endorsed Lauren for Congress.

Today, she is one of the only nurses in Congress and the youngest African American woman ever elected to the House. That has made her a powerful elected advocate on health care issues. Your own experience doesn't just drive your passion.

When you share it, as Lauren does so well, it can help others better understand you and want to work with you. That's how you build a movement and build support for a cause.

There is another story I have to share, about Senator Tammy Baldwin—one that I wasn't even aware of until she ran for reelection in 2018. I know Senator Baldwin pretty well. We talk regularly and have become good friends. But even women who have been in politics for years, fighting tough fights, can learn the value of sharing their passion to help accomplish their agenda even when it's personally difficult. Tammy has always been a groundbreaker. She was the first openly gay first-time candidate to win a seat in the United States House— and when a US Senate seat opened up in Wisconsin, I urged her to run, despite the risks and the huge number of skeptics. I was so proud when she won, becoming the first openly gay US senator, and I am even prouder of the work she has done since taking office.

For years, Senator Baldwin has fought to end our nation's opioid crisis. She has been a relentless advocate for getting additional resources to communities not just in Wisconsin but around the nation. Tammy has been in Congress fighting the challenges of opioid addiction for years, and I always assumed it was because that was just the right thing to do for her state and the country. She hadn't been comfortable enough, even with me, to share all of her own personal story.

During that reelection campaign, Tammy chose to share with voters something she had rarely discussed openly. Her own mother had battled addiction throughout Tammy's childhood. Tammy told the story straight to camera. It was honest, strong, and vulnerable. I am not telling you that you have to share your most difficult personal stories; not everyone is willing to and that's all right. But Tammy was willing to do that during her reelection in 2018, and it was so powerful. It gave people a more personal understanding of who she is and why she is driven to make change. I remember her calling me to tell me she was going to go up with this ad. It was so brave and I was so proud. Even in writing this, my heart fills up with emotion. It is hard to show even your closest friends what drives you and what scares you, but telling the world is another level of bravery. Revealing your passion (and the reasons for it) shows voters that you are supporting a policy or agenda for the right reasons.

I've seen bravery in so many of the women I've worked with in politics. An unthinkable tragedy drove Georgia Representative Lucy McBath's commitment to gun violence prevention, making her an activist first and then a member of Congress. Lucy lost her seventeen-year-old son, Jordan Davis, to gun violence when a man shot into his car at a gas station after complaining about the "loud rap music" Jordan and his friends were playing. Lucy turned this unspeakable tragedy into advocacy, as a Faith Outreach coordinator and national spokeswoman for Moms Demand Action for Gun Sense in America, a grassroots arm of Everytown for Gun Safety. Working with other volunteers in Florida, Lucy lobbied successfully against bills that would have allowed guns in schools and airports in her state.[4]

Lucy kept fighting while Congress failed to address the growing gun violence problem, but she knew it was time for more extreme action after the 2018 shooting at Marjory Stoneman Douglas High School in Parkland, Florida. She decided to stand up and take her advocacy and leadership to the next level. She ran in a right-leaning district for a seat held by a Republican and once held by House Speaker Newt Gingrich. Lucy herself noted, "Absolutely nothing—no politician and no special interest—is more powerful than a mother on a mission." Lucy's passion took her all the way to the US House, where she fights every day to protect kids like Jordan.[5]

Each of these women identified the issue that mattered most to her and the people she loved, and she used that issue to anchor a successful campaign. And these women's campaigns earned them jobs that allowed them to act on their passions.

Putting your personal story on display is never easy. Lauren's talking about her health challenges, Tammy's talking about her mom's addiction, Lucy's talking about her son, Jordan—these were all hard things to do. But everyone has hard times, and trusting people with your story helps them trust you in return. So let me try to do what I ask candidates to do all the time and tell you about one of the hardest things I've ever been through.

I lost my mom to breast cancer in 2007. She was a really great mom. I am the oldest of three by a lot. My brother Charlie is seven years younger, and my baby brother (he loves that), Jonathan, is nearly ten years younger, so I always felt a bit like the mother hen even when Mom was around. My mom had so much energy and passion for people, but she also loved quiet time with a good book. I think I get my half-introvert/half-extrovert mix from her.

Her first bout of breast cancer was in 1994 while I was in college. Her older sister had already battled and survived her breast cancer, so though it was serious, we felt really positive. Mom was a trouper and as a college kid, I was supportive but living states away. She pulled through, and for nine fabulous years she was in remission. But in 2003, the cancer came back, metastasized in her liver, and knocked us all down. I found out as I was packing up a moving van to leave for Burlington, Vermont, where I would start my new job as the finance director for Howard Dean's presidential campaign.

I seriously considered turning down the job to find something that would be easier to do and let me be closer to Mom and Dad, who were living in Overland Park, Kansas. But my dad and my aunt Linda both said the best thing to do—the thing my mom would have wanted—was to continue on with my life. So I did. She battled and battled for years, but in the summer of 2007, her body finally gave out. By that time, now three years further into my career, I was serving as chief of staff for Senator Jon Tester, whose campaign I had managed the previous fall. I spent most weekends and the final three weeks with my family. It was one of the greatest honors, and saddest times, of my life to be with my mom and my dad at the very end.

This experience changed my priorities and influenced the

issues that matter to me. I know firsthand the importance of increased research to end all cancers, which I do fully believe we can do. I am a passionate supporter of hospice and the angels who do that work. I am always so grateful to our women candidates who fight for these programs, and to the many women elected officials who are breast cancer survivors as well. These are tough women, just like my mom; Aunt Sue, my mom's oldest sister and a breast cancer survivor, who is doing great; and my mom's twin sister, Aunt Jean, who is in a long battle with metastasized breast cancer herself. I am so lucky to have been raised by these absolute warrior women.

These are the women whose shoulders I stand on. They taught me to be strong, to never give up, and to fight for those who have less, particularly when it comes to basic health care.

That is one of the reasons I do what I do and what burns inside me every day. I want to make them proud, and that passion makes it easy for me to love my work. These are the stories that connect us all together.

So I urge you to think through all the reasons you really want to be in this fight. Because if it happened to you or your family, it is happening to other families, too. If you could spend your time focused on one thing, what would it be? What is the thing that would make your family proud? These questions can help you better understand what you're really passionate about, and once you figure that out, you can work out a plan to have an impact.

I am lucky—I get to be the woman who runs the organization that empowers women. It's a passion—and believe me, my team doesn't doubt my passion when we have big wins or disappointing losses. But I want to do more than get women elected (although I'd like to do a lot more of that, too). I want to change the culture of politics with women leaders. More women leading organizations, more women-owned political consulting firms, more women quoted in news stories. I think about these things all the time and work with my team on how best to lift up the great work women do in politics and how to help them get ahead. In fact, that's one of the reasons I decided to write this book. I'm hoping you take these lessons and give me great examples to talk about moving forward.

COMMITMENT

Running for office is tough. So is being in office. The problems our government has to solve are complicated and require hard work and dedication. So when my team at EMILY's List talks to potential candidates, one of the first things we try to figure out is whether they have a commitment to service and to something bigger than themselves. Candidates must have the commitment to take on huge challenges and change the world. For many of our candidates, before they even start running, they have already found a way of turning their passion into a commitment to fix an issue. Now we want those women to take that commitment to the next step. Through elected office they will earn the authority to achieve that broader goal and effect meaningful change.

Some candidates start with a deep commitment to public service through government employment. For the last few decades, we've heard from people in power—and in the last few years, from President Trump—that government is bad, that it does no good in our communities, that government officials are corrupt, and that the swamp must be drained. In my experience, this couldn't be further from the truth.

The government—federal, state, and local—is full of people committed to making our society work better, from the military to our health care, from educating our youth to taking care of our seniors and making sure our communities reflect our collective values. I personally know so many government employees whose skills could have taken them anywhere. They chose to serve the public, not for power, not for a title, and definitely not for money, but to do some good and make change. And they take their deep knowledge and expertise with them into service.

Mikie Sherrill was a Navy aviator who became an assistant US attorney and then a member of the US House from New Jersey. Senator Kamala Harris of California was a prosecutor, a district attorney, and an attorney general who enforced the laws before she decided it was time to help write them, and before she became the first Black woman and Indian American woman to be nominated for vice president. Abigail Spanberger served as a CIA officer before she ran and won a House seat in Virginia. Haley Stevens was a government staffer, serving at one point as the chief of staff to President Obama's Auto Recovery Task Force, before she flipped a Republican House seat blue in Michigan. Each of these women was committed to making change through public service within the government, even as her role evolved along the way. And knowing them all personally, I know each and every one of them could have chosen a career outside of government, probably for a bigger paycheck and without the enormous stress of life in the public sphere. But they are all driven by a commitment to public service, and that is really key.

Then there are the women who are driven to take on the government, who want to make change so much they are willing to fight the authorities and create power in a different way. Patty Murray, the highest-ever-ranking Democratic woman in the Senate, is one of my all-time favorite stories. Patty was a community college instructor who was protesting cuts to a key preschool program in 1979 when a male legislator told her, "You can't do anything; you're just a mom in tennis shoes." That was exactly the wrong thing to say to Patty, and his dismissal only added fuel to her fire. She organized a grassroots coalition of thousands of parents who fought together to save the program. Though she hadn't considered running for office before, through this experience Patty found she was a natural leader and organizer. She served both on the town of Shoreline's school board and in the Washington state senate before she became the first woman to serve as a United States senator from Washington State.[6]

When she ran in 1992, the first so-called Year of the Woman, Patty still faced skepticism from the establishment, despite having served in elected office before. Like many of the women you'll read about in this book, Patty learned how to absorb the attacks on her. She used those tennis shoes as a symbol for who she was and whom she would represent. As *The New York Times* noted in 1992, Murray's campaign was "sneered at by many political insiders in Seattle" but "succeeded by playing on a nonpartisan image of a harried mom—caring for two children and aging parents, while holding a job and making dinner several nights a week."[7] Talking consistently about her commitment to child care and education, and with the support of EMILY's List, Patty was elected to the US Senate and has served as the secretary of the Democratic Caucus.

My commitment to Democratic values and electing women has driven me for many years, but perhaps never so much as in the last year or so. That's because I experienced something that knocked me down and reminded me how much it can take to get back up. While I was writing this book, I had a stroke.

I have to be honest; I wasn't sure I was going to open up about this, in this book or ever. I am still getting my head around it. I was worried people would think less of my ability, and that scared me. Frankly, the whole thing scared me. I was a healthy forty-six-year-old, running the most powerful women's organization in the country, heading to a work meeting in a Lyft. It was a beautiful morning and I was excited about a fairly unusual stretch with no travel and an upcoming dinner date (also sometimes too unusual for a single gal with a busy job like mine).

Then, boom! The next thing I knew, I couldn't feel my left side. The first moments were terrifying—and a bit of a blur. I remain incredibly grateful to my guardian angel Eric, my Lyft driver, for recognizing something was wrong and getting me to the hospital. While in the car, I started to understand what was happening and called our executive director, Emily Cain, who kept me calm even when I was struggling to get words out or understand what was going on. Emily jumped right into action and somehow made it to the hospital before me to take my hand and get me into the ER. My best friend, Christa, came to spend the whole day in the ER with me while we waited for test results and for my dad to arrive from Kansas City, Kansas. The first few days were full of uncertainty and more waiting for tests until I was discharged without a conclusive diagnosis. And it was still scary, maybe even scarier, once I learned what had happened—that a blood clot in my brain had caused a stroke.

I was incredibly lucky. My stroke was relatively minor, and I had good health care and the support of my team and my amazing family and friends to get through it. Honestly, I can't imagine having gone through any of this without my dad, who must have been beyond worried and never showed it as he stayed with me in the hospital. I wish I could say I was right back up on my feet, but the healing process was not easy. I was angry and I was scared. I had to commit the time to heal, staying completely away from work while I learned my own limitations.

I spent a month out of work before getting the green light to slowly come back to the office. And not a moment too soon; there was work to be done!

At the time, EMILY's List was in the middle of Virginia legislative elections. I knew my health was fragile, but I couldn't fathom missing the chance to support all our brave women candidates who were getting ready to take the Democratic majorities in both chambers in the commonwealth's legislature. So I went out and did speeches just six weeks after my stroke to rally canvass volunteers. And, shocker, I was *exhausted*. But I also knew I was up to the task and that these candidates needed my help.

You'll hear later about my support network throughout this process and what it meant for me.

But the work and my support network have kept me going. Even months later, back to work full-time, I could feel the fatigue that so often comes with stroke recovery. I learned quickly that every stroke is different and the timeline for healing varies dramatically. There were days I thought I was back to 100 percent, only to be hit with a wave of fatigue that would slow me down again. But even as I made the necessary changes to my schedule and lifestyle to focus on healing, I never lost the drive to fight through it, because I knew that this election in 2020 would be critical to the future of our world. So I fought through, committed to the work and to the women running for office across this nation.

No matter what that issue or life challenge is for you, it is the commitment to make change that matters most deeply. It is the commitment to the work, to the mission, to the job, that keeps you going even when things are rough. All of us should be driven by a commitment to something bigger than ourselves. It is our North Star, the thing that brings our focus back when the days are long and we're not sure why we're doing this very hard thing. That commitment is a vital part of changing the world.

ENERGY

Campaigns are exhausting. A successful campaign requires months, sometimes years, of hard work. Integrity defines how you should run. Passion and commitment speak to the why. But to maintain energy over the course of an entire race is, simply put, incredibly difficult. Anything worth doing takes hard work, and campaigns are no exception. But if you're willing to train for it and learn what you need to know, I'm here to coach you through it.

Every campaign, every job, takes a different amount and kind of energy. They also require different strategies to reenergize. Here are a few examples from my own experience, and a few from our candidates, about finding energy when the going gets tough.

Do You Have the Physical and Emotional Ability to Do This?

My first campaign job was in 1996. I was the finance director for Mary Rieder, who was running for Congress in Minnesota. I picked up some good and bad behaviors in that race. The finance shop was at her home in the country outside a little town called Eyota, while the rest of the campaign was headquartered in Rochester. This was great when we were making calls, because we had peace and quiet to raise money. But the isolated office was pretty hard on my psyche. I like a balance of being around people and having my own space. For me, being alone from eight A.M. to sometime between ten and midnight every day was emotionally draining.

I had to figure out how to take care of myself and get the job done at the same time, so I started building strategies to lighten the emotional load. I learned that taking a few short walks during the day helped my outlook immensely, and during the last six, most intense weeks of the campaign, I would even take a twenty-to-thirty-minute nap in the middle of the workday. Yes, I napped. It was incredible. And most important, it saved my sanity and my energy at a time when I needed them the most. You have to find what works for you.

Since that first experience, I have honed some of my emotional recharging skills, though it is a constant work in progress. For me, I still need to go outside and walk even for ten minutes every day during the day. I am a good sleeper and make it a priority to get seven to eight hours a night, though that does get challenging as things ramp up at the end of the campaigns. I have a group of go-to friends for pep talks and bitch sessions (more on your support system in chapter 5). And when I can, I get away for a day to hike or just be by myself, because I am actually more introverted than not. I love people, like I said, but I need Stephanie time.

You need to figure out how to do this for yourself and find what makes you work at your best.

Of course, not all my coping mechanisms are positive. I'm a stress eater and often gain weight on campaigns. In my twenties and thirties, through a series of stressful jobs, I really gained, and I promised I wouldn't do that again. Now, during stressful times, I watch my food intake carefully, though my current EMILY's List staff knows that I just spent the last few years losing what I called the Trump 20, which had been on top of the Hillary 15. Knowing your weak points is just as important as identifying your most effective strategies for stress relief.

Do You Like People?

When we tell our candidates that they have to have the energy to run for office, what we mean is that they have to have the emotional and physical energy to take on this huge and all-consuming effort. Campaigns, like many goals we set in life and as leaders, are grueling and take discipline and hard work, balanced with knowing how to go the distance in a healthy way.

When you are a leader, you are going to be listening and talking to people *all* the time. Changing the world is not a job easily done from a closed office. Running for office is about engaging with people, first and foremost. One of the first questions we ask our potential candidates is: Do you like people? Because at their core, campaigns are about the voters. If you are the type of person who values alone time above everything else or has a hard time seeing the good in people, I'll be honest, this is going to be hard for you. Really hard.

To run for office, candidates have to connect with people

all day every day. There are voters to listen to and convince, donors to approach, volunteers to inspire, staff to motivate, and family members to comfort. This is a people job. Depending on the office, you will communicate in different ways, through speeches and town halls, in small rooms, or on doorsteps asking for votes. It sure helps if candidates are genuinely curious about the concerns of voters, interested in their families and the challenges they face, and willing to work with them to solve problems.

How often do you get frustrated when an elected official isn't connecting with you in some real way, or they seem like they are in it more for themselves than for others? It can be maddening and disappointing. Of course, there are definitely elected officials who aren't good at talking to people, but that is harder and harder to sustain these days. We are in an era where voters want authenticity—you have to put yourself out there to let voters get to know you and vice versa. *That* takes a *lot* of energy. You have to know that you have at least enough emotional energy to listen and to share.

Are You an Introvert or an Extrovert?

This gets to another important question: Are you an introvert or an extrovert? Do you get energized by being around people? Or do you need space to reenergize your mind and body? There is no one right answer. You just have to really know the right answer for you so you can build supports around you to restore your energy levels.

You don't have to be an extrovert or a natural public speaker to be a candidate or lead an organization. An introvert can certainly lead people and organizations, even though those roles usually require things that may be tough for them, like public speaking and networking. An introvert has to be willing to work their way through those challenges and learn how best to address them.

If you've ever seen Stacey Abrams of Georgia speak, you know she's something special. When Stacey was in the Georgia legislature, we knew she was a rock star in the making and named her the first EMILY's List Gabrielle Giffords Rising Star Award winner. Since then, she's run an amazing gubernatorial campaign, written a bestselling leadership book (on top of her eight novels), been touted as a presidential contender, and started an organization to fight for all Americans' right to have their votes counted. It might surprise you to learn, then, that Stacey will be the first one to tell you that she is a total introvert. She has had to work to overcome her shyness and push herself to be comfortable in front of big crowds. She also makes sure she has time to herself to reboot. And in that process, she's become one of the best speakers in politics today.

There's a broader, practical lesson here. Most introverts get exhausted by the constant communication required by campaigns, as opposed to the extroverts, who feed on that kind of constant contact. It's important to know where you fall on that spectrum. For introverts, you need to be very clear with your team about when you hit your exhaustion point and when you need to recharge. If your staff is full of extroverts, they may not instinctively understand

Introverts may need more, or more thorough, prep when headed into certain situations. For example, it's easier to feel comfortable at an important meeting if you know something about each of the people who will be there or have spent more time focused on your goals for the meeting. Some introverts feel more comfortable with more structure around meetings or occasionally relying on email or conference calls as alternative methods of communication.

I fall right in the middle—I can get tired from being "on," but I love being with people. Frankly, since my stroke, I really need to know when I am about to hit the wall. In the first six months of recovery I've found it harder to bounce back as quickly as I could before. I still use the same recharge strategies—I may just need to go to the gym or watch TV, or, if I really need to take a step back, I get outside, breathe fresh air, and hike. And, of course, sleep.

Each person will have different ways to recharge at different times in their life, and what works for you today may be different ten years from now. Be thoughtful and intentional when you consider your own needs and how they evolve, because running a campaign and then holding office will take months and years of sustained energy. And you won't be able to do it if you never give yourself a break.

Find Something That You Love

Maintaining energy requires looking inward, but I hope something on the campaign trail also energizes our candidates—otherwise it is really hard to run. For me, nothing is better than a canvass kickoff. A canvass is when volunteers get together to knock on doors for a candidate or cause in a specific community, and I love to fire up the team. Put me in a packed field office or a volunteer's garage, talking to excited volunteers picking up their lists of voters for door knocking and devoting their weekends to getting out the vote, and I feel like I could go forever.

I also am the odd leader who likes to raise money. I like the challenge of it. You get to start with a person you don't know and then try to persuade the person to make an investment in you, your candidate, your organization, what have you. When you get that yes, it feels like the world has just given you a trophy. And when you get a no, you just have to decide to try again. Sometimes I compare it to fly-fishing. Now, I am not an avid fly-fisherwoman, but I know enough to say it is all about the right cast. You keep casting the line over and over again until, in a beautiful moment, the fish bites. I do a lot of fly-fishing fundraising, making many calls and having many conversations with the same person before they say yes. I don't mind. I get to know the person along the way, and then it's a real accomplishment to finally get the yes. I love it.

For some candidates, it's all about door knocking, engaging with voters face-to-face. Many of our women thrive under pressure, so winning a debate fuels their fire. And for others, they get their energy from seeing their kids at the end of a tough day. Some women, like Abigail Spanberger, just need to know that Election Day is coming. She told journalist and author Caitlin Moscatello that her response to people who asked her about self-care was, "I'm running for Congress. I'll take a nap in November. Do you want me to win this or do you want me to go to yoga?"[8] Whatever it is for you, identify it and find more ways to treat yourself to those energy boosters.

While my EMILY's List team deals directly with everyday campaign tasks, my role is more often as a coach and cheerleader for our candidates as well as my staff. What I repeatedly remind them is to try to enjoy it. It may sound hokey, but this country is full of the coolest, most interesting people, and you meet the most amazing individuals on the campaign trail. If you are open, you will be educated, inspired, and awestruck every day by their resiliency. You meet the parents, the workers, the nurses, and the teachers. You learn about things going on in your community. If you go in with curiosity, win or lose, you come out a different person, a better person, with a better understanding of your community and the people who make it. Take it in. You'll get the best stories to share with others.

WILLINGNESS TO LEARN AND ASK FOR HELP

Every candidate has to run a first race. That means they have to learn how to do an entire new job, from fundraising to giving speeches to doing press interviews. They have to figure out what kind of staff they need and how to set up an organization from the ground up. They all have to learn the rules governing campaign finance and disclosure.

No matter how many races a candidate has run, while the fundamentals stay the same, there is always more to learn. The rules change for different offices, sometimes district lines shift, even the unwritten rules and technologies change. When you're doing big things, you need to know what you know and what you don't know. You need to build your skills every day. And you need to ask for help, all the time.

To put it more simply:

Step one: Admit what you don't know.
Step two: Ask for help.
Step three: Learn and then practice.

Simple, right? From our jobs to our hobbies to the most basic things in our life, someone had to show us or teach us what to do first. You may be a pro in the spin studio now, but think back to when you were little, just wanting to learn how to ride a bike.

I begged my dad to teach me to ride a bike, particularly after my Big Wheel finally wore out (Gen Xers will know what I am talking about). He talked to me about the basics, including balance, and then he ran behind me as I wobbled on my first ride. It was exhilarating. First through the streets of my neighborhood, then over dirt trails. I was a bit of a "tomboy," as they called it back then, so I had to prove I could take the jump like all the boys. I practiced and practiced.

The truth is, it's never too late to learn something new, even well into adulthood. And if you haven't done something in a while and you're a little rusty, you can still refresh your skills. But the first two steps are always the same: Admit you need to learn something and ask for help.

Why would you know how to make a fundraising call? Or how to walk up to a voter and ask for their vote? If you don't give speeches every day, why would you be any good at it the first time? Get over yourself and your fear of showing there are things you can't do—yet. No one is born knowing how to do these things. The good news is—and trust me on this—you can learn. It starts by pushing away the toxic assumptions that other people know more than you do, that you should already know what you're doing, or that asking for help shows weakness. Because you can learn everything you need to know if you're just willing to ask and do the work.

Every job I've ever had, I've had to ask for help and learn new things. And I'm grateful for every one of those opportunities. My goodness, how boring life would be if we didn't get those chances to learn.

In 1997, I took a job as the finance director for the South Carolina Democratic Party, despite the fact that I'd never lived further south than DC, having spent most of my young life in Montana and Minnesota. At that time, South Carolina had a number of prominent Democrats in office, including former Senate Commerce Committee Chairman Fritz Hollings, who was up for reelection.

Anyone in politics will tell you that each state's political environment dances to its own tune. There are always adjustments to make when jumping from one state to another. In my first weeks, I felt completely out of my depth, so I started seeking out advice as soon as I got to South Carolina. Admittedly, there was some advice I didn't take, like one very kind gentleman's suggestion that I would raise more money for the party if I wore more skirts. I decided I liked wearing pants too much and ignored that particular pearl of wisdom.

I realized quickly that South Carolina was far more diverse than anywhere I'd been before to that point. And it wasn't just politics. I will always be grateful for the time State House Minority Leader Gilda Cobb-Hunter spent educating me, helping me better understand what was happening with race in South Carolina and, by extension, America. When I started working with her, I didn't know what I didn't know. She and the Reverend Joe Neal, a state representative and pastor, were gracious to begin my education—which still continues today. They took me to my first Black church experience, where I found the kindness and sense of family overwhelming. They showed me the great income disparities in the state and how those disparities were too often drawn along lines of race. I had my first experience with Southern poverty and communities that had access to almost nothing. Democratic leaders like Representative Cobb-Hunter and Reverend Neal were working full-time to get better schools and jobs for all communities across the state, made up of families that deserved better opportunities. I learned by recognizing my own ignorance on certain issues and asking thoughtful questions with the aim of understanding and connecting. It's a lesson I've carried through my career and a skill I continue to foster and value in myself, my colleagues, and our EMILY's List candidates.

The first big jump in my career came in 2007 when then-Senator-elect Jon Tester made me his chief of staff. I had a huge learning curve. I had never worked on Capitol Hill in any capacity and suddenly I was responsible for setting up an organization of over forty people spread across nine offices, all with very different functions than a campaign. I knew I had some of the skill set and a good relationship with the senator, but without the willingness of Montana's then-senior Senator Max Baucus's staff, particularly his chief of staff, Jim Messina, I would have been all sorts of lost.

Messina, who later ran President Obama's reelection campaign and served as White House deputy chief of staff, gave me valuable insight and helped me understand everything from how the Senate worked to how the senators worked with the Montana government. I now know so much more about the state I love, its elected officials, and its place in the United States government than I could have ever imagined. The most valuable lesson I learned was how to lean on people around me, including the incredible staff that we hired, to get the job done.

There isn't a group of nicer people than Senate chiefs—from both sides of the aisle—and in my experience, they will always take time to help each other with the day-to-day job. You may fight on policy, but when it comes to making the place work, everyone is willing to help when asked.

My second gigantic jump was when I started in my current job as president of EMILY's List. I knew that I needed media training immediately, so I reached out to some experts, including Christina Reynolds, who joined the team at EMILY's List eight years later and is helping me with this book. I have been in my current role for over ten years and I still bring in a coach for major speeches and ask my staff to practice with me before TV interviews. I am always training—trying new things and working to be better. It's okay not to know everything—I am living proof you can learn on the job.

Even When You Think You Know, You May Not Know—Be Open to Change

EMILY's List is a really good place to learn, because we have access to great teachers and innovators. The need for that teaching and innovating became immediately clear after Donald Trump's election, when EMILY's List saw an explosion in the number of women who wanted to run for office. All of these women needed to learn how to run and win a campaign, and it was our job to teach them how to do it. We had been training women to run for office for years, but we knew we were about to scale up in a serious way.

We started with the 2017 Women's March, offering a training the day after for all of the women looking to take their activism to the next level. Like the march itself, the number of women at the training shocked all of us. The room was filled with hundreds of inspired and inspiring women, and there were just as many on a waiting list to get in. It was, for lack of a better word, awesome, and perhaps the balm for the soul we'd sorely needed since Election Night 2016.

If that training hadn't been a strong enough indication, our inbox was the next sign that women everywhere were waking up.

In the entirety of the 2016 cycle, from the day after the 2014 election up until Election Day 2016, 920 women reached out to us about running for office. That number was far above previous years, and we called it the "Hillary bump." Various members of the staff (including me) were excited about the increased engagement but worriedly assumed that it would be temporary—an outlier that would return to normal once Hillary Clinton was in the White House.

Then, in the dark days after she lost the election, we worried that women would not want to ever run for office again. The sexism, the chants of "Lock her up," the feeling that she could never get a fair shot, just felt so impossible to overcome. I was deeply worried.

I was also deeply wrong.

In the days after the election, prospective candidates kept reaching out, saying they had signed up on the website. Which was a bit confusing, as our campaigns department didn't even know there was a way to sign up on the website. After some looking, we discovered an old link, not readily accessible from the main page, that hundreds of frustrated women had searched for until they found a way to do something. This was one of those moments when you have to open your mind to something new. It was time to get ready for change.

In the first month after the election, more than 1,000 women (more than the entire cycle before) signed up, saying they wanted to run for office. By the inauguration on January 20, that number had more than doubled to 2,442. By the end of January, more than 4,000 women had signed up. By Election Day 2018, an almost unimaginable 42,000 had reached out to EMILY's List. That number has grown well past 55,000 as of this writing.

That kind of growth takes some serious maneuvering. So our organization began to innovate. We didn't have a playbook for this, so we had to adjust and really start thinking outside the box. EMILY's List created a department to manage training and community engagement, and we blew out our training schedule, expanding our Intro to Running for Office course, or Campaigns 101, if you will, all across the country. Those trainings included future members of Congress like Lauren Underwood of Illinois and Lucy McBath of Georgia.

One woman we trained in these early days was Chrissy Houlahan, a Pennsylvania Air Force vet and business leader. Chrissy is the mom of an LGBTQ daughter. She turned to EMILY's List because she worried about what Trump's election would mean for her community and her daughter's rights and wanted her family to be represented fairly. Chrissy knew she needed help in taking the next step, so she asked for it. She replied to a $3 EMILY's List fundraising email, attaching her résumé and asking if we thought she could run for local office. A member of our team received her email and forwarded it to our campaigns team. We took one look at her experience and where she lived and knew she should run for Congress. Our team jumped in to do what they do with women candidates every day: They worked to get Chrissy started on her campaign and coached her all the way to the House seat she now holds.

There were so many future candidates stepping forward, all acknowledging they didn't know how to run for office but wanting to learn. We gave them the basics, the same lessons you're reading now, and supported them along the way. Many of those women have already run, and even more of them are planning to run soon.

That's why we created the Run to Win program, our effort to make sure that these thousands of women have the tools they need when they are ready. Our staff leads webinars and Facebook Live sessions on key campaign topics where they answer questions from women who—you guessed it—want to learn more. We also invite those women to join a private Facebook group that might just be the happiest place on the Internet. Beyond the support systems created in the group, it is also a place for new candidates to ask questions and others to share tips from the campaign trail. We started this broader outreach in the wake of 2016. It continues to grow and expand so that the next generation of leaders can learn, ask questions, and get the support they need.

The thousands of women who went through initial trainings

during the 2018 cycle and joined our Run to Win program will not all run for office right away. But they represent a pipeline of women leaders for years to come, all because they had the courage to raise their hand and ask the first question.

Candidates don't need to know exactly what they don't know. They don't need to have all the answers. They don't even need to have all the right questions. They just need to understand that they still have more to learn and, more important, that there are experts and specialists like EMILY's List out there, ready to help. Be willing to listen and ask questions. And remember that like me, you don't have to accept all the advice you receive, but you should at least listen openly to those who have been working in this world a long time.

I didn't know how much I'd learn in that South Carolina job, but I was open to advice from well-intentioned people who knew more than me. I didn't know how to be a chief of staff, but I asked a million questions. And I surely wasn't 100 percent ready to be the president of EMILY's List, but I knew my abilities, and I knew how to ask for help.

When the world turned upside down, I was willing to open my mind to a new way of doing business. I brought in good people to help innovate new programs, and we changed how EMILY's List did business. Every step of the way, I have learned new methods to work and succeed because I have been willing to ask, listen, and be open-minded around change. I have also had an army of people willing to help—and so do you.

None of us can be leaders completely on our own. No matter what you're trying to do, we all need guidance, coaching, and support from trusted friends and colleagues. They make us better. So it's on each of us to find the people who can make us better and ask them for help. Think through the people who are most knowledgeable about the issues that matter to you, the people who are most trusted in the communities you care about, or the leaders you'd want to emulate. Find as many ways as you can to learn from them. Ask them thoughtful questions. Follow their work and listen when they offer opinions. Be brave enough to ask for the help you need.

THE TOPLINES

In campaigns, we work with a lot of opinion research as just one tool to understand what voters are thinking. Polls in particular are full of all sorts of data, so pollsters pull out the most important points, called the toplines. I thought I'd do the same for you at the end of each chapter. Think of it as a handy reference tool to give you the key points when you need a quick refresher.

And a reminder: Every time I write about a candidate, I could be talking about you and the leap you want to take in your job, in your community, in your activism. Whatever move you want to make, these steps are here for you—just as they've been here for me. I hope you give them a try as you go about your business, taking the leap and changing the world.

So, with that said, here are your toplines for our first step, making the decision to stand up and lead.

■ Nobody's got a secret playbook for how to change the world, because there is no secret playbook.

■ The ingredients for a successful woman leader are clear.

  ✦ Integrity, or doing what's right regardless of the cost.

  ✦ Passion, for an issue or a movement.

  ✦ Commitment, to a cause, to public service, to something that matters.

  ✦ Energy, both physical and mental.

  ✦ Liking people, or at least wanting to help them.

  ✦ A willingness to learn and ask for help. You don't need to know everything. You just need to be willing to learn.

  ✦ The ability to be open-minded when the world changes around you—that is when the best innovation can happen.

■ Add up these ingredients and your own hard work and you've got this!

CHAPTER 2

Ask Yourself the Right Questions.
Be Honest About the Answers.

ONCE A CANDIDATE has decided she's ready to run, the hard work begins. I have to warn you: This is when things get real, because it requires you to be honest about what you want and what you're willing to do. Any woman can make herself a good candidate, but as we discussed a little bit in the last chapter, if you're going to put yourself forward as a leader, you have to figure out if this is the right time, if you have the right motivation, and if you're in the right situation to get the job done well.

Every day, women reach out to EMILY's List wanting to run. Some join us in trainings, some come in through our Run to Win website, some simply give us a call. And while we support every woman who stands up to make her community better, we encourage all of them to ask the tough questions first. I'd like to share these questions with you, because figuring out the answers is vital for all of us, no matter how we want to change the world.

WHAT MOTIVATES ME?

We've already discussed the fact that you'll need to have a passion and commitment for making some kind of change. So you've likely already figured out the key issues that motivate you. But motivation is about more than just political or social issues. It's about what wakes you up every day, what gets you going, and what gives you energy. It's about your values and how you want to live your life.

Over the years, we've seen some women motivated by outside forces and events, as well as women driven by issues that impact them or their families. Let's take a look at a few examples.

External Motivation

Sometimes there's a pivotal moment, a movement of people, or a shift in our society that drives us to act. We've definitely seen that a few times during the history of EMILY's List.

In 1991, President George H. W. Bush nominated Clarence Thomas to be a Supreme Court justice. Thomas was a right-wing conservative who drew fire from Democrats and allied groups for a number of reasons. There were concerns about his views on reproductive freedom and his stance against affirmative action. Despite those objections, Thomas appeared to be sailing toward confirmation. Then news began to spread that at least one former coworker had been sexually harassed by Thomas. And though a Democrat-led Judiciary Committee knew of Anita Hill's allegations that Thomas had sexually harassed her, the committee had not called her as a witness. And so women took action.

Backed by key feminist groups, Representatives Barbara Boxer, Barbara Kennelly, Nita Lowey, Patsy Mink, Pat Schroeder, Louise Slaughter, and Jolene Unsoeld, and Delegate Eleanor Holmes Norton, literally marched across Capitol Hill to the Senate and demanded they delay a confirmation vote until Hill's claims could be investigated.[1]

Following those women's actions, Anita Hill was called to testify before the Judiciary Committee. But during her testimony, the all-male Senate panel degraded and belittled her and dismissed her accusations. It was so frustrating to watch them treat this brave young woman with such contempt. For many women across America, this was a galvanizing moment, their anger driving them to the campaign trail as candidates. In 1992, women candidates shattered many records. Eleven women were nominated by major parties for Senate races and 106 women for the House.[2]

The results were also record-breaking. Four new EMILY's List–endorsed Democratic women were elected in the Senate, including Washington Senator Patty Murray and California Senator Dianne Feinstein, who still serve; Senator Barbara Boxer, one of the courageous women who marched across the Hill to demand change; and Senator Carol Moseley Braun from Illinois, the first African American woman elected to the Senate.[3] EMILY's List also helped elect twenty new pro-choice

Democratic women to the House that year, the most ever in a single election at that time.

Women voters were enraged and mobilized, too. I myself had watched the Anita Hill hearings and felt the same anger and frustration at the way a panel of old white men had treated a brave and accomplished woman of color who was raising an important issue. To be honest, I had never heard anyone verbalize what sexual harassment was, and I was stunned by her testimony. Not being in the workplace yet, just heading to college, I hardly knew how to digest what I was hearing. It was gross and shocking, what Thomas had done to Hill.

I was just as disgusted to watch what those senators did to Hill in order to dismiss her. I was one of millions of American women who were asking the same question: Where were the women on the committee? Senator Barbara Mikulski, who was one of only two women in the Senate at the time, and the only Democratic woman, noted that the lack of support from the men on the committee sent a troubling message to any survivors and whistle-blowers. In 1991, Mikulski said, "To anybody out there who wants to be a whistle-blower, the message is: Don't blow that whistle because you'll be left out there by yourself. . . . To any victim of sexual harassment or sexual abuse or sexual violence, either in the street or even in her own home, the message is nobody is going to take you seriously, not even the United States Senate."[4]

The 1992 election was the first one in which I was old enough to vote. I looked toward my eighteenth birthday like most teens looked toward their sixteenth and getting their driver's licenses. But even as someone who followed politics, I wasn't fully plugged into how many women were running and didn't understand the seismic shift of those women's victories. Let's face it: I was in college and I did not have CNN on in my dorm room, though maybe it wouldn't surprise you if I had, knowing what you know about me now. There was no real access to the Internet yet and no social media, so even though it was a huge deal, I didn't know how many women were running across the country. Most people didn't know.

That external motivation, sparked by the Clarence Thomas nomination, was powerful in 1992 even without social media. And of course, EMILY's List was there to help lead the way.

As I've worked with women in politics, I've often wondered how different that year could have been in an era of social media, a network that, despite its dangers and shortcomings, allows us to connect and harness the power and fury of women around the country.

Today, we are living in a supercharged environment, and now we are finding out what determined women are capable of with the connective tissue of social media.

Since 2016, we've seen movements driven by inspiring women and in spite of despicable men. During the 2014 cycle, a few of the women we tried to recruit told us they were waiting to "run with Hillary" (and some of them did just that the following cycle). As the first woman nominee of a major party, Hillary Clinton was no doubt an inspiring figure for many of the women who ran during the 2016 cycle. At EMILY's List, we were thrilled as hundreds of women reached out to run at that time.

These are examples of powerful external motivations driving change. Over the decades, those external forces have been wars, economic downturns, and civil rights battles. But it seems abundantly clear that for women, nothing has been as motivating as the current direction of our nation since the 2016 election.

We were shocked when those fifty-five-thousand-plus women came knocking on our door after Trump won, looking for help in running for office. Many of those women were worried about what Trump would do in office and knew that they couldn't sit on the sidelines and hope someone else would take care of things. They also watched as an unfit and unqualified blowhard managed to beat one of the most qualified candidates ever to run. If anything will make you realize that you are qualified to run for [insert office here], it's the fact of President Donald Trump.

We have seen incompetence and corruption from the White House, a dangerous rise in hate crimes and hate speech, more frequent gun violence, and a staggering number of mass shootings. We have watched as children have been separated from their families and held in cages, refugees have been denied entrance, immigrants have been demonized, and the response to a global pandemic has been botched and bungled. We have seen protests and demands for action after the murder of too many Black Americans at the hands of police and watched in horror as Trump made and applauded racist statements. Women today are inspired by each other's bravery, made evident by the #MeToo movement. We watched as powerful men who abused, assaulted, and harassed women were being called out and even, at times, held accountable. Women stood up and demanded their voices be heard and believed, and they stood up to amplify the voices of others. We saw firsthand how badly our systems needed to be fixed, and we saw how loud and undeniable a chorus of women could be, speaking together, demanding change.

These things came together to create a second so-called Year of the Woman in 2018. It was a year in which women were inspired, externally motivated, and, in the end, elected. And yet, I have to admit, I share Barbara Mikulski's views on the notion of a single *year* for women. As she put it in her trademark feisty style, "Calling 1992 the Year of the Woman makes it sound like the Year of the Caribou or the Year of the Asparagus. We're not a fad, a fancy, or a year."[5] I'm with Barbara. As we like to say at EMILY's List, that wasn't a pink wave. It was a sea change. After all of the successes in 2018—with the most women in Congress ever, the most diverse Congress ever, the first state legislature that was more than half women, the reelection of Nancy Pelosi as Speaker, and on and on and on—all of that was a start, not an ending. Women have stood up and demanded the power and leadership we deserve. And though we won't win all the races—and sadly, we still haven't cracked that highest glass ceiling, the presidency—we are never going to be made to sit down again.

Internal Motivation: Is There a Specific Problem I Want to Solve?

This is a question many candidates have asked themselves over the years, and without a clear answer, they typically don't run. The question admittedly got easier to answer in the period after Trump's election, as so many of the challenges we face have become worse and more urgent, and others still have become more obvious. Women may get initially motivated by external forces, but it's the deep-seated desire to change something specific that gives candidates the energy to run a competitive campaign.

I likely don't need to explain to you why health care has mattered so much in recent elections. Women feel the urgency of this issue acutely. Beyond our frequent role as caregivers, women have specific health concerns that are too often ignored or downright misunderstood by the men in office. Women's reproductive health is a critical issue that motivates women voters and candidates alike. And yet, before Obamacare, pregnancy was a preexisting condition that could cost you more or result in a denial of coverage. And in the years since, Donald Trump has used the judicial system and even a global pandemic to roll back women's rights and their reproductive freedom. In a nation where we already have a terrible record on maternal deaths, particularly among African American women and Native American women, we can't afford to go backward.

We've each got our own personal health care story.

I told you earlier about Lauren Underwood's health care experience. Lauren cared so much about quality health care for people like her, she worked in the Obama administration helping to implement the Affordable Care Act. So after 2016, when Lauren's local Republican congressman promised at a town hall that he was "committed to voting no" on any plan that denied coverage to anyone with preexisting conditions, she was grateful. But when he later broke his promise and voted for a bill that would jeopardize the care of people with preexisting conditions, Lauren decided she would go after his seat. EMILY's List was proud to support Lauren as she flipped a very Republican seat in Illinois and became the youngest African American woman to serve in Congress.

Lauren is only one of the many women who ran in 2018 because she was motivated to protect health care. From Washington Congresswoman Kim Schrier, a pediatrician and a diabetic who knew the importance of health care policy, to Michigan Congresswoman Elissa Slotkin, whose mother died too young of a cancer that went undiagnosed because she had no health insurance, women all over the country found their internal motivation in the urgent issues of their own health and that of their loved ones.

My first driving internal motivation was the deep desire to get rid of nuclear weapons—when I was about ten years old. This is, perhaps, a heavy calling for a child, but I grew up during the Cold War era in Montana, which was (and still is) one of the major launch sites for nuclear Minuteman missiles.[6] I remember doing nuclear bomb drills in elementary school.

Thinking on it now, I'm not sure hiding under our desks would have protected us in case of a real nuclear emergency, but those drills are a vivid memory.

One day when I was at church with my grandma, they handed out a book called *The Hundredth Monkey*, which is based on the idea that at a tipping point we can make the societal change needed to stop nuclear proliferation. I was overcome by the possibility of doing something that would, well, change the world. Something that could make it better and safer. I may not have succeeded in ridding the world of nuclear weapons (yet!), but I believe with the right leadership in the world, we one day will.

That copy of *The Hundredth Monkey* is still on my bookshelf. It has been well read.

Other things have driven me over the years, and many different drivers will motivate you, too. I am motivated by a deep belief that if our world has equal governing representation by women and men, we will change everything for the better. This core belief drives me on the hardest days.

If you're going to take on a serious challenge like running for office, you must have a powerful motivation. "Because it's the next step" or "Because it seems like a cool title" will not sustain you through long days and late nights and political attacks in the same way that "Because I want to protect my children from gun violence" or "Because I want to make sure my mother has health insurance" will. Your best work comes from efforts that require your head and your heart to work together.

WHAT DO I HAVE TO OFFER?

Too often, we paint in our minds a picture of what makes someone perfect for a job. For elected officials, we envision a lawyer or someone who majored in political science at a top college as the natural candidate. For too long, and in too many industries, we've pictured a white man as the natural candidate. That's a problem EMILY's List is working to fix. The reality is, you don't have to be a lawyer to make the laws. And you don't have to have studied political science to be an effective politician. As we've seen time and again, women of all backgrounds have something fantastic to offer. Let me give you a few examples of the diverse backgrounds of four women whom EMILY's List helped to elect in 2018.

Iowa Representative Abby Finkenauer was one of the first two women ever elected to the House in her twenties. The daughter of a pipe fitter/welder who belonged to a union for forty years, Abby was elected to the Iowa state legislature at the age of twenty-five as a champion for workers and Iowa's working families, a responsibility she later took to the US House as one of the first two women elected to the House from her state.

Connecticut Representative Jahana Hayes was a teenage mother who worked to further her education, starting with community college, then went on to get her bachelor's, then her master's, then advanced degrees. Before becoming the first African American woman ever elected to Congress from

Connecticut, she was an educator for fifteen years and was named National Teacher of the Year in 2016.

After losing her son to gun violence, Lucy McBath changed careers to work full-time for advocacy groups on gun violence prevention. Before that, she was a flight attendant and the daughter of civil rights activists. She is also a two-time breast cancer survivor and a proud rider of Harley-Davidsons.

Abigail Spanberger grew up in Virginia's Seventh Congressional District, earned an MBA, and is a mom of three. She's also a former CIA officer who gathered intelligence around the world to keep us all safe for nearly a decade before running.

Abby, Jahana, Lucy, and Abigail all bring very different and valuable understandings to Congress, from the work that they've done to their lived experiences. It is perhaps the best part of our democracy, because where else can four people who are so different succeed in the same job and sit at the same table? From a mother who has suffered the hardest loss any parent can endure, to a young woman who has served her community from an early age, to an award-winning teacher, to a CIA officer, they have very little in common. They grew up in different parts of the country, in different kinds of families, and they've built completely unique lives for themselves. The inclusion of their voices will change every debate they participate in. It's a lesson for the entire country that their differences make them a stronger team and not a weaker one.

It reminds me of a story Senator Jon Tester once told me when I was serving as his chief of staff. Jon is a third-generation

Montana dirt farmer whose family went without health insurance some years and in the worst of times had hardly any income to speak of. He arrived in Washington missing three fingers (via a meat-grinder accident from childhood) and sporting his characteristic flattop haircut. Shortly after getting to the United States Senate, Jon was at a meeting with then-Senator Jay Rockefeller, a scion of one of the country's wealthiest families. Together they marveled at this great country that allowed a dirt farmer and, well, a Rockefeller to stand together as senators, joining in a mission to serve the people.

Their shared job gave them a lot in common, but those two men represented huge economic and experiential differences. Both brought important, unique perspectives to every issue they debated. I still feel this way every time I look at the class of women we elected in 2018. Just knowing that for the first time, Native American women have someone speaking from experience on their issues in Congress is powerful. Knowing that they are working with, among others, a former cabinet official and university president, a single mom, veterans, and so many more—that's what a truly representative Congress should be as it handles issues for all of us. I know firsthand how much better we are for those differences.

Of course, there are similarities that our women candidates share that are vitally important. These are passionate women with strong values, including the idea that everyone in this country has the right to health and happiness. While they may sometimes differ on what they see as the best path to achieving these goals, I know that each of these women is working to ensure her community is healthy and safe, and that the inalienable rights of her constituents are protected. They all bring a commitment to and understanding of what the families in their districts need to survive and thrive.

The lesson here is that we all have something important to offer. Whether it's experience from your career, or an understanding of an issue, or familiarity with a district, or a formative life experience, you have something to add to the debate. And there are people like you who need a representative at the table. You have a story to tell and something only you can contribute. Figure out what that is and where it can be most useful.

You don't think you fit the mold for that office or job or project that interests you? Great. Break the mold. If they've never seen someone like you, my goodness, it's a sure sign they need you. If they aren't including people like you in the conversation, then how can they speak for people like you or value your perspective?

You may have heard of a statistic that says men will apply for a job if they meet only 60 percent of the qualifications required in a job description, while women will only apply if they meet 100 percent of them.[7] Here's the thing. Short of age or residency qualifications, there's only one hard-and-fast qualification for running for office: wanting to change things for the better for the people around you. If you've made it this far, we know you've got that, and, as you now know, you can learn everything else.

Do not doubt that you have plenty to offer your community. The real question is where and in what role you can best make the difference you want to make.

AM I READY?

This is one of the toughest questions you'll face, in part because there are real considerations to account for that are outside of your control. While my team and I help women manage all sorts of challenges, only you can answer how big and unwieldy your particular situation is. You have to be prepared to be fully honest with yourself.

Of course, even if you *are* ready, you might not *feel* fully ready to do a big thing—whether that's running for office, taking a big risk, or helping fix things in your community. There's always going to be something standing in the way. Here are just a few of the reasons we've heard why women can't run right now.

A family member is sick.

A kid is just starting school, entering their last year of school, or facing issues in school that require more time from you.

You're getting married or getting divorced.

You lost a partner, a parent, or a child and are working through your grief.

You're starting a new job or up for a new promotion.

You're a business owner who employs people who would be impacted by a change in your work.

You're facing an illness or living with a disability that could make campaigning harder.

You don't know if you can financially afford running or winning.

These, and other personal issues like them, have a real impact on your life and, yes, on your ability to run a good campaign. And the hard truth is that only you can decide whether it's the right time in your life for a big move. Some of us want to work through troubled times; some of us need time to regroup. Sometimes you can lean on your support system or look for ways to better juggle, while other times you know that the issue you're facing simply won't allow enough time to do the work or that your body just isn't physically up for it.

It may surprise you, but I'm not going to tell you that the answer should always be yes. Sometimes there's just no way around the challenge you face. At EMILY's List, we've helped candidates sort through these questions and we know that sometimes the obstacles are just too big. We've worked with great candidates who needed to wait a cycle or two and others who decided to find another way to serve. Not running is a valid answer and can be a brave one.

On the flip side, for many women, the things that make their lives complicated are their exact reasons and motivations for running. In those cases, what they need is logistical help and maybe a bit of encouragement. And we've got lots of that. Because if you are waiting to run until you have checked off every item on the to-do list, solved all of the problems, and gotten enough sleep, you will be waiting a long time. (If you are a magical woman who has accomplished all these things, please call me and tell me all your secrets.)

I've done a lot of recruiting in my years in politics, particularly during my time at EMILY's List. The conversations with women often go a certain way. First, those women ask the same types of questions I do when I'm faced with a big task. How can I get this done? The questions are all about tactics and campaign logistics.

Can I win? (Good question, but we'll work with you to figure that out.)

How do I raise the money? (We can teach you!)

How do I put together the staff? (We've got a résumé bank and some help on questions you can ask, where to look, and so on.)

Should I hire this kind of consultant first? Where do I need to put my resources? Etc. Etc. Etc. (We can work with you. Everything is teachable . . . please see chapter 1.)

This is the doable part. Logistics are our specialty, and we've got all the answers you need. So my team and I know how to answer those questions pretty easily. That lets us dive into what's really holding the candidate back. It's what I call peeling the onion of recruitment—it's where we get to the sticky questions that can really drive a decision.

Sometimes it's a political question. Is this the best race at the right moment? I have asked so many women to run for office, and I always tell them, they can tell me "Not now" but not "Not ever." I've had that conversation with many of the women we've tried to recruit over the years. One of them was the great Stacey Abrams. After she faced significant voter suppression while narrowly losing the governor's race in 2018, we hoped Stacey would consider running for Senate in Georgia in 2020. Instead, in typical Stacey fashion, she decided it was more important for her to work for voters everywhere. She set up a new organization called Fair Fight that is fighting to protect voters' rights across the country. I have no doubt her name will be on a ballot again someday, but she knew that she had a more urgent battle to wage right now.

Sometimes those questions are about personal concerns. "Can I pay my mortgage and pay for child care if I take this challenge on?" "Will I be able to be around for the big events in my kids' lives, or the small ones?" "Can I continue to care for my neighbors or family members who need my help?" "Is my spouse or partner ready for this?" Those are real, serious questions that no one else can answer for you. We can talk it through and offer advice, but sometimes the answer is that a candidate can't do this right now, because it's not right for their family. That's real life, and we respect it.

One of the toughest questions we get is how to stay afloat financially while running a campaign. "Can I afford to do this?" It's a very real concern, since campaigning for some offices can be a full-time endeavor that doesn't fit in easily with many day jobs. The even tougher part is that for a state or local job, many of those offices pay little or even no money. And for state legislative offices, as with Congress, you may be needed in a city far away from home for months at a time. If you live in El Paso, Texas, it may take you just as long to drive to the state capital as it does to travel by plane to the nation's capital.

Plenty of campaign experts will tell you that you need to quit your job as soon as you start running, arguing that you'll need all of your time for the campaign and that you don't want to risk having any conflicts of interest or having to do anything that might run counter to your campaign. At EMILY's List, we try to recognize that that's not always possible. Most of us simply can't afford to have no income. And considering many state and local offices are only part-time, most elected officials can't quit their jobs even if they win the campaign. Frankly, we need more elected officials who actually live like most Americans, having to balance a personal budget, in office. But it can make the commitment all the more daunting.

For too long, government was only for the wealthiest Americans—in fact, owning land was once a prerequisite for voting.[8] That's not a good way to govern a diverse nation. A democracy only works when it includes the voices of all of the people it represents, including those who are living paycheck to paycheck. That's why we try to work with candidates to find a variety of options to keep the family budget intact while running an effective campaign.

I want to drill down on what I believe is one of the biggest challenges facing potential candidates. In so many fields, from law to business, academia, medicine, science, and so on, if we want to attract and keep good people, we must pay them. Yet in many state governments that decide so many important issues, we pay elected officials next to nothing. And for candidates who are running a campaign, we expect them to go without a paycheck for up to two years. When you think about people who are able to do that financially, you have to wonder if they have the most informed perspective for deciding issues like raising the minimum wage, taxes, or health care. This inequity weighs on me as the leader of an organization that asks women to make this sacrifice. I hope that the smart women who read this book will join me in thinking about how best to solve this problem—how to ensure that candidates can take a salary from their campaign (currently an option for federal candidates but not all state or local candidates).

One example is North Carolina State Representative Sydney Batch. Sydney is a child welfare advocate, social worker, and family lawyer who practices in a small law firm with her husband. While she had been recruited to run for judge in the past, she knew that the best way to address all of the issues she had dealt with in the child welfare system was to run for the North Carolina General Assembly. Sydney is a mom of two, so she thought very carefully about how best to manage her family and financial responsibilities before she decided to run for the state house of representatives.

Over the years, we've seen more working moms of school-age kids running for office. As we did with Sydney in those early days, we talk through how each candidate is going to balance work and family life with the campaign, rather than how they can just erase part of them. We know that's not possible. Each campaign is different, so my team works with candidates like Sydney to build the strategies that work for them. We take into account their specific family needs and then organize around them. If it's important to make bedtimes or soccer games or court cases, then we build the schedule around their top priorities. There will be plenty of tough decisions, and some sacrifices to make, but there are no hard-and-fast rules for work-life balance during a campaign.

Sydney's run got more complicated throughout the campaign. In the summer of 2018, headed toward her first election, Sydney was diagnosed with breast cancer, which meant her treatments unexpectedly became the new top priority. While Sydney would often note that she was lucky to have a loving partner, supportive family, and good health care, cancer treatments aren't flexible. Whether or not to continue with the campaign while undergoing treatment was a decision that only Sydney could make. But we were happy to help her consider her options and build a new strategy that could work.

Sydney announced she was taking several weeks off the

campaign trail, so her whole team made a plan to ensure that the campaign kept going while she was having surgery and in recovery. Of course, Sydney being Sydney, she was already making phone calls a few days into her recovery. Considering her impressive determination and dedication, it was no surprise to us that she won her race, or that she has fought on behalf of all North Carolinians in the legislature ever since.

Yes, the life questions, the work questions, the financial questions, can be tough. As can questions around how to be a parent and be in office or how to maintain your old job while taking on this new one. But thankfully we have more and more role models each year balancing life with their candidacy, providing blueprints for future women trying to make it all work.

I see this nearly every day at EMILY's List. The women who first ran years ago are more than happy to offer advice to the ones going through it now. I've put candidates on the phone with moms in office to talk about how best to handle kids and Congress. We've asked women who went through certain challenges (a death in the family, an illness, financial hardships) to offer advice and guidance to candidates dealing with the same thing.

This is something we can all be doing. Your mentors and teachers are so important to your journey. Make sure you're seeking out people with a variety of experiences they can share with you. Find people whom you admire or who have traveled a path you want to travel and ask them how they did it. You have nothing to lose by asking.

Understanding that life is complicated, it's important to recognize when questions about your future are really just masking issues of confidence. When women ask the question "Is this the best time for me to run a campaign?" what they are actually wondering is, "Why would anyone vote for me?" or "What do I have to say that would be better than what we're hearing now?" Trust me when I say that if you are a motivated, passionate woman with a desire to change her community, your voice is important and needed.

Then we hear the comment that burns me up the most: "Surely, there's someone better than me out there." Often, that's coupled with a concern that running could cost the party or her community a great opportunity because she believes there must be someone better than her for the job or more likely than her to win.

Our own executive director, Emily Cain, has a story like this. In 2004, Emily was twenty-four years old, just finishing graduate school, and hoping to land a job in education policy in Maine. Emily reached out to her local state senator, a woman named Mary Cathcart, and asked if she could pass along her résumé, hoping for a job in the statehouse or state department of education. To Emily's surprise, Mary responded by asking her to run for the legislature. Emily replied with an email saying, "I'm sure you are talking to a lot of qualified people. Let me know how I can help them." Mary had a very specific idea for how Emily could help—by becoming the candidate and the great elected official she knew Emily would be. She told Emily, "I wasn't joking. Just say yes." Emily went on to serve five terms between the house and senate, including one term as the youngest woman ever to lead the minority party in Maine (and then she helped Democrats take the majority back!). She was qualified from day one, but she didn't know it. All she needed was a push.

I hear stories like this all the time, and the question I always ask is: Why? Why do you assume there's someone better? Different, yes. And sure, they may bring a different perspective that also matters. But they are not inherently better, nor is their perspective. In fact, with a federal government that's currently only one-quarter women, every woman has an even greater reason to run and to offer her perspective. We owe it to each other to ensure our voices are in the debate and that we've taken our place at the table.

IS THE RACE WINNABLE?

This can be one of the tougher questions to figure out, because as anyone can tell you, every cycle there are candidates who win the unwinnable district and conversely ones who lose the races that should have been easy victories. It's also a tough question because it's not just about you. There will always be variables outside of your control. The key is identifying as many potential issues as possible before you begin. Understanding the full picture is crucial to your success.

Here's what you need to know.

- **What's the partisanship of the district?** It's easier to win the general election in a place with more people who belong to your party than the other party. Even in 2018, when Democrats picked up forty-one seats, plenty of good candidates didn't win because some districts are just too Republican. That doesn't mean those candidates shouldn't have run, but the gravity of partisanship does still have a pretty strong hold.

- **What's the general political environment like?** This one may not be fully knowable until closer to the election, but you need to think through whether you'll be running into the wind or with it. For example, is this a change election (and if so, do you represent change or the status quo)? Is the economy in good shape or headed in the wrong direction? Do people like the leadership of the city, state, country, party? Is there a key issue driving the news? Is there a moment or a wave you can ride to victory? Representative Kendra Horn got elected to a very red congressional seat in Oklahoma by understanding the political moment in 2018 might matter more than the partisan breakdown of her district. Kendra watched as others in her community dealt with health care issues and massive cuts from Oklahoma's government, and as a teachers' strike, one of the results of those cuts, generated huge support from the voters, and knew that it was not going to be party politics as usual in her district. She was right.

- **Will this be a high-turnout election or low?** The answer will help determine what kind of field program you run and whether the votes are out there for you. It will also give you a sense of how big a campaign and how much advertising or mail you'll need, and how much you'll need to spend to get out your voters.

- **Are you running for an open seat?** This is still the best place to be running unless the partisanship is *really* out of whack. Why? Because the voters have to get to know everyone and aren't tied to someone who has been serving them for a while. I love open seats—and I really love electing women into those open seats.

- **Are you running against an incumbent from a different party?** These are the pickup opportunities that the parties care the most about. From city council all the way up to the presidency, when it's Democrat v. Republican, you have a pretty clear debate about values and the direction of the community.

- **Are you running against an incumbent in a primary?** This one can cut both ways—an incumbent might have cast a bad vote that the voters don't like or represent the status quo in a change electorate, but they have also run before, have likely brought home some accomplishments, and start with more name ID and both a voter and donor base that you likely don't have.

- **Are you bringing a community of voter support with you or will you need to build it?** The same question applies to your donor base: Are you starting with lots of donors or do you need to find them? The good news on this one is that the work continues to pay off. Every time you run, your previous run gives you a foundation, a springboard even, for your next run. Washington House member Pramila Jayapal had served as executive director for the largest immigration advocacy organization in Washington State, a great base of activist support.[9] Virginia Congresswoman Jennifer Wexton built on her successful campaigns for the Virginia state senate to jump-start her campaign, while Minnesota Congresswoman Angie Craig ran a close but losing campaign in 2016, so she had a good list of voters and volunteers that helped her win two years later.

- **How is the district changing?** While gerrymandering (the partisan drawing of a district to benefit one party over the other) has made many districts far more partisan than they should be, many over the last decade have seen changing demographics that are altering the partisanship and helping support your run. Texas is a great example of a place that is becoming more diverse, younger, and, thus, bluer. What kind of growth or shifts has your district seen and what does that mean for your likely voters?

- **How are you connected to the district?** Typically, the more connected you are to the district and the people who live there, the better. For some people, that means having grown up there. For others, it means building a life there or doing work that draws a bridge between you and the people there. Choosing to run for office in a place where you have a strong personal connection may seem like common sense, but it's important to consider.

■ **Does your opponent face any specific problems?** We've already talked about Illinois Representative Lauren Underwood, whose opponent broke a promise to protect people with preexisting medical conditions. We've faced opponents who had #MeToo problems or other ethical issues. These issues can become a major focus for voters and the press and therefore can have a major impact on elections.

■ **Will you have party support or be running against the establishment?** If you've watched the news in the last few years, you know that you *can* beat city hall, so to speak. But it's not easy, and the question of whether you'll have support, indifference, or opposition from the state or national party or key groups is something to consider. If you're running against the party or the current leadership, is that something you want to highlight, or will you want their support after you win the primary? If they're not with you, who will be and how will you get over the organizational disadvantage?

At EMILY's List, we've supported pro-choice Democratic women on every side of all of these questions. We've had many tough conversations with candidates about the challenges they'll face. We've also helped many women develop plans and skills to help tackle those challenges. We've moved from consistently having to fight the establishment to get women nominated, to working with the national and state party committees and others on recruitment and support for candidates. It's a great sign that women candidates are often the party favorites these days (at least on the Democratic side), but we're still willing to take on the establishment when necessary.

Danica Roem was a Virginia journalist, part-time member of a rock band, and stepmom who decided to run for office because of a burning passion to fix a problem plaguing every family in her district: traffic on Route 28. Living in Virginia, I know firsthand how bad that traffic is! But as a transgender woman, she would be breaking new ground by running for the Virginia legislature, never an easy thing to do. Danica's opponent tried to use the fact that Danica is a trans woman against her. Bob Marshall was a long-serving extremist legislator who proudly called himself Virginia's "chief homophobe."[10] As a proud member of the LGBTQ community, Danica represented exactly what Marshall had actively worked against for decades in Richmond. She knew the challenges, but she also knew she was talking about issues that actually mattered to the voters in her district. She knew she could build the organizational and financial support to be able to communicate about those issues.

I'm thrilled to tell you that Danica sent Marshall packing. She was one of eleven women to flip Republican seats in the 2017 Virginia election, and since being in office, she has helped expand Medicaid to give more Virginians health care, worked to increase teacher pay, and yes, taken steps to improve the traffic.

Wisconsin Representative Gwen Moore was another groundbreaker who identified the obstacles she faced in her campaign and built a plan to handle them. Earlier in her career, Gwen helped found a credit union to help low-income people looking to start small businesses secure loans. She took her problem solving and hard work to the Wisconsin legislature, serving two terms there, and then became the first African American woman elected to the Wisconsin state senate in 1993, serving until 2005.

Gwen already knew something about tough fights, but when she decided to run in a crowded primary for a retiring Democrat's US House seat in 2004, she was facing the former Wisconsin Democratic Party chair, backed by the establishment. She was also running in a district that, thanks to redistricting, included a larger population and a different demographic than the voters who'd elected her to the legislature. Gwen did not have a high-dollar network, which was understandable given her past work, but it caused others to doubt her ability to raise what she would need.

Gwen understood these challenges and addressed them head-on. As our founder, Ellen Malcolm, notes in her book *When Women Win,* with Gwen's tremendous skills and experience and some help from EMILY's List in training staff and raising money from our members, Gwen defeated the establishment pick in the primary with 64 percent of the vote and has been a hero for women and working families in Congress ever since. She was also replaced in the Wisconsin state senate by a woman—I love it when that happens!

When you are looking to run for office, or taking on a tough fight of any kind, you should know what you're up against. You need to know what lies ahead to be prepared, to feel confident in your plan, and to make a sound and comprehensive strategy. Sometimes you'll find that you're at the bottom of a pretty daunting climb. Sometimes you'll think a race is unwinnable. And you know what? Sometimes you may be right.

That doesn't always mean you shouldn't run. The truth is, every campaign matters. Even if you don't win, you'll likely engage in a debate or a discussion of issues that wouldn't have happened without you. You may have forced your opponent to take a better position on an issue that matters, or energized voters or volunteers to your cause. And every woman who runs—whether she wins or loses—helps more people see women as viable candidates and valuable parts of our political system. And that makes it better for every woman who runs in the future.

WILL I DO THE WORK NEEDED?

Yes, here I go again, talking about how hard this will be. But it's the most important question here: Are you willing—really willing—to work exactly as hard as you need to?

Depending on the race, you'll likely hire staff. And you will have volunteers, friends, and family to help. But running for office takes a lot of work that only the candidate can do. The hardest job in the campaign is that of candidate. And it's not just candidates who should internalize this. We all face real problems every day. If you want to make change, we need your smarts and your sweat, your head and your heart.

Are you willing to give it everything you've got?

THE TOPLINES

You've decided you're going to do something great. Now we get to the hard parts. First is asking yourself tough questions. Be real, be honest, be thoughtful, as you work through these questions:

- What motivates me?
- What do I have to offer?
- Am I ready?
- Is this fight winnable?
- Will I do the work required?

In the end, some of the answers may not be easy and the path may have more obstacles than you'd hoped, but answering these questions honestly gives you a clearer path to getting the job done.

CHAPTER 3

Break the Rules,
Break out of the Box

IF YOU WORK on enough campaigns, you learn the playbook by heart. You learn what separates successful candidates from unsuccessful candidates and what makes winning and losing campaigns different. You figure out which voters you need for a victory and how best to reach them.

And while there are differences from district to district, state to state, race to race, and election year to election year, there are certain campaign lessons that apply across the board. I believe strongly in those lessons. But I also want to make sure you understand that one of the most important parts of knowing the lessons and unwritten rules is figuring out when you can and should break them.

For the sake of my compliance and legal team, I'll note: I'm not talking about laws or federal, state, or local election rules. Those laws and rules are *not* to be broken. They're there for a reason, and if you want to be elected to make laws, it's generally a good idea not to break them. And a disclaimer to that disclaimer: I am, of course, not including acts of protest or civil disobedience here. Some of America's most important changes have been a result of people's staging sit-ins or protests, thanks to civil rights or environmental protestors literally putting their well-being on the line to impact change. As the late, great Georgia Representative John Lewis, a man who'd been arrested for protesting dozens of times, often noted, there is such a thing as good trouble.

What I am talking about are the unwritten rules that tell candidates, particularly women, how they should behave, how they should dress, what their backgrounds should be. The ones that say that there's only one path to victory, only one way a candidate should look. The ones that say you can't do certain things as a woman or can't win certain races because of who you are or where you come from or what university you went to. Those are the rules that set arbitrary limits. In today's world, we've got no time for rules like that.

You may ask why someone who came up in the political system and works in a large organization within that system wants you to break out of it. It's quite simple: This system wasn't designed for women like us.

It's not just politics, of course. Everything from CPR and crash-test dummies to military equipment and space suits was designed for men. Those may seem like minor issues until you read studies showing men have significantly better odds when in a car crash or requiring CPR.[1] A study of medical research of the last twenty-five years shows that while progress has been made, women are still underrepresented in studies of cardiovascular health, digestive health, and more. And that progress likely only came because Congress had to pass a law in 1993 to require government-funded research to include women and people of color.[2] Women still face a gender pay gap and often pay more for everything from certain medications to razors to cars.[3] And don't even get me started on tampons and pads—another version of a pink tax!

So why are we still worried about fitting squarely in a system that couldn't imagine us when it started and hasn't adapted quickly enough to our arrival? Instead, let's break the mold, change the rules, and take this system over.

CHANGING THE TEMPLATE ON WOMEN CANDIDATES

After years of women being forced to fit into a very specific mold to be a candidate, it has been so powerful to see women in recent cycles reject that template, run as themselves, and win.

When I started in politics, women looking to lead had to be perfect—and there was a very specific definition of *perfect*.

The idea of perfection applied especially to our appearance. We had to fit into a certain box in order to be successful. Quite simply, our leadership had to look masculine, because up until that point, only men had held positions of power. This was the birth of the pantsuit—and not the stylish ones we see today, but the ones with straight-cut pants and jackets with broad shoulder pads in navy blue, gray, and brown. I know what I'm talking about here; I had a ton in my closet, and that brown one was a doozy.

When I was working for Mary Rieder's House campaign in Minnesota in 1996, I gave her lots of advice that was standard at the time. I told her to cut her hair, change her glasses, look a certain way. When she wasn't in the pantsuit, there was the matching skirt suit, with which she always had to wear pantyhose. Part of my job was carrying an extra pair in case she got a run. I told her that she couldn't wear jeans at parades and had to wear the standard "parade politician" blue shirt and khaki pants—again, not yet made for women at all. There was a uniform for women running for Congress, and most women candidates didn't deviate from it. That's what the playbook told us we had to do and what voters had come to expect.

Look at any picture of the few women in office in decades past and you'll see women in that uniform—the pantsuit and a similar short haircut or long hair pulled back. By the late 1990s, we could add pearls!

But in the last few years, that uniform has finally changed. Take a look at pictures from the amazing women sworn in in early 2019 and you will see what it means to trade uniformity for diversity. We saw New Mexico Congresswoman Deb Haaland, one of the first Native American women ever elected to the House and a member of the Laguna Pueblo, wearing a traditional Pueblo dress during her swearing-in. In highlighting her heritage, Deb noted, "As a kid, I never could have imagined today. I will leave the ladder down behind me so girls of color know they can be anything they want to be."[4] And while women of color still face more roadblocks and higher expectations, Congress has moved beyond the white woman politician's nineties bobbed hair to include Minnesota Congresswoman Ilhan Omar—one of the first Muslim women in Congress— wearing a hijab and Massachusetts Congresswoman Ayanna Pressley's Senegalese twists. That definition expanded even further with Ayanna's moving video in 2020 announcing that while she had long been identified with her braids, the onset of alopecia meant she had to grapple with going bald and wearing wigs.

This is also where we have to thank a number of women who came before us. As much as I complained about the pantsuit, women like Senators Barbara Mikulski, Carol Moseley Braun, and Nancy Kassebaum helped change the standard in the Senate enough to allow women to wear pants in the first place. So this has been a fight for a long time.

Of course, it's not just by our appearance that women are unfairly judged, and it doesn't just happen in politics. Women have been trying to fit in certain specific boxes since we've been allowed to assume public leadership positions. That has meant trying not to show what men might consider weakness or trying not to offer any reason for people to question our commitment or ability to get the job done. No CEO had appeared on the cover of a business magazine while visibly pregnant until September 2019.[5] It could be that other CEOs and entrepreneurs didn't want to lose seed money, as other businesses had when word of a woman founder's pregnancy plans got out, or they worried about what investors would think about their commitment to or ability to do their job.[6]

Today, those long-standing cultural rules and biases are finally crumbling, thanks to the brave women who were willing to charge right at them. Of course, women of color still face unfair judgment and rules about their hair and their clothing, among other things. But with women standing up to those injustices and even more women running on a platform of being themselves, we are making progress at changing the norms and confronting societal bias.

I remember once telling a man I was working for that he would need to cover up his tattoos. It was for the same reason I suggested Mary Rieder get a shorter, almost masculine haircut. I knew voters expected candidates to look a certain way, and at the time, that did not include tattoos. For years, the same would have been even truer for women. But in 2018, Texas House candidate and veteran MJ Hegar didn't just show her tattoos, she put a spotlight on them in a television ad. It was a powerful message—some of MJ's tattoos were cherry blossoms on her arm, designed to cover up the scars from when her helicopter was shot down in Afghanistan.[7]

We are seeing women run in dresses and jackets and jeans . . . and yes, when they want to, in pantsuits. We've watched New York Representative Alexandria Ocasio-Cortez explain policy while making dinner in her apartment and New York Senator Kirsten Gillibrand working out at the gym (with some impressive guns). We've even watched many of the new women in the House take to wearing their congressional pins—lapel pins with a rough edge made to go through men's suits—as necklaces instead; Representative Lauren Underwood explained, "[There were] holes in all my clothes, all my blouses."[8]

Don't get me wrong: Voters still judge women incredibly more harshly than men for their appearance. Women are still held to far higher standards of perfection. Let's be honest: It's hard to imagine a woman running for president with wild hair or pit stains while standing on top of a counter somewhere, like some of our recent male candidates. And yes, every woman who runs for office will, at some point, hear from a well-meaning supporter about how she "needs to do something about that hair." But we've made huge progress, and the more women who run, the more progress we'll make. In the 2020 election cycle, it was clear the women candidates were picking their own uniforms: Elizabeth Warren in her black pants and colorful jackets (and tennis shoes for those long selfie lines), Kamala Harris in her pantsuits, Kirsten Gillibrand and Amy Klobuchar in their bright dresses for debates. They all looked like someone unique, like themselves. It may seem like a small step, but let me tell you, it was a hard-fought victory.

Of course, assumptions and judgments about our appearance are not the only ways women are written into a certain narrative in campaigns, or in leadership.

Think back to typical campaign ads from previous elections, and you'll see a few of the same images, no matter who the candidate was: a candidate behind a lectern, sitting at a dining room table with an older couple talking about health care or Social Security, walking with their family. The only difference between them was the geography. If you were in Montana, you saw mountains in the shot; in Iowa, a cornfield or a tractor; and so on. These ads credentialed candidates as a member of their community, someone who knew and cared about the issues, and a member of an upstanding family.

We ran those ads because that's what voters expected. Women couldn't take big risks or try something new when their gender was "new" enough for many districts. But even when they did what was expected of candidates, voters still questioned the women's actions. At EMILY's List, we'd hear focus groups tell us they needed to see a woman behind the podium to credential her as "serious," but then we'd hear in other groups that when a woman was behind a podium, she was not relatable and seemed "too far away." It sometimes seemed as if the women just couldn't win. Even when they followed the unwritten rules of what a candidate was supposed to do and say in an ad, they still were viewed as lacking in some way.

But in recent elections, we've seen women candidates cast aside those rules, shake things up, and bring their whole selves, their whole personalities, into the campaign. We've seen ads and videos that introduce our candidates not as cookie-cutter politicians who fit with what voters are expecting but as individuals. MJ Hegar made a powerful video telling her story through the art on her arms. For one of her ads, former California Congresswoman Katie Hill free-climbed on the side of a cliff while a drone camera recorded her. We watched Kansas Congresswoman Sharice Davids show how much of a badass she was through her MMA fighting experience. We heard Florida Congresswoman Debbie Mucarsel-Powell highlight the importance of supporting climate efforts while scuba-diving in a completely underwater ad.

These women took the risk of showing themselves as individuals instead of the generic model of a candidate we've gotten used to.

And yet, despite this progress, there is still a long way to go. Massachusetts Senator Elizabeth Warren was mocked and pilloried for drinking a beer on Instagram to celebrate a successful campaign launch. Elizabeth was called inauthentic, even though those of us who know her know that she does genuinely enjoy a beer after a good, long day. But as Elizabeth persisted, and continued to put herself out there for voters to see, more and more Americans came around to Elizabeth's authentic self over the course of her campaign.

I've had to learn this lesson myself, and being authentically you is not always an easy thing to do. When I was only a few weeks into my tenure as president of EMILY's List, I went on a fundraising trip out of town. I was still very much learning on the job, so when I got a question at one of my events that I couldn't answer, I told the truth. I told the woman asking the question that I didn't know, but I would make sure we got back to her with an answer.

I don't remember what the question was, but I do remember

the feedback that came shortly thereafter. A well-meaning friend told me that I couldn't ever do that again. She said that I would always need to know the answer because I would have to show strength. Uncertainty was a show of weakness, she said, and that was something I could never allow.

I know how ridiculous that sounds. But my friend was basing her advice on an unfortunate reality. For too long, women weren't allowed to show any weakness. We had to be perfect or else risk losing respect and authority. Men are more easily forgiven, of course, but women have never had the luxury of uncertainty. I feel lucky to have lived through a change in that thinking. No one has every answer, and I have come to learn that honesty gets you much further than bluffing. I am not afraid to admit when I don't know it all, and neither should you be.

Women were told for years, for decades, in politics not to show emotion. Not to show weakness. The only option is strength and acting like you know everything. But even in that moment, ten years ago, I knew my friend's advice was wrong. Bluffing is not how you build trust among voters, partners, allies, even your team, and it wasn't the way I wanted to lead. To me, leadership is about showing vulnerability and trusting that people will understand and appreciate your honesty. It's about having the confidence to know that people will accept that you don't, and couldn't, know everything.

This change—accepting women who acknowledge a weakness, a difference, a vulnerability; loosening the rigid standards we have held women candidates to—has come on fast, and not a moment too soon. We've had a generational shift in the way we judge women candidates, largely because those women have stood up and demanded not to be judged more harshly than their male counterparts. That shift is good for all of us, in all the work we do.

THE FIRSTS, AND SECONDS, AND THIRDS

Perhaps my favorite unwritten rule–breakers are the brave women who become the firsts. From Jeannette Rankin, the Montanan who was the first woman elected to Congress, to more recent firsts like the first Native American women and the first Muslim women elected to Congress, we are still seeing women of all races, ages, religions, and more break through barriers that no one has broken before, deciding to take a leap that literally no one else like them has ever taken.

Imagine that for just a moment—doing something that no one like you has done before. These women had to figure out how to do something big without an example of how to do it. They had to break the mold of people's expectations, which had never included someone like them. And they had to show the voters why breaking that mold and adding a new voice was important. I've seen it many times at EMILY's List: The women who break through—the firsts, seconds, and thirds—they do the work; they get to know people in their community and help them understand that we are far more alike than we are different. That's when they find success.

And that success matters for all of us. Those firsts expand the opportunities for everyone. There's power in the adage "If you can see it, you can be it," and that power is made possible by the groundbreakers. Their wins prove to everyone that elected office and leadership are possible, no matter what your story is. And everyone's lives are made richer by having that diversity of voices in our system. It's true in politics, and it's true in so many aspects of our society, from schools to businesses: We are better and often more effective when we have a diversity of voices in the conversation.

And I'm not just saying that because it's the right thing to do (although it certainly is) or because we believe in the power of diversity (although that's true, too). Having more women at the table makes things work better. As *Harvard Business Review* noted, several studies suggest "having women on the board means better acquisition and investment decisions and less aggressive risk-taking," which means better rewards for shareholders. One theory was that the women balanced out the overconfidence of male CEOs,[9] though there could be many explanations. Having women in elected office makes an equally important difference. Hardworking women looking to change the world get so much done.

We know that having more women in leadership roles is good for America. But America's elected leaders have mostly been men. That's why when many Americans picture a president, a senator, a CEO, a leader, they see a man. To change that, we need to change the norms. We need the firsts and the seconds and the thirds, and the tenths, because each one is a vital step on the road to progress. And though we have a long way to go, we're ready for the time when it's so normal to see women in those roles, we don't have to celebrate each victory. It's just what we expect.

Of course, as Stacey Abrams once noted, gaining power means you can be the "last" woman to deal with political, racist, or sexist nonsense. When EMILY's List awarded Stacey the first-ever Gabrielle Giffords Rising Star Award in 2014, Stacey said, "I am tired of being first. I want to be last. . . . We will populate the heavens and we will all become last! And the first to say thank you."[10]

Florida Congresswoman Stephanie Murphy was another one of those firsts. She was the first Vietnamese-American woman elected to Congress. Stephanie's life started very differently than that of any representative before her. Stephanie was the daughter of Vietnamese refugees. Her family escaped Vietnam on her father's boat when she was a baby and eventually were rescued by the Navy when they ran out of fuel. They lived in Malaysian refugee camps before making their way to Virginia, doing a variety of blue-collar jobs to stay afloat.

Stephanie put herself through school and eventually went into corporate consulting, but after 9/11, she decided to work as a national security specialist.[11] We helped recruit her in 2016 for Congress because of her strength in national security and her incredible story. This mom of two took on a twelve-term Republican incumbent and unseated him in 2016, with EMILY's List proudly by her side.

Illinois Senator Tammy Duckworth was a first several

times over. As a pilot in the US Army, Tammy suffered severe wounds in a helicopter crash in combat and became the first female double amputee in the Iraq War. Tammy ran for Congress in 2006 and lost, later serving a senior role in the Obama administration's Department of Veterans Affairs and eventually winning a seat in the US House in 2012. In doing so, she became the first woman with a disability and the first Thai-American woman elected to Congress.

Tammy had her first daughter near the end of her first term, and when she was weighing running for Senate a few months later, there were political experts who argued that a woman with a young baby couldn't get elected to the Senate. At EMILY's List, however, we knew Tammy could do it and that being a mom was part of the reason she was running. And yet, it was enough of a concern among some people that we did focus groups to prove to the skeptics what we already knew—that voters were open to having a new mom in the Senate. Tammy didn't just win that election. She won decisively, becoming only the second Asian American woman ever elected to the Senate (after Hawaii Senator Mazie Hirono and at the same time as California Senator Kamala Harris). She broke another barrier just a short time later, when she became the first woman to give birth while serving in the US Senate.[12]

Tammy's not the only candidate who has been told what she couldn't do. When you're not what they're used to, people assume that the job isn't made for you. There's never been someone like you in a role, so there must be a reason for that, right? That role must be better suited for someone else, or people just won't accept [a woman, a mom, a young person, a person of color, you name it].

So many of our historic firsts have heard this. We've already talked about the first transgender woman elected and reelected to the Virginia legislature, Delegate Danica Roem, but she's far from the only LGBTQ candidate to face serious skepticism. When Wisconsin Senator Tammy Baldwin was a Dane County commissioner deciding to run for an open US House seat, she was viewed as the long shot, running against two men and most of the establishment.

EMILY's List was proud to stand with her, knowing that she would be a terrific congresswoman and a groundbreaker as the first openly gay member elected to Congress. Despite her win, her great work in the House, and her leads in the polls, when Tammy ran to be the first openly LGBTQ elected US senator, people wondered whether she could actually win in a midwestern state. Thankfully, those pundits underestimated Wisconsin voters' ability to see Tammy for exactly who she was: a proud member of her community, and a great legislator who happened to be a historic groundbreaker. She proved doubters wrong by winning the election and broadened the perception of who a senator could be.

In politics, the argument that you can't win because no one like you has won before is often framed as questioning your "electability." Throughout the entire 2008 election, political experts questioned openly whether America would elect a Black man named Barack Hussein Obama. As you know, voters elected President Obama handily and then reelected him four years later, so now we no longer question the "electability" of a Black male president.

Unfortunately, the opposite effect can occur. Some pundits and candidates have turned Hillary Clinton's 2016 loss into a weapon against the women who ran for president in 2020. They ignored the fact that Hillary actually got nearly three million more votes than Trump, and suddenly it was as if sexism were the only reason Trump was president, suggesting that the sensational women candidates were unelectable out of hand, using Hillary's loss as evidence.

Here's the truth: Every election victory is made of thousands of decisions, the mood of the electorate, breaking news, economic turns, and thousands more things that are out of your control. It's rare when you can pinpoint one thing that caused a candidate to lose or win, and people who tell you they can are often just fitting the campaign into their own narrative. This challenge will still exist for every woman trying to be a first. People will continue to doubt it can be done because no one has ever done it. Elizabeth Warren put it so well at the end of her presidential campaign: "We'll know we can have a woman in the White House when we finally elect a woman to the White House."[13]

So the next time someone tells you that you can't do something because people like you never have, just remember every other first who heard that no and did it anyway. Let those firsts inspire you, and don't give the naysayers the power to stop you. What if there's never been someone like you in the position because *you* haven't tried it before? For every leadership role, someone has to be the first of their kind to step up to the challenge. And then someone else has to be second, and then third.

And if you're still doubting yourself and your ability to be the first, think about California Senator Kamala Harris. The daughter of immigrants, Kamala was bused into a new district as part of an attempt to integrate schools in the 1970s. She is one of the very few presidential candidates to have attended a historically Black university (Howard University) and credits her Indian mother and her alma mater as having had a huge impact on her life. She has been the first in nearly every job she's taken.[14] She herself said it best in an inspiring moment during a September 2019 Democratic primary debate:

You know, every office I've run for, whether it be district attorney or attorney general, I was told each time, it can't be done. They said nobody like you has done it before, nobody's ready for you. When I ran for DA, I won and became the first black woman elected DA in a state of forty million people, in San Francisco. When I ran for attorney general of California, I was elected—because I didn't listen. And I was the only . . . woman black elected attorney general in the state—in the country.

And each time, people would say, it's not your time, it's not your turn, it's going to be too difficult, they're not ready for you, and I didn't listen. And a part of it probably comes from the fact that I was raised by a mother who said many things that were life lessons for me, including "Don't you let anybody ever tell you who you are. You tell them who you are."

And when I look around the town halls that we do in this race for president of the United States, and I look at the meetings that we do and the community meetings, and I see these little girls and boys, sometimes even brought by their fathers, and they bring them to me and I talk to them during these events, and they smile and they're full of joy, and their fathers tell them, "See, don't you ever listen and let anybody ever tell you what you can or cannot be." You have to believe in what can be, unburdened by what has been.[15]

CHANGING THE RULES

Sometimes, rather than breaking the rules, we need to fight to change them for ourselves and generations of women to come.

Of course, many women decide to fight city hall by running for mayor. At EMILY's List, we're here for you if that's your choice. Remember when I asked you to consider running a few chapters ago? That won't be the last time you hear that request. But running for office is not the only way to make systemic change.

Women have been demanding change since this country began—even when women lacked the rights and voices they have today. From Harriet Tubman, a woman born into slavery who later risked her own freedom to become the most famous "conductor" of the Underground Railroad,[16] to Frances Perkins, the first woman to serve as a US cabinet secretary, credited as the chief architect of much of the New Deal;[17] from Rosa Parks, a civil rights activist whose iconic act of refusing to move on a city bus launched the Montgomery Bus Boycott,[18] to the early suffragists who fought for passage of American women's right to vote, women have often been the backbone of resistance in this country.

Women like Anita Hill (the law professor who testified that Clarence Thomas sexually harassed her), Christine Blasey Ford (the professor who testified about an attempted assault in high school during Brett Kavanaugh's Supreme Court confirmation hearings), Tarana Burke (the founder of the #McToo movement), Ai-jen Poo (an American labor activist who cofounded the National Domestic Workers Alliance), Dolores Huerta (the labor and civil rights activist who cofounded the United Farm Workers of America), and so many more have stood up for themselves and for women like them. They've spoken their truth, fought against the tide, and changed the rules in the process.

Like these women, and so many more, we must continue to push against the status quo. We see the rules that limit our rights and our opportunities, the laws that violate our values, and we know what we need to do: change them. Let's review a few examples of brave and powerful women who have done just that.

While Congress has had many members who are the fathers of young children, it's only been in recent years that mothers with young children have been elected. In fact, as of

2020, there were more than one hundred men in Congress with children under eighteen, while there were only twenty-five moms of kids the same age—meaning those moms make up only 5 percent of Congress.[19] And that number is actually double what it was just a year before, in 2019.[20]

It's still unusual enough that every one of the moms in Congress with school-age children or younger frequently gets asked, "Who's going to take care of your children?" or "How will you manage that with kids?" It probably will not shock you to learn that male candidates almost never get asked these same questions. One candidate even told me about how after she got elected, people asked her, "Are your children okay?" as if being a congresswoman might make her suddenly forget that she had kids to raise.

Choosing to be a mother affects women in every field. While having children is rewarding for many, it can also be costly. One report shows that the average mom's income drops 4 percent for every child she has, while the average man's income rises 6 percent when he has a child. Women also have more to balance after having a child. One study showed that women spend thirty-two hours a week on housework and child care while men only spend eighteen hours.[21]

It should be no surprise that dealing with child care becomes a major challenge as soon as a woman starts campaigning. Liuba Grechen Shirley was a young mom when she decided to run for Congress against long-serving New York Republican Peter King. Facing $22-an-hour child care expenses for her two- and three-year-old children, totaling hundreds of dollars a week just from her time at campaign events, Liuba decided to ask the United States Federal Election Commission to allow child care expenses to be considered a campaign cost. With the support of twenty-six members of Congress, Hillary Clinton, and two advocacy groups, Liuba successfully convinced the FEC that the child care costs were the direct result of the campaign and won the right to pay for the costs out of her campaign funds.[22] It was a major victory for any woman to come after her.

Liuba did more than provide a great example for young moms—she offered a potential solution for how to be a mom and a candidate. "I've been told by a number of women recently that they've been inspired to run. People are realizing you can do it with small children," she said.

Though she lost a tough fight for that congressional seat, Liuba is still innovating, now using her experience to help other women. In 2019, she founded Vote Mama, the first political action committee aimed solely at helping women with children under eighteen get elected to office. Vote Mama will both raise money for progressive moms and also pair them with moms in Congress as advisers to create a support system.

The fight doesn't stop when the campaign ends. Congress might be even less kid-friendly than elections are. But women have been questioning and changing the rules there, too.

In 2018, Tammy Duckworth became the first senator to give birth while serving in the Senate. She had to fight convention and Senate rules in order to bring her daughter Maile to the Senate floor. Duckworth worked with Minnesota Senator Amy Klobuchar, the senior Democrat on the Rules Committee, to help make the change.

Although the final rule change was unanimous, Klobuchar reported that there was some resistance. There was a concern that this kind of change could multiply: Utah Senator Orrin Hatch wondered, "But what if there are ten babies on the floor of the Senate?" Amy's response was perfect: "That would be wonderful and a delight." Amy also pushed back on an opposition effort to make this exception only for Senator Duckworth, arguing that it sent the wrong message to other women and the nation. She was right, and I couldn't have been prouder of both women when Maile joined her mom as Tammy became the first senator to cast a vote with her newborn along for the ride.[23]

That's not the first time Congress has been forced to make changes as its makeup has changed. Congress was built for men, as were its facilities and its rules. It took the first woman Speaker of the House, Nancy Pelosi, to make the push to install the first lactation room in the Capitol in 2006. And again in 2018, when the newly elected women in the House included many moms of young children and one single mom of school-age kids, they worked with House leadership to try to set more specific schedules with fewer late-night votes. In 2019, Speaker Pelosi worked to change the rules against wearing hats on the House floor in order to allow Minnesota Representative Ilhan Omar to wear her hijab at work.[24]

Statehouses still have work to do as well, and the growing

influx of brand-new moms is forcing that change to happen quickly. In 2017, when women flipped eleven seats in the Virginia house of delegates, that included mother of four Delegate Kathy Tran and Delegate Jennifer Carroll Foy, who found out she was pregnant three weeks into her campaign. Some people doubted whether Jennifer could campaign while becoming a new mom—of *twins*, no less—but she proved them wrong, winning a seat while also spending many nights with her premature twins in the hospital. Those twin boys are happy, healthy, and thriving—and I bet they're as proud of their mom as we are at EMILY's List.

Maine was another place that showed what kind of difference it makes when women are in charge. Under the leadership of then–Speaker of the Maine house Sara Gideon and then–Maine Majority Leader Erin Herbig, the Maine statehouse opened its first breastfeeding room. When the room opened in 2018, Sara noted that because the unpredictable hours of the legislature often deter women from pursuing an elected office or serving in leadership, "we need to create a culture that is welcoming to everyone—and that includes the practice of making it a place that works for people's lives, and a perfect example of that is a warm and accessible nursing room for mothers."[25]

We've worked with women who have shattered the rules outside of campaigns as well. MJ Hegar served in the Air Force for twelve years,[26] as a mechanic and then as a pilot. In 2012, she was one of four military servicewomen who sued then-Defense Secretary Leon Panetta to end the Pentagon's ban on women serving in direct combat jobs. While all four women had served tours in Iraq or Afghanistan and two of them, including MJ, had even earned a Purple Heart, they brought suit because the women who had fought in battles with men were not allowed to attend combat leadership schools and were denied a chance at positions that were stepping-stones to promotions.

As then–ACLU Women's Rights Project lawyer Ariela Migdal put it, "The servicewomen who have been spending the last ten years trying to accomplish missions in Iraq and Afghanistan are coming back and seeing there really is a brass ceiling."[27] While the case has not yet been resolved, MJ and the other women made change when Secretary Panetta felt the pressure and reversed the ban in January 2013, giving women a path to units and ultimately promotions that had largely been closed to them.

MJ saw a rule that was keeping women from advancement (even while they were serving on the same battlefields with men), and she fought it. As she noted in the campaign, she knocked on doors everywhere in the effort to do that, including the door of her congressman, Republican Representative John Carter. Even though she was a constituent with a real concern, Carter ignored her—and so after MJ got the rule changed for her and women like her, she came home and ran for Carter's House seat. While MJ didn't win her first time around, I know we'll see her continue to lead for years to come.

WHEN YOU DON'T FIT IN THE BOX, BREAK OUT OF THE BOX

There is another unwritten rule you should break. It's the one that tells you there's only one way to win. A model campaign plan you must follow, the one politicians and pundits are accustomed to. But if you still believe that you should follow the rules just because everyone else always has, you haven't read this chapter closely enough. Maybe the established way isn't an option for you. Or maybe you just see a better way to do things. In business, innovative companies don't just try to sell the same products or services to the same people—they look to expand the market or change their offerings.

Too often, we listen to the naysayers who would limit us to only one way to campaign and tell us there is but one path to victory. New candidates are encouraged to follow the same conventional wisdom, make the same assumptions, and use the same road maps. It's one of my biggest pet peeves—too often, we are trying to run the same race as the last time. The bad news is that most of the time, that's a mistake.

At sixteen years old, I saw firsthand how powerful creative campaigning can be. It may not surprise you to know that I was a kid who always wanted to be engaged and consistently got involved to try to do some good. I joined clubs, I ran my church youth group, and as a Girl Scout, I always wanted to be the best cookie seller in my troop (and I was often number one, still a point of pride). I'm betting this might sound familiar to a few of you . . . for many of us it starts young!

In high school, I ran for class president every year. And the first few tries, I lost. High school elections are more of a popularity contest than anything, and I learned early that ambitious women, especially at that age, are not always the popular ones. Even after losing the elections, I would still sign up for student council because they needed worker bees and I was certainly that. I was the one who'd put the homecoming float together, or chair the junior prom, or work the bake sales. But I knew that wasn't enough for me. I wanted to lead, so I figured out a way to win. I needed to change the electorate.

As I approached my senior year, my last chance at student leadership, I realized that if I ran for student body president instead of class president, I'd expand the electorate to the entire school. That way, while my own junior class margin was split between all four of the candidates running, I could focus my attention on the freshman and sophomore classes. Normally, the senior candidates would ignore the underclassmen, so the younger students appreciated the outreach. And when I secured the endorsement of the younger sister of one of my opponents, they had validation from one of their own. With their votes secured, I finally won the presidency. Well, the student body presidency of Butte High School, but still.

All those experiences, the losses and the win, taught me a valuable lesson, and one the media and political pundits should remember as they debate how Democrats can win and which voters they should target: You are always better off if you can expand the electorate. Bringing in new or infrequent voters is good for democracy—we build a better system when we're all participating in it.

Recent elections have taught us not to assume that only certain people can get elected in certain places. Just ask all the people who thought America, and particularly the South, would never elect a Black man president (thank you, Virginia and North Carolina, for casting your electoral votes for President Obama). Or the people who assumed that a Virginia district that had elected a homophobe for years would never elect Virginia's first transgender delegate. Or those who assumed that Kansas wouldn't elect a Native American former MMA fighter. We assume that Republican districts with mostly white voters won't elect women of color, but three women broke that rule in 2018: Sharice Davids in Kansas, Lauren Underwood in Illinois, and Lucy McBath in Georgia.

Sometimes when you make a plan, you figure out the numbers and you realize that you will come up just short. Some people see the writing on the wall and give up. I've seen many campaigns end that way. But others see that moment as a chance to get really creative to find ways to bridge the gap. And you know what? That's when it gets really fun.

Pennsylvania Congresswoman Susan Wild ran a race like this. She was fighting an uphill battle in a six-person primary for Pennsylvania's Seventh District against Northampton County district attorney John Morganelli. He had huge name recognition and a seemingly insurmountable lead. Morganelli was no average Democratic primary opponent. He was anti-choice and anti-immigrant—he'd even tweeted at President Trump, seeming to ask for a job—and he'd been elected in the district in other positions. So how to turn around an unwinnable race against this opponent? Well, EMILY's List figured out that the voters didn't really know what he stood for and just needed some education.

Susan ran a great campaign, leveraging every tool and ally she could. She built a huge network of volunteers to help define her policies and her opponent. And at EMILY's List, we pulled out every tool in our toolbox as well. We pulled together allied groups for events to help generate press. We did digital organizing. And our independent expenditure arm found as many ways to reach voters as we could, including a small TV station on the edge of the district. Against the odds, all of those efforts combined for a victory for Susan in the primary, and then again in the general election—and now she's making us proud every day in Congress.

The history of EMILY's List is built around ignoring the naysayers and finding ways to shift the conventional wisdom and change the script. The election of New Mexico Congresswoman Xochitl Torres Small is another success story that had the odds stacked against it. Xochitl was a former Senate staffer and water rights lawyer who knew her district and its issues. And when the Republican incumbent in her very red home district ran for governor, creating an open seat, Xochitl saw an opportunity. So did EMILY's List. Even though many experts doubted a Democrat could win the district, we all saw that she was doing the work she needed to do, convincing voters by talking about local issues. It helped that her opponent was unpopular. We all knew Xochitl was the right candidate and we invested in her, in terms of spending and staff, with roughly a quarter of our office clearing out to New Mexico to knock on doors and help out. She pulled off an impressive victory, to the surprise of the pollsters and pundits.

And then there's Georgia. Democrats have had a rough time in Georgia over the past couple of decades. The Republican voters there are more reliable, thanks to years of voter suppression, particularly in midterm elections. So when Stacey Abrams told me she wanted to run for governor in 2018, I was afraid the numbers wouldn't add up, even for a candidate as talented and qualified as Stacey.

I was not the only person concerned that the Georgia governor's race was just not winnable. Conventional wisdom, particularly among white Democrats in Georgia, told Stacey the only way to win was to persuade right-leaning voters who might consider the "right" Democrat to vote for her. The catch—no Democrat had been the mystical "right" Democrat in two decades, not since 1998.

But Stacey had a strategy. She wanted new voters, voters who had been left behind by a decades-old system of intimidation, lack of registrations, and disenfranchisement. For years, she had worked out a program to register and mobilize all those ignored and excluded voters. But she also knew that her opponent, Brian Kemp, was willing to use his position as secretary of state to help him win and continue that long tradition. During the cycle, he would end up putting 53,000 voter registrations (thought to be of likely Abrams voters) on hold.

In the 2014 Georgia governor's race, 6 million people had been registered to vote, but only 2.55 million had cast votes. Stacey and her team decided their margin of victory would come from "irregular" voters, including some of the 760,000 voters who voted for Hillary Clinton in 2016 but didn't come out for Democrat Jason Carter in the 2014 gubernatorial race, and more than one million voters whom the Abrams team labeled as Democrats or left-leaning independents who didn't vote regularly. Naysayers told Stacey she should be aiming at "persuadables"—those likely to vote—but her team had only identified 90,000 truly persuadable voters, which would leave them short of the deficit they needed to make up.[28]

When faced with these impossible odds, Stacey didn't give up. She reframed the race and the playing field. They did mailings to those voters and built a large field and political team to do outreach. As a result, she outperformed any Democrat in Georgia in years (including President Obama). Her plan did exactly what she'd promised and effectively engaged those irregular voters.

And yet, Stacey still lost. You might wonder, then, why I included this story.

First, though she didn't win the race, I believe firmly that without Republican voter suppression, Stacey would have beaten the odds and won. I *know* that Georgia would have been better off as a result. And second, you don't just learn from victories. Sometimes you can learn more from a close loss than a blowout win. Just because outside forces were too big for Stacey to combat in this case, that doesn't mean her plan wasn't enormously effective. And now she's taking all of those lessons learned and turning her skills, attention, and desire to break the unwritten rules to fight against an issue that will impact all Americans: voter suppression.

So how do you get creative? How do you figure out how to bridge the gap, grow your market share, and change the expectations? I get asked this question all the time and there's no one right solution. But there is a good rule of thumb: Take risks.

We see it all the time in politics. The front-runners play it safe, because they know what's worked for them in the past. They're not playing to win; they're playing not to lose. That usually does work if you're in an easy district or running so far ahead you can't be caught, but too often, that's not the kind of race that we women will face. But at EMILY's List, we love the hard races. Because where's the fun in playing it safe? The best campaigns—and certainly the most interesting ones—are run by innovators who are constantly aiming high and trying new things.

Of course, it's not just politics where innovation matters. Apple didn't stop after the success of their first computer. Netflix had a popular service when they mailed DVDs in those red envelopes, but they kept adapting to the market, and now we can watch their own original content on our phones whenever we want. Speaking of, I love black and white movies, but

I'm glad we've added color. New Coke might have been a huge flop, but Coke Zero has some staying power.

In 2003, I went to work for a little-known Vermont governor looking to run for president. Vermont is a solid blue state in presidential elections but at the time was thought of as too small to support a presidential run (although clearly Senator Sanders's two recent runs might disprove that theory). But then-Governor Howard Dean had spoken out against the Iraq War at a time when I believed that was the tough but right thing to do. I was sold.

In the early days, no one gave us a chance. I was the finance director, not an easy job for a start-up candidate from a tiny state, with a governor who, as is typical for governors, didn't have a huge financial base of support. But we decided to take some chances. We doubled down on both fundraising and organizing online, putting us on the cutting edge of using either for campaigns. We worked with lawyers to help us figure out how to do a partnership with Meetup.com, hoping to give local people a way to organize their own Dean gatherings. We built an incredible network of supporters that raised more money than anyone had anticipated from small donors and volunteers.

Governor Dean not only allowed us to take those tactical risks but spoke openly about—even empathized with—the anger so many Democrats felt at that time about entering into the Iraq War. No one was really willing to go as far out on this issue as Howard was, and it worked. He also did something simple and brilliant—he convinced people they had the power to change the country by making their voices heard on this issue. The campaign, led by Joe Trippi, made a vote for Howard Dean about more than just him as a candidate, and it paid off financially and with new supporters.

Then momentum started to build and we seemed to be winning. We took our foot off the gas. Not on the fundraising—we were always willing to try new things there because the establishment money wasn't coming in, even after Howard became the front-runner. But the pressure of suddenly leading the race changed our thinking. The campaign and the candidate decided that our lead was not worth jeopardizing with risky strategies—even if those were the strategies that had gotten us there. When we started winning, we started running a more traditional campaign. And once we looked like every other campaign, we lost our edge. We ended up losing the nomination. It was a lesson learned the hard way.

More recently, I've had the pleasure of working with another innovator. In 2019, Elizabeth Warren planned to end candidate-driven high-dollar fundraising events for her primary campaign and only raise at the grassroots level. It gave her a hard job, and she had plenty of doubters. But Warren stuck to her guns and used the time she saved by not doing big fundraisers for things she found more important. She took selfies with every supporter at her events who wanted one and talked to them all individually. At one large New York event, Warren stayed for nearly four hours, shaking hands, taking pictures, and making contact with voters who hadn't paid a dime to meet and speak with her. And after a few months of working her own campaign plan, Warren found herself moving up in the polls. She was raising money overwhelmingly via small donations from people impressed with her campaign and her decision to take a harder road that showed commitment to her values.

Innovation can only happen after companies, leaders, and campaigns stop playing it safe and try something new. The only way to move forward is to shake up the status quo. That's especially true when you are facing what looks like an impossible fight.

Break those rules, and you may be surprised by the result.

THE TOPLINES

The system wasn't made for us women, so let's stop assuming that playing by the system's rules will help us get ahead. Unwritten rules that exclude women need to be broken, and we should all be grateful for the brave women who have been knocking down those barriers for decades.

Learn your lesson from those women:

- Run your own smart campaign, work your own plan, and ignore the naysayers.
- Wear what you want to wear—whatever makes you feel confident—and speak how you want to speak.
- Be yourself, and use your individuality to your advantage.

- Don't be discouraged if no one like you has done this before. It's not easy to be a first, or a second, and so on, but it *is* doable.

If the rules don't work for you, work to change them. Use the courts, ask elected officials, build a crowd, raise your voice: Do whatever it takes. Your efforts will help you and the women who come after you.

When the odds are stacked against you and it seems there's no path to the finish line, get creative:

- Throw out the old playbook and find a new way to get the results you want.
- If you can, expand the market and/or move to a new playing field.
- Run your race, not someone else's.

★★★

CHAPTER 4

Know Your Story,
Learn How to Tell It

CAMPAIGNS ARE ABOUT all sorts of things, from policies, to field plans, to poll-tested messaging, to debates, to candidate biographies. But years of working in politics have taught me that the best candidates are great storytellers, and the most compelling campaigns—and most of the winning ones—are all about stories.

Virginia Woolf once said, "Indeed, I would venture to guess that Anon, who wrote so many poems without signing them, was often a woman." Writer Rebecca Solnit put it well when she noted, "Some women get erased a little at a time, some all at once. Some reappear. Every woman who appears wrestles with the forces that would have her disappear. She struggles with the forces that would tell her story for her, or write her out of the story, the genealogy, the rights of man, the rule of law. The ability to tell your own story, in words or images, is already a victory, already a revolt."[1] Women haven't always been able to tell their stories, but that time is over. History is being made every day by women. The revolt is happening. The voices of women are changing the world. Yours can, too.

Good stories can inspire us. They can move and motivate us to take action, to reach for more. They can help us better understand why an issue matters or how it impacts us directly. And whether you are running a campaign, trying to win people over to a cause, or even running a business, the first step is learning to tell *your* story.

Here's the reality. We live in an era when the personal is political. Social media allows and almost forces us to put more of ourselves out there. We expect to not just understand our leaders' policy positions but get to know their families and be behind the scenes in their lives. We see what motivates and guides them. Because of this expected transparency, introducing your own stories into your arguments and platforms has become almost a requirement for any public figure. That's why the first thing we teach candidates in our trainings is how to tell their stories. Even if you're not the candidate, communicating your story is one of the most important life skills you can hope to learn.

You may be thinking that good storytelling depends on the story, not the narrator. You may be worried that you don't have the right thing to say or the most interesting life to talk about. But that's just not true. Every one of us has a good story inside. How you got here and what you learned on the way, your family history and your experiences—you've lived a life that's worthy of discussing. Don't doubt that. We've all lived experiences that can teach something to others.

The mark of a good—and, more important, an effective—storyteller is not the story itself but how they tell it, and how they engage their audience. Can people relate to what you have to say? Is there a resolution or an action that feels fulfilling? Do you use your story to present listeners with a clear call to action and an ask to get them involved? In campaigns, stories come down to four parts:

- **Your situation.** This is what drives you to run. It's the challenges you've faced, the issues that you know you need to fix, the problems facing your community.
- **Your reaction.** How did you deal with those challenges? How did you respond to the problems at hand? How did it make you who you are today?
- **Your resolve.** This is where you move to the next level. How can your reaction help other people? What's the next step, and how can you help others who find themselves facing the same situation you've conquered? This is where you show how your campaign will matter to the voters.
- **Your ask, connected to your values.** Quite simply, this is what you want your audience to do after hearing your story and why their involvement matters. In the case of candidates, this is when you ask for their vote, their support, their money, or their help volunteering. What you

are really looking for is an emotional connection that results in a vote, support, a dollar, or time. It is the emotional connection of sharing stories that makes us human and drives our desire to do things together to make change. That is why this is so very important.

These four pieces of effective storytelling allow you to explain who you are, why you're running, and some of what you'll do in office. They also clarify to anyone listening why it should matter to them and what you need from them if you are going to win. They allow you to engage voters and end with an ask to take that engagement into action. That last part, the ask, is both the most important part and the part most candidates forget. And it allows you to wrap that story up in a compact package that gets something done.

The ability to tell a story, and specifically to land all four of these parts successfully, is not just important for a candidate. It's also vital to convince people to make change, talk your way into a job, organize a movement, ask for a raise, and so much more. A great story is how we win people over to our side and how we begin to change the world.

EMILY'S LIST WOMEN TELL THEIR STORIES

During my time at EMILY's List, we have worked with thousands of women running for office. Each one of them has a different story—some are epic and some are tragic. Some are family sagas and others triumphant underdog stories. But there are some less dramatic stories, like mine, for example.

I mentioned earlier that I grew up in a middle-class family in Butte, Montana—a small town by most states' standards, but a real city in Montana. Butte is a town where the community comes together around the local sports teams and where neighbors pitch in to help neighbors. I think the house next door actually had a white picket fence. But amid all this classic Americana, my hometown also put me in the middle of an issue to which I attribute my political awakening. Growing up in Montana, I realized at some point in elementary school, during the most tense years of the Cold War, that my state was the home of the Minuteman nuclear missiles. Not irrationally, it scared the crap out of me. I was worried we were going to get blown up by the Soviet Union and then the United States would blow them up and the whole world was going to blow up. I think a lot of people shared that fear in the 1980s, and for good reason.

The situation and the fear it caused made me passionate at a young age about getting rid of all nuclear weapons. Even as a child, I saw politics as a way I could make that change. Now, clearly I did not succeed in that goal (yet!), but it's a mission that ignited my passion for government, and action through policy.

That's part of my story, one that I've honed over time. I tell it and retell it, so when I introduce myself to someone and make my ask of them, I feel confident that I'm conveying my core narrative. But that's just one example.

I also talk frequently about being raised by a Vietnam veteran who had to fight back some ghosts of his trauma to become my superdad. My deep respect and support for our military comes from my family's generations of service, including both of my grandfathers, who served in World War II. Each of us is knit together by patches of experiences. That is what I want you to figure out—what makes up your patchwork of experience, and how do you share it with others?

Some of our candidates were raised by teachers or members of the military, some saw or lived an injustice and wanted to fix it, and some realized that they had to make things better for their communities. Every story is compelling, whether born in trauma or born in generosity, because they all make a connection between a human story and a desire to make things better. Telling a good story is a way to harness the power of what connects us to each other.

If you're still wondering what story you have to tell, maybe you'll be inspired by examples from women we've seen run and win over the last few years.

Minnesota senator and 2020 presidential candidate Amy Klobuchar stands out for so many reasons. At a September 2019 debate, when asked to describe a time she showed resilience, she told her story. See how she used this story to give voters a reason to support her.

When our daughter was born, I had this expectation, we're going to have this perfect, perfect birth, and she was really sick, and she couldn't swallow. And she was in and out of hospitals for a year and a half. But when she was born, they had a rule in place that you got kicked out of the hospital in twenty-four hours. She was in intensive care, and I was kicked out. And I thought, this could never happen to any other mom again. [HER SITUATION]

So I went to the legislature, our state legislature, not an elected official, a mom, and I advocated for one of the first laws in the country guaranteeing new moms and their babies a forty-eight-hour hospital stay. And when they tried to delay the implementation of that law, I brought six pregnant friends to the conference committee so they outnumbered the lobbyists two to one. And when they said, when should it take place, they all raised their hands and said now. [HER REACTION]

That is what motivated me to go into public service. And when I got to that gridlock of Washington, DC, I got to work and passed over one hundred bills [HER RESOLVE], and I know a lot of my friends here from the left, but remember, I am from the middle of the country. And I believe, if we're going to get things done, that we have to have someone leading the ticket with grit, someone who's going to not just change the policies but change the tone in the country, and someone who believes in America and believes it from their heart because of where they came from, that everyone should have that same opportunity. [HER ASK—FOR SUPPORT][2]

As we've mentioned in past chapters, many women are driven by and center their story on a health care experience.

Those women, like Illinois Congresswoman Lauren Underwood, who is a health care professional with a preexisting condition, or Washington Congresswoman Kim Schrier, who is the only woman doctor in the House and also has diabetes, connect their own experiences to the fears and concerns of their constituents. We have worked with a number of people whose stories are tied to their concerns about education, from Nevada State Representative Selena Torres, a twenty-four-year-old high school English teacher,[3] to North Carolina State Representative Julie von Haefen, a former PTA leader concerned about cuts to local schools.[4]

Sometimes you tell your story in service of an issue. For example, read below for Georgia Congresswoman Lucy McBath's use of her powerful story and personal tragedy to push for passage of legislation to prevent gun violence. McBath was chosen to give the Weekly Democratic Address (the response to the weekly White House address) in February 2019. These addresses are short and must get to the point quickly and drive a message. As you can see, Lucy managed to tell each of the key parts of her family's tragic story while promoting the legislation.

As many of you may know, gun violence is an issue that is deeply personal for me. In 2012, my son Jordan Davis was shot and killed by a man who opened fire on a car of unarmed teenagers at a gas station in Jacksonville, Florida. My son Jordan was 17 years old. Jordan would have turned 24 this past weekend. [HER SITUATION]

After my son's death, I dedicated my life to advocating for commonsense gun safety solutions. But it was the shooting at Marjory Stoneman Douglas High School in Parkland, Florida, last year that finally motivated me to run for Congress. [HER REACTION]

The pain of losing a child to gun violence never ends. It is that pain which drives my work to prevent gun violence.

These stories are vitally important as we work to pass commonsense gun safety legislation to keep families like ours from experiencing the horror and the heartbreak brought on by gun violence. [HER RESOLVE]

The overwhelming, bipartisan support for universal background checks symbolizes the power of advocacy and the incredible power of the survivors, family members and students who have shared their stories as they advocate for commonsense gun safety solutions and demand that we act to address gun violence.

House Democrats are taking action to make sure our communities and our nation are safer.

We need commonsense legislation to prevent gun violence and ensure that mothers and fathers have one less reason to worry. This gives students one less thing to fear when they walk into school. Most importantly, it makes our communities and our nation a safer place to live.[5] [HER ASK]

These are just a few of the powerful stories from a handful of the EMILY's List women who have run in the past few years. Those stories could fill a book of their own.

WE CONTAIN MULTITUDES

When we talk about telling your story, it's important to remember that your story is not just one incident or memory; it's a lifetime of lessons. If you're going to run for office, you'll need to be able to mix things up. If you've followed campaigns, you know that the best candidates tell many stories. Lucy McBath talks about her son's tragic death, but she also tells audiences about her experiences with the health care system while she was dealing with breast cancer or about her concerns with trade deals as a Harley rider. (See? We contain multitudes!)

When I started at EMILY's List, on my path from becoming the staffer behind the scenes to becoming the face of an organization, I knew that I would need to be able to tell many stories—and so will you. My team and I sat down around a conference table and I went through a variety of stories from my life. I told them about being involved in my church, the first place I learned activism. About running for student council and what I learned in both victory and defeat. My time in athletics, when I learned you play to win, not just to participate. My first campaign experiences, and so many more.

Putting my stories into buckets allowed us to think through which examples might work for different audiences. That way I can tailor my remarks to different groups while sharing the real me and make sure I'm not always telling the same story.

I recommend this kind of activity for anyone who's going

to have to speak often in front of groups. Beyond the fact that it will help refresh your memory of all the amazing things you've accomplished and lived through, it's an uplifting project that will remind you that you are really interesting. If you are concerned that others won't find your life exciting, try doing this on your own and you'll be amazed at what you've done and experienced.

Listeners don't really want to hear what you stand for and what you want until they know a little bit about who you are and how you got there. That is the purest human nature. That is why the best politicians, leaders, CEOs, teachers, and professionals are the ones who make themselves a bit vulnerable and offer a little transparency through sharing their story.

TELLING THE TOUGHER PARTS OF YOUR STORY

Not all stories have a happy ending. Or sometimes to get to a happy ending, you had to go through a terribly difficult experience. It's your life and your story, so only you can decide if and when to share those really hard chapters.

Running for office is a choice to step into the public eye. For your own privacy and sanity, it's important to find which personal stories you are willing to share with the world. It's important to be intentional about what you reveal and what you decide to keep private.

Remember the story of Senator Tammy Baldwin. She wasn't ready to share those intimate details about her mom until later in her career. That's okay. Authenticity and honesty are the only real ways to build some common ground between you and your audience, but you have to be comfortable with what you open up about.

In recent years, women have shared their stories of sexual harassment and assault en masse, encouraged to come forward as strength in numbers grows. Our society has spent centuries ignoring, denying, or dismissing women who accuse men of sexual misconduct. Women who did manage to tell their stories risked being blamed themselves for the assault they were trying to report.

That time is ending now. We are living through the revolution, witnessing the brave women who stood up first and told their stories alone—an almost impossible thing to imagine, particularly before movements like #MeToo and Time's Up. We watched as generations of gymnasts stood up to an abusive doctor and an organization that ignored abuse and their needs. We saw candidates and elected officials like California Congresswoman Katie Porter and Michigan Governor Gretchen Whitmer talk about the violence they suffered as a way to help change policy and put a face on abuse. While in the legislature, during a legislative debate about abortion, Whitmer told her own story of being raped in college. Several minutes into a speech, she put aside her written remarks and noted that she couldn't ask other women to tell their stories if she didn't have the bravery to share her own.[6]

So many stories feel impossible to share. The loss of a child or a parent, getting through an illness, losing a job, making a mistake that you've had to come back from—these are just a few examples of the parts of your story that carry very real emotion and can be tough to tell. But all of these hardships contribute to who you are and are likely a part of what makes you a compelling and effective leader. No one's life is without struggle. Life experiences like these tie us all together.

I've watched many women share their stories over the years. I can tell you that there's no best way or best time to do so. Some women find strength in sharing. Some find acceptance that makes any negative feedback feel small in comparison. You are the only person who can decide when it makes sense to share so much of yourself with the world, and it's not a decision to take lightly. What I can give you is a few examples of our candidates who have been glad they've shared their stories. And I can help you think through how to frame your story effectively.

In recent years, we have seen a revival of the concerted effort to undermine reproductive rights. More and more states are passing legislation that would effectively end the right to an abortion. In Georgia, State Senator Jen Jordan wanted to make her colleagues better understand the issues they were going to decide on, so she did something powerful. She made it personal.

In her floor speech, which has since been shared and viewed thousands of times, Jen talked about how she had been pregnant ten times but had only had two children, losing the rest to miscarriages. Instead of sticking to the usual political talking points, she offered an emotional example of what women like her could face under the bill. She illustrated with her own experience how hard it was for women to lose wanted pregnancies and reminded the legislators of the complexity and human consequence of the laws they were trying to pass. With our government still so overwhelmingly dominated by men, we need women like Jen in the room to get loud about women's perspectives. After making her case, Jen asked her colleagues to vote against the bill.

Though we lost that particular fight in Georgia, Jen's speech made national news and fundamentally changed the conversation around reproductive rights. She chose to make use of her grief and tragedy to help people better understand an issue.[7]

Women candidates often feel compelled to use their own stories to personalize an issue and make it more relatable and understandable to voters. As lawmakers on the right attempted to demonize abortion, Washington Congresswoman Pramila Jayapal came forward with a story she'd never told publicly before. She had to end her second pregnancy with an abortion due to health concerns. Pramila wrote in *The New York Times,* "I have never spoken publicly about my abortion. In some ways, I have felt I should not have to, because it is an intensely personal decision. But I have decided to speak about it now, because I am deeply concerned about the intensified efforts to strip choice and constitutional rights away from pregnant people and the simplistic ways of trying to criminalize abortion." In telling her story, Pramila also ended with an ask: that we allow every pregnant person to make a decision for themselves.[8]

Watching other women tell their stories can make a candidate ready to tell her own. We've seen this time and again. As more women use their voices and share even their hardest and most private moments with the country, other women feel safer in doing the same.

During the 2020 presidential primary, Elizabeth Warren often told the story of having to leave her teaching job when she became pregnant. When some critics nitpicked the details of the story, women around the country told their stories to the media or even their own families about the challenges they had faced at work after becoming pregnant. These women weren't necessarily newsmakers, but they helped many people understand the prevalence of a fairly recent phenomenon that hadn't been widely discussed.

These are just a couple of the ways in which women have used their stories to help move opinion and generate more understanding. Storytelling is one of the most powerful tools you can use, in whatever way you want to lead.

TELLING THE STORY OF YOUR FAMILY

There are so many challenges women candidates (and, frankly, women in every profession) face with regard to families. If you have children or a spouse, people will wonder why you aren't with them more, or they'll wonder how they feel about what you're doing. If you don't have a spouse or children, they'll ask why not instead. Answering those questions is something you need to be able to do. It may not be fair, but that's the hard truth of the matter.

Before we go on, let me clarify something. I believe the definition of *family* is very broad. We all have families, though maybe not in the traditional sense of the word. Some of us have partners or spouses, some have children, and some are taking care of parents. I'm a single gal with no children, but I couldn't love my nephew more and have lots of stories about my younger brothers. I often talk about my parents—they are who made me who I am.

I must never forget my late grandmothers. My grandma Grace Schriock lived to ninety-five years old and showed me how to foster a deep compassion for people. She was the grandma who would hug me so hard I couldn't breathe and would tear up every time I left, waving until our car finally turned out of view. She was full of love for her family, something I try to always carry with me.

Then there was my grandma Nancy Fairbanks, my mom's mom. While I was writing this book, she celebrated her one hundredth birthday, but then we lost her a few months later. Grandma Nancy was a woman who was born in the wrong era. She was a truly stubborn Iowa farm wife who had four daughters and, without realizing it, raised them as strong, independent, tough women. She was well-read and would have been better educated had she been born fifty years later. Grandma Nancy was so liberal that she made me look conservative (well, almost) and had lots of opinions about politics. EMILY's List would have run this woman for office if they'd caught wind of her. She wasn't a "hugger" like Grandma Schriock, but she did her duty always and cared for those around her. I sure got my independent streak from her, and I will miss her. She was born into a nation where women couldn't even vote, and I will always regret not delivering a woman president during her lifetime, but with some of that tenacity she taught me, I know I'll never stop trying.

Then there are the families we build. Some of us have the community we've found for ourselves at a church, work, or school. For some of us, it's the friends we couldn't live without, like my best friend, Christa, and some others who get me through the good times and the bad. When I talk about family, I mean anyone you count as your family. Your love for them is the only thing that matters.

When you start talking about your family, you start figuring out who you are and why you do the things you do. What better way is there to connect with an audience who often have shared experiences?

Talking about family, however, gets a little more complicated when you are talking about children. When you start to talk about your children publicly, you are making a decision for them, to enter them into the public consciousness. Many questions arise: How should I talk about my family? Am I talking about my kids too much? Or not enough? How can I protect my children from unfair yet unavoidable public scrutiny in the age of social media?

The Obamas were famously cautious with press and other

public appearances with their daughters, in order to protect their privacy and security. Parents with kids old enough to check the news themselves are also dealing with children old enough to have an opinion about which stories Mom can tell about them. These are issues that all parents—moms and dads alike—will have to balance. But there are many reasons talking about children can be particularly complicated for women, who are often judged more harshly on their parenting than men.

In politics, we find that women are judged and questioned for their parenting significantly more than men are. Moms get asked on the campaign trail who is taking care of their kids or how they will get it all done in ways men are not. When women do choose to discuss their children in the campaign, they risk raising those biased questions in voters' minds as well. It's a ridiculous dilemma, in my opinion. Parenting and leading is not an either-or proposition. I can think of many moms who have run for office knowing that their experience as parents has made them better and more confident leaders. And we don't question whether or not men can do both. But it is something women have had to consider for years—in politics, in business, in far too many careers and venues.

You may have heard the old saying in law firms that women can be on the mommy track or the partner track, but not both. It was often the same for candidates. Even once women could run for office, it was clear that the candidate track and the mommy track did not mix. And you couldn't even think of having a baby while in office. When Jane Swift was running for lieutenant governor of Massachusetts in 1998, a *New York Times* headline said it all: "A Pregnant Candidate Discovers She's an Issue."[9] In 2012, not all that long ago, I remember us at EMILY's List pitching a story to the press about the moms of school-age kids running for Congress. It was a big deal that we finally had a small handful of them, and it sounded like a story.

Fast-forward less than a decade and so much has changed for the better. Juggling parenthood and elected office is still a big challenge for women, don't get me wrong—and we still need more working moms in office to show just how possible it is—but we have evolved really quickly.

Part of that is social media, which has made all of our lives open for discussion. People now expect to know everything about a politician. They know that when entering the public arena, a person is expected to enter with their whole life open wide for examination. Now, if I had a magic wand, I would change this element of American politics. In my opinion, to expect our politicians to be so public about everything is an unfair demand. But since I don't have a magic wand, our recommendations for women running for office have shifted.

The best solution is to find balance in talking about your family. Find ways of being open about yourself and your children but set boundaries, and make it part of your story. As women, we still have to be intentional about that balance, because a lot of folks can't get their heads around working moms and everything they have to do both professionally and in the household.

For women who don't have children or a spouse and are questioned about it constantly, you, too, can and should share the parts of your life you are comfortable with. Depending on where you live or where you're hoping to run for office, not having children may be seen as unrelatable to voters. As a leader who doesn't have children, I've gotten this question hundreds of times—in addition to unsolicited advice on how and when to freeze my eggs. Times are changing, as are the makeups of our families, but this may come up when you tell your story.

And I urge you to remember what I said about *family* having a broad definition. During the debate over passage of Obamacare, I got a call from my sister-in-law explaining to me that when my nephew was born, they had no maternity coverage because they couldn't afford the rider every month. We joked that with a nearly $15,000 bill, my nephew was the cost of a small car. Though we joked, we knew this was a serious matter and a key example of what is wrong with our health care system. I may not be a mother, but I still love that kid (who, by the way, is happy and healthy today), and I shared that financial concern with my family. That became a part of my story, too.

The good news about the changes in both our society and our elected officials is that we're moving toward normalizing all kinds of families. I believe the more our leaders and all of us talk about our different family structures, the better our society will be.

THE PRESS AND THE PUBLIC:
TIPS ON DELIVERING YOUR STORY TO THEM

Your story has impact when someone hears it and is moved by it. And whether you're looking to spur them into action or spark a feeling within them, as a candidate and a leader, you need to learn how to deliver your story to a broad audience if you want that impact to be big. That means getting comfortable with doing interviews and with giving speeches.

If that thought gives you heart palpitations, you're not alone. Fear of public speaking is so common, there's a name for it. If your fear is so significant it causes you problems at work or in meeting your goals, it's called glossophobia.[10] So now that we've named it, let's work on managing it. There are proven ways to contain your anxiety and actually improve your skills at public speaking.

I will confess that getting up and speaking to a group has never bothered me. I think it came from so much practice as a kid. I learned that for me, overpreparation was the key to feeling calm and confident. I gave plenty of presentations in Girl Scouts and spoke up constantly in school. Between that, serving on the Montana Episcopal Church statewide youth board, and student government, I've spoken in public for most of my life, and at this point it comes naturally.

That's not everyone's truth, though. Some people were never comfortable talking in front of the class. Or maybe the last time you spoke in public was in front of a high school civics class and it's a distant memory. Don't worry. Remember my promise? All you need to bring with you is integrity, commitment, and energy. I'm here, and my experts at EMILY's List are here, to coach you through the rest. With a good speech, a lot of practice, and a clear story to tell, you can become a good—and even comfortable—public speaker.

The first step is having a speech that you like. A good speech tells a story that reflects you and that sounds like you.

Great speeches do two things: They make listeners feel something, and they give them something to do. That means great speeches aren't always the longest or the most eloquent—after all, the Gettysburg Address was fewer than three hundred words long.[11] The *best* speeches also say something and leave you with something to think about. That something doesn't have to be overly complicated. One of the most famous feminist speeches in history came when then–First Lady Hillary Clinton went to China in September 1995 and made a speech declaring that "human rights are women's rights and women's rights are human rights, once and for all."[12] What a radical idea.

Once you've determined what you're trying to say, you have to figure out how best to say it. Remember that structure is key. You might not need the whole speech in front of you, but unless you're a pro, you should have something organized and prepared ahead of time. At the very least, I recommend you have an outline that includes the point of your speech and the case you want to make, your supporting facts and stories, and finally your ask. Yes, that's right—a speech must contain an ask as well. After all, if you have a chance to speak to a big group of people at once, why not make good use of your time?

For some parts of the preparation, you'll need to figure out your own process. Some people like writing out a speech in longhand first but use only outlines or bullets to practice so it feels more natural. Some people want the full text printed out as they're speaking.

The materials I use depend on the event. For longer speeches or when I'm introducing something new, I like to have the entire speech in hand. If I'm doing something shorter or an event like a canvass kickoff where I'm trying to rally the troops, I just like a few bullets to keep things looser. The more you practice, the more you'll feel comfortable with a specific method—it's just a matter of finding what works for you.

Now that you've got the content, you've got to work on nailing the delivery. I find a big part of that is tapping into your emotion. The first meaningful speech I remember giving was during my campaign for student body president my junior year in high school. I was one of the last ones to go, so I had the benefit of watching as my opponents gave a variety of forward-looking speeches. These speeches were very full of content and agendas and were all very serious.

I looked around at the room full of my classmates and saw that they were bored out of their minds. I knew the room was completely done, so I realized that instead of the brainy speech I was going to give, one that mirrored the other candidates' and was full of policies and programs, I needed to call on emotion. I took the microphone off the stand (my own TED

Talk before the concept existed), and I essentially led a pep rally. It was all excitement and emotion, and seeing the reaction, I knew even before I put the microphone back down that I was going to win. Today, my team calls me "Coach Stephanie," but I think that stage is where she first appeared.

Emotion matters. Yes, we want people to care about our content, we want them to be moved by policy, but the reality is that most people react to your delivery more than anything. That's just human nature. Every speech doesn't need to be a pep rally, but whether I'm giving a forty-minute address at a law school or a canvass kickoff speech, I think about how I'm going to connect to the people in the room and make them believe in my mission and want to join the action.

Writing your best speech also means figuring out what kind of speech works best with your delivery and personal style. I'm a simple speaker with simple language, so shorter sentences work best for me. I'm not President Obama or Hillary Clinton, who can make long sentences with complicated ideas and big words flow naturally. I listen to them in awe, but that doesn't play well coming from me, something my speechwriter and I have figured out together.

All of this requires practice and lots of feedback from people you trust. This is one of those times when you need to know when to ask for help. After decades in politics and ten years at EMILY's List, I am very comfortable giving speeches. And yet I still work with an actress from New York once a year before my biggest speech, just to nail the delivery. She doesn't work in politics, which helps ensure that her focus is on the emotion, not the specific policies I'm discussing. We always work on the physical presentation as well. How you are standing, your facial expressions, and even what your hands are doing are important to the viewer.

Of course, in order to nail a good speech, you don't need an actress to coach you, but it is helpful to find some people who will tell you the truth with honest (but not brutal) feedback.

Some people are naturals at giving speeches. Some can do it easily and it doesn't bother them. They can command a room and speak off the cuff. But for most of us, even those of us who are relatively comfortable with public speaking, it just takes practice and a little good advice. Here are some of my best tips for giving a speech:

- Wear something that makes you feel good. You don't want to be distracted by how you look or something that's uncomfortable or unflattering. You want to focus on your speech. That includes shoes. Make sure you're not wearing shoes that are going to make you wobble or sway at the podium. Be mindful of the backdrop—you don't want to be a floating head because you wore the same color as the background. And if you're going to be on camera, solids are your safest bet.
- Plant your feet firmly and stand up straight. Too often, women shrink themselves. They hunch over, cross their arms over themselves, or twist themselves into a pretzel to take up less space. But you need to project your voice and confidence, and good posture is essential to both. If

it helps, I often remember the advice I've heard on *The Marvelous Mrs. Maisel*, in which the lead character's agent tells her, "Tits up!" before she goes onstage. It may sound crazy, but if you push your chest out, you will have a straight back—and maybe a little chuckle when you need to cut some tension.

- Mind your face. Generally speaking, you want to smile, or at least offer a warm expression, but you also need to keep in mind both what you're saying and your natural facial expressions. I've seen warm and caring women who appear grumpy or overly concerned during speeches even when they're not. I have a different problem: I have resting smiley face. My face is in a constant smile, particularly when I'm nervous. Not the worst thing—most of the time, it's actually positive—but there are times when I'm talking about a serious issue or telling a story about a tragedy and need to actively control my expression.

- If possible, practice the same way you'll give the speech. If you'll be standing at a lectern, try to practice with one. If it's you on a stage with a wireless mic, practice that way. If you are using a teleprompter, try to do a run through with both the prompter and the person who will be running it.

- Think about your audience. People can tell when you're speaking at them instead of speaking to them or with them. Try to engage with them as best you can—look some of them in the eyes like you are sitting across the dinner table. Looking around and speaking to audience members instead of just reading your speech is really key.

- Find a way to relax before the speech. Whether it's taking a five-minute walk, meditating, or drinking a cup of tea, do something that allows you to clear your head and take your heartbeat down a bit if you can. Some people I know like to shake out their nerves and tension literally—they go off by themselves and shake their arms and get the jitters out. Others like to run through the key parts of the speech with someone else in a private space. My team knows that I need a five-minute warning before a speech. I take that time to head to the restroom, look in the mirror, and run through the topline points of the speech. Bonus: It gives me the chance to check my makeup, reapply my lip gloss, and see whether there's food in my teeth.

- Take a few good deep breaths before you go on. When we're speaking, we often forget to breathe, which makes our voice go higher and makes us sound breathless (because we actually are). The experts will tell you that you should speak from your diaphragm. I'm sure as a singer, my number two at EMILY's List, Emily Cain, would agree with that sentiment—and she might be able to tell you why it matters and how to do it. But if I'm honest, I couldn't even identify a diaphragm, let alone figure out how to "speak from it." So I'll just leave you with: Breathe deeply.

- Remember that you've got a great story to tell. Confidence is contagious.

MEETING THE PRESS

If you're a woman who wants to lead, you know that you need to be able to crush an interview. For many of us, that includes press interviews. This is another thing that gets most people nervous. Perhaps it's something about the fact that the press buys ink by the barrelful, controls the airwaves, and influences public opinion.

I get it. I've already told you that being the face of EMILY's List was the thing I needed the most help with when I started, because I was so scared of the press. Put me in a room of a thousand people and I'm great, but put me on MSNBC and I am completely panicked. But after training, practice, and starting small, then moving my way up, I have learned how to do interviews well. I do them all the time, in fact. From print to podcasts to TV, I actually feel pretty comfortable speaking to the press . . . most of the time.

As with making speeches, the best way to get better is to practice. Only you can make the time and find the people who can help you do that. Here are some tips from my own arsenal for how to use the press to help you tell your story to a broader audience.

- **Do your research.** You wouldn't go into a job interview unprepared. The same rules apply here. When you're doing an interview with the press, you need to figure out what the outlet and the reporter have said about you, your issues, the race you're running, etc. You should check out the reporter on social media (most reporters are on Twitter) and see if they've offered any thinking on the news of the day or issues that you care about. Also, presumably you know the general topic of the interview. Make sure you dig into that topic and that you have a solid grasp on all the important details, and on your position.

- **Think about your goals.** What's the headline you want? The idea that any press is good press is, well, wrong. You shouldn't say yes to an interview just because it's offered. You should say yes if you believe it gives you an opportunity to deliver the message you want to the audience you are trying to reach. You need to walk in understanding what that goal is and what the ideal headline would be if you could write it. You can't write it, of course, but you should know what you're aiming for.

- **Figure out what messages you want to deliver.** The reporters control the questions, the placement and the framing, and whether or not they cover you. You only control your answers. Luckily, that's the most important part. You should know going in what messages you want to deliver and have no more than two or three specific things on that list. If you go in with a top ten list, you'll have a hard time delivering a concise and simple message. But if you focus on two or three talking points, your position will seem clear and strong.

- **Plan for the questions that scare you.** The two biggest fears we hear from candidates around interviews are that the reporters will ask tough or uncomfortable questions, or that the candidates won't be able to find the perfect answer on the spot. The best way to overcome those fears is to think through the questions you really don't want to get and then work out answers you're comfortable with. They may not be great answers—sometimes there are just bad questions. But this process will ensure that you actually have an answer to fall back on. Keep adding to this list, and practice periodically. But a tip for the prep: Try to avoid prep sessions that are exclusively the bad questions. That's just too tough on your mental well-being.

- **Practice—out loud.** That's right—I keep telling you this will be hard work. You have to practice for interviews in whatever way is best for you. If you need to start by writing down answers or talking to yourself in the car to better drill them in, that's fine. But however you begin your prep, you *must* also practice answering the most likely questions out loud, either in front of a mirror or with a trusted friend or staffer. It's awkward sometimes, but it's the only way to know which answers don't sound quite right, which words get you a little tongue-tied, and which messages ring false. Preparation is the best way to calm your nerves, as I know from experience. I do this before every single interview.

There's no magic wand to make press interviews less nerve-wracking, particularly when you're getting started. That's why I recommend starting with more forgiving formats if you can—taped TV interviews are less pressure than live or live-to-tape TV pieces, interviews with smaller outlets will have lower stakes than those with your most important validators, and so on. You may make mistakes, but remember that no one is perfect and mistakes are rarely as bad as we think they are. You *will* get better if you keep practicing, ask for help, and listen to feedback.

For me, I expanded my press outreach as I built my confidence. Though as a campaign manager for two big Senate races I had done a couple of print interviews, I really was green coming into EMILY's List. When I got the job, I started with print interviews with reporters I knew and with whom I felt comfortable sharing the big news (my new job). Then my communications staff had me do a couple of progressive radio station interviews—safe ground—to talk about our candidates. After every interview, my press team and I listened to it together and talked through ways to improve.

Then came TV. The first TV interview I did was Bonnie Erbé's show on PBS, where I was on a panel. It was really hard, made more challenging by sitting next to the great House delegate Eleanor Holmes Norton of DC. I found myself just watching how good she was and forgetting that I had to talk, too. I also forgot which camera to look at during the interview. It was rough, but I learned a lot. We moved to C-SPAN, which provided more time to give longer answers. We went back to radio, which I enjoyed doing, and print, where we knew more about the topics and could prep, and then eased into cable. Now I feel comfortable enough to prep well, trust my team, and focus on some of the finer points (like working on what my former comms staffer Marcy Stech called my tendency to go "squinty face").

So, start with practice. Then go to easy print and radio interviews. Then find smaller TV opportunities—for some that would be local access. And one last word to the wise: Don't assume university papers are easy. I always get some of my toughest questions from school newspapers!

THE TOPLINES

Telling your story is a vital part of changing the world. These days, our society demands every part of us, and so learning how to best tell your story and leverage it for your issues is critical.

When you're trying to move people or convince them of something, you should break your stories into four parts:

Situation: What you're facing

Reaction: What you've done about it

Resolve: What you'll do to take your response to the next level

Ask: What you need from the audience

If you want people to actually hear your story, you need to be able to give a speech. That requires the right content, but especially the right emotion in your delivery and your story. In order to do that well, you should:

- Wear something that makes you feel good.
- Plant your feet firmly and stand up straight.
- Mind your face. This is particularly important if you wear a permanent scowl or, like me, a permanent smile.
- Practice, ideally the same way you'll give the speech.
- Speak directly to your audience. Know who they are, understand what they want to hear, and talk to them, not the piece of paper on the lectern. Find a few friendly faces in the room to go back to if you need encouragement.
- Find a way to relax before the speech. Take a few minutes to run through the key points, do a mirror check, or whatever will make you feel ready.
- Take a few deep breaths and breathe from your diaphragm.
- Be confident. Audiences feed off it. They'll respond better to you and your great story.

Dealing with the press is another way to get your story out. Here are a few ways to nail an interview:

- Know what the reporter and outlet have written about you, your campaign, or the issue and the topic of your interview.

- Go in knowing the headline you want to achieve and the audience you want to reach.

- Figure out what messages you want to deliver. You should have no more than two or three message points that you want to drive home. Think about how you're going to work those into your answers.

- Brainstorm the tough questions that keep you or your team up at night, as well as answers for those questions. Practice them periodically.

- Practice. Out loud. You can guess the first question or two—say out loud how you would answer them.

★★★

CHAPTER 5

Build Your Team

NO ONE CHANGES the world all by themselves. You may be the candidate, the leader of the movement, the first and only person to stand up for your cause—but you won't get very far if you're by yourself.

Hillary Clinton was right: It takes a village. *Village* can mean a lot of things, and can speak to different types of teams and support systems.

The World Cup–champion US women's national soccer team needs every player to win the game on the field and to challenge the sexist pay gap in American professional soccer off the field.

"The Squad" has been making news since they got elected. They are a group of four dynamic and progressive members of the House of Representatives: New York Congresswoman Alexandria Ocasio-Cortez, Minnesota Congresswoman Ilhan Omar, Massachusetts Congresswoman Ayanna Pressley, and

Michigan Congresswoman Rashida Tlaib. These four women of color, including the first two Muslim women in Congress, have stood up to Trump continuously since they took office. They have been threatened frequently and attacked publicly as a result. But through it all, they've had each other's backs and amplified each other's voices.

You may also have heard of "the Badasses," a group of women who took their national security experience to their successful campaigns for Congress and then to the House floor. New Jersey Congresswoman Mikie Sherrill was a Navy pilot and assistant US attorney. Pennsylvania Congresswoman Chrissy Houlahan served in the Air Force. Virginia Congress-woman Elaine Luria served as a Navy officer on surface ships and carriers for years. And Michigan Congresswoman Elissa Slotkin and Virginia Congresswoman Abigail Spanberger are both former CIA officials.

While they were not the first women with national security service experience to run for office, they are still some of the first. These women decided to help each other through the process. Through their campaigns, they lifted each other's spirits and validated each other the same way many of us do: with text chains, and glasses of wine on the rare occasion they were in the same city. That support continues now that they are in office. In fact, when they decided to support convening an impeachment investigation in the House, they did so standing side by side, along with other veterans in Congress.[1]

Every successful leader creates her own village in order to run, to lead, and to succeed.

And it starts by acknowledging that you can't do it yourself. Please take a minute to do so now. I mean it. You cannot do this on your own.

No campaign is a one-woman affair. And the best campaigns and the best organizations are led by women who delegate well and make the best use of all of the people and tools at their disposal. It's not just having a team; it's providing strategic direction and then utilizing and trusting that team to do their jobs. That's real leadership.

So what should your team look like? Well, that depends entirely on what you're trying to accomplish. It could be a few very scrappy volunteers and supportive family members, or a kitchen cabinet of close friends. Or it could be something a little more professional, like a team with a paid staff resembling a start-up business. Regardless of what your operation looks like, though, you need people to play specific and clearly defined roles. Let's dive into how you can build the best team possible.

YOUR CAMPAIGN

The size of a team can vary, from the literally hundreds of people on presidential campaigns to just a handful of volunteers you recruit to help you run your local race. Instead of talking about the exact titles and positions, let's talk instead about the key jobs that every campaign needs to fill, and then more generally about what types of people can get those jobs done.

Deciding the size of your team is the first step. In some small offices, one person handles multiple responsibilities, while in larger ones there may be many people assigned to one task. You've got to find the best way to get this done for you, based on what you are trying to accomplish. Rightsizing an organization is very important, particularly for your financial bottom line.

Campaigns are the original start-ups. They start from nothing; build to a fully operational organization very quickly, within months or a whole year if you have it; then reach Election Day and shut down, just like that. It's like building a big business barreling toward a one-day going-out-of-business sale where everything must go, and go exactly right. When you think about it, it is kind of crazy. You spend all these months getting the right people on your side, talking to voters, and raising the money to achieve one simple goal: Getting votes. Enough votes to win. And when the voting is over, the campaign is over, and everyone packs up and heads home.

But as you build your campaign, you have very little time and even less money to figure out your available audiences, how to reach them, and how best to move their support to you, or your candidate, or your cause. Your campaign requires all of the work of a business, but thanks to its having less money and a very definite timeline (you can't move Election Day), it requires a great deal of innovation and creativity and a near-perfect game. Campaigns move fast, and people have to be smart, nimble, and strategic to keep up, operating within a system that allows them to do their best work. It's something we should all remember when thinking through what we need on a team in any aspect of our lives.

As you read the following list, I still hope you're thinking about running for office. But as much as I want everyone to run, I hope this also illustrates just how many roles there are for you in politics, no matter who you are or what your skill set is. My roles thus far have included the volunteer, the finance director, the campaign manager, and the chief of staff. Then when I arrived at EMILY's List, I became the front person— the chief strategist, chief fundraiser, and chief spokeswoman. Working for or volunteering on campaigns is incredibly ful-filling, fun, and an important part of changing the world.

Whether as the candidate, a staff member, or a volunteer, you'll see a wide variety of specific jobs that need to get done on a successful campaign. No matter what your skills are, they can be put to use in politics. Read below, and think about where you'd best fit in.

Who Decides What the Organization Will Look Like?

First, let's talk about the plan. I always remind people that this isn't rocket science; it's putting a puzzle together. You just need to know what the pieces are. EMILY's List has a lot of resources to help you organize no matter what level of office you are engaging in. The smaller the office, typically, the fewer financial resources you will have with which to hire people and consultants. With a bigger office, the necessary budget and the ideal amount of people you need can look infinite. Both extremes, and everything in between, require careful and realistic planning.

Start by researching how much a typical race for this particular office costs. What did the most recent campaign for this position cost the candidates? Are we talking a $50,000 budget, a $1 million budget, or a $5 million budget? Someone should be responsible for deciding what you need, how many roles you can pay to fill, and how to manage that process. Sometimes that will be the candidate, but many times, a campaign manager or campaign professionals like us at EMILY's List can be brought in to make those early decisions. Don't be afraid, women of America, to call EMILY's List for advice. Early wrong decisions can cost you big-time in the end.

Simply, you, a manager or consultant, or organizations like EMILY's List can help lay out what your budget and structure should look like. Let's talk about some specific roles you could see on a campaign, depending on its size.

Managing the Team and the Process

You need someone in charge. If you have a staff, they need to be managed and they need to get paid. They need health care, they need email addresses, and so on. This is the business side of the work. Someone needs to make sure your campaign is following all of the relevant laws, including human resource regulations and the applicable election rules. Someone has to deal with the office space, the travel (as needed), the technology, finding and paying vendors, and more. If that technology doesn't include strong security against hacks and other interference, you haven't been paying attention for the last few years. Someone needs to make sure that each of the key members of the team is communicating with the others and they're all working well together—not always an easy job when the team is working too many hours with too few breaks. I'll remind you now, long hours are just part of it.

I put this category of tasks first on purpose. The person or people who manage the process are the unsung heroes of any campaign effort. They are the people whose jobs often aren't noticed until there's an issue or a problem, but we rely on everything they do to keep things running smoothly.

- Who fills these roles: campaign manager, treasurer, chief administrative officer, chief operations officer, chief financial officer, human resource director, chief technology officer

Strategy and Messaging

Campaigns are all about figuring out why people should vote for you, why they should support your cause, and how you're going to convince them to do it. Your strategic plan and your message are the foundation on which the entire campaign is built. They should be informed by research and an understanding of the district and the electorate. And they need to be flexible and adapt to changing circumstances, just like your campaign.

Your message is not just a slogan but the underlying argument for your candidacy. Though, of course, slogans can be highly effective at communicating your message: It's *Hope and Change*. It's *Stronger Together*. It's *Change Can't Wait*. It's even *Make America Great Again*. But the underlying argument that backs up these slogans, as well as your plan to deliver that message to the voters, is what's going to matter in the long haul. Why are you running? And what are you going to do to make voters feel good about their future? That is the backbone of a campaign.

Once you've decided on your message, you have strategic decisions to make. Are you going to engage or ignore your opponent? Do you have the resources to mass-communicate? Even digital communications cost money, and TV, which still works with a number of audiences, is really expensive. So if you can't personally knock on every door in your district twice and get to know your voters firsthand, how will you raise money to communicate more broadly?

Then you need folks who can help you think through the way to get to 50 percent + 1, as we like to say. Or 52 percent, as I like to say, because recounts suck. Are you going to try to go big by spending early resources in delivering your own story and message via TV? Are you going to start by disqualifying your opponent via the media or TV and digital ads? Are you going to focus your time on events and meet voters literally where they live? Do you want to ignore attacks (a great way to deprive them of oxygen), or do you want to face attacks head on and turn them into a weapon against your opponent? These are just a few of the questions you might consider in developing and implementing your campaign strategy.

The key is that you have to tell voters who you are and the good that you are going to do for them, while contrasting yourself with your opponent to show why their plan is bad. A campaign plan includes what you are going to say (your message), how you are going to communicate your message to voters (door-to-door field, TV, digital, direct mail, phones), and how you are going to pay for all this (your budget).

Communicating who you are and why you are running is a great place to start. Nice and positive messaging to introduce the candidate is usually a safe bet. But elections are competitions. That means someone is going to win and someone is going to lose. The voters need the contrast to understand the choice, and defining yourself in contrast to your opponent is a valuable tool as well.

And this is worth saying again: Your strategic plan and your message are the foundation on which the entire campaign is built. They should be informed by research and an understanding of the district and the electorate. And both need to be flexible and adapt to changing circumstances, just like your campaign.

- Who fills this role: campaign manager, pollster, ad maker, general consultant, communications team, and sometimes help from party entities and organizations like EM-ILY's List

Communicating with Key Audiences

If you're going to do big things, you will need to figure out a way to make use of all three kinds of media: paid, owned, and earned.

Paid media is just what it sounds like. It's TV, radio, print, literature, or digital ads, or sponsored online content that you pay for. You get to decide exactly what you put out there and where you put it (which shows, newspapers, websites, etc.), but you have to pay for that privilege.

Owned media describes the platforms or accounts that you have total control of. This is your Facebook, Twitter, and Instagram accounts; campaign website; email list; etc. The only cost to your campaign for this type of communication is in staff time. That's not nothing, since building and motivating that following is hard work. It's well worth it, though, because once that following is built, you have an army of evangelists. The important thing to remember is that these advocates need information to get engaged. Activists are amazing. But they will veer off your message if you don't give them some guidance.

The final form of media is earned media, and like the name suggests, you're going to work for it. This involves the media and journalists on platforms you don't control, which generally means they're viewed with more credibility by voters. If you're going to run for office or change the world, you're going to want to get some press around to cover it, which means someone has to talk to the reporters, pitch the podcasts, convince the editorial boards. These days, the world is one constant news cycle, fueled by reporters who need to create more and more content, presenting both more opportunities and more challenges.

■ Who fills this role: communications director, digital director, press secretary, social media director

Raising the Necessary Resources

Campaigns cost money. Even the most people-powered campaign still needs a way to pay the staff, build the website, or pay the rent on the offices where volunteers meet and make phone calls. But there's good news on this front, particularly if you, like me, want to see the end of the influence of money in politics. While big donors can still make a huge difference (and I'm certainly grateful for the generous Democratic ones who put money behind electing women), grassroots donations are becoming an increasingly important part of campaign fundraising. Other than the advent of social media, this is the thing that has changed more than anything in my years of campaigning.

It's not just campaigns, of course. Nonprofits need donors, companies need seed money and shareholders, your local NPR station needs listeners like you. We all need resources to do big things, so whatever your effort, you need to think about how you're going to get funding and from whom.

- Who fills this role: finance director and necessary staff support, digital team (for online, social, and email fundraising), and, yes, the candidate herself

Building Allies

Every successful campaign has influential allies, groups (large and small) who support you by giving you credibility, donations, and/or volunteers—the elected officials and community leaders who lend validity (and hopefully their own lists and support systems) to your race. That kind of support doesn't often come looking for you. You and your team have to do the work in seeking out smart partnerships, and then the even harder work of winning them over.

This is a part of every organization and every history-making, world-changing enterprise. If you want to make change, you need to figure out how to win allied groups and people to your side, how to get them to step out of their comfort zone and try something new or take a risk by publicly standing with you. You have to convince them that they have reason to stand with you because you share the same values and goals, and because you will always stand by them in return. That's what being an ally is all about.

- Who fills this role: political director, campaign manager, and, again, the candidate herself

Convincing and Mobilizing the Voters

By the end of your campaign, every person on your team—paid, unpaid, family members, college roommates, that neighbor who offered to help, and so on—will be talking to voters. This work involves figuring out the plan and answering the key questions: What is your vote goal? Who are the voters you need to reach, and how do you best convince them?

I know it seems obvious, but you do not need to win all the votes to win the race. Ultimately, you need 50 percent plus one vote, but like I said, try to build for 52 percent at least. You'll need to figure out what the turnout is likely to be and how many of those voters can be persuaded to vote for you. Too many Americans don't vote, especially in state and local elections, so you have to make your best educated guess as to how many will turn out for the upcoming Election Day. That gives you a base number to work from. After that, you'll need to determine what percentage of likely voters can be persuaded to cast their ballots for you. Some people are just not going to vote for you, no matter what. But that's all right. You don't need them all to win, so focus your efforts on the ones you can convince, while still giving attention to voters you consider a "sure thing."

Know your margins, set reasonable goals, and don't spend time chasing votes (support, donations, etc.) that are not winnable. Work on the available field, not the whole field.

- Who fills this role: campaign managers, field directors, analytics team

Chairwoman of the Board

The chairwoman of the board is the leader of the whole operation. Of course, the candidate is the inspiration and the motivation, the reason for the entire team, but they are also the person who sets the values and norms of the organization.

Knowing how to delegate is the key to being a successful leader. By hiring good people in the other roles, you are free to be the motivation that both the staff and the voters need. That job, by the way, is exhausting and often underappreciated. It's a tall order to maintain a joyous presence all day, every day, with energy that is contagious. Therefore, staying focused on the bigger picture and finding a team that you trust to manage the important support work is the key to the whole thing.

- Who fills this role: Only the candidate can do this. And I'm sincerely hoping that person is you. Don't worry, you've got this. Keep reading.

This list can seem overwhelming, particularly if you're running for a local office or planning something that won't allow for a large staff. But keep in mind that this is a list of jobs that need to be done, not necessarily individual positions that you need to hire for. In any effort, you'll need to figure out how to do each of these things, with your campaign team, your own hard work, and volunteers.

In fact, every one of these roles may be filled by volunteers. Volunteers can be the best fundraisers, leaders, spokespeople.

Volunteer-driven efforts can be effective and powerful. Volunteers are golden, if trained and empowered, and they can take on many of these roles—but they need to be treated with the respect they deserve. Small campaigns—just like many grassroots efforts—depend not just on volunteer help but often on volunteer leaders, those amazing people willing to give up their time and effort to change the world.

So now you need to decide how each role is getting filled, how each role is getting done, how responsibilities will be handed out, and who will make decisions at every level. It's a planning process that can make or break a campaign. Many candidates want to sign off on everything; many campaign managers want the same. Nothing can stop movement faster than an unclear or overly burdensome decision-making process. The best campaigns are smart, strategic, and nimble. You need to figure out how to be all three.

When I took over as the campaign manager for a then-floundering Senate race, I was told by concerned local allies, leaders, and even hired consultants that I needed to clean house and fire the entire senior team so I could start over with a clean slate. But I took a beat, got acquainted with the campaign and the senior team, and tried to diagnose the root problems before I took any drastic action.

What I realized very quickly was that this group of talented campaigners did not have a clear structure or plan. They were trying to make decisions as a group, and they had overlapping responsibilities. As a result, decisions were made way too slowly. Some small things got too much attention, while important jobs fell through the cracks. Junior staffers weren't exactly sure whom to ask about what, particularly in moments of crisis (and there are many of those in campaigns).

So instead of firing the team, I went to work reorganizing. To start, I simplified the workflow and gave them each a clear lane. Then I streamlined the decision-making process. And because they were grown-ups who knew the campaign was not running as well as it could, they trusted my decisions, even when those decisions were harsh. I had to demote some staffers, but instead of bristling at what could have been viewed as lesser roles, they flourished in them.

I believe when we won that race, it was not in spite of those staffers I was told to fire but because of them. I think back to that example often to remind myself that everyone needs a clear definition of their role and an understanding of the path forward to be able to do their best work. I'm still so proud of that team.

A Few Thoughts on Management and Leadership

Throughout my career, I've managed two successful statewide campaigns, a House race, a large department on a presidential race, a brand-new Senate office, and a major national organization. Each offered different challenges, but in all these varying positions, these two things remained true: Good management is vital, and good management takes time and effort.

No matter what you're doing in your life—organizing activities for your kids' school, running a nonprofit, planning the neighborhood watch, or taking a leadership role in a business—surround yourself with people you can trust and who know what they're doing. And if they don't know what they're doing at the outset, they must be willing to learn. Especially on a mission as singular as a campaign, don't expect your team to be perfect or know everything at the start. Just be sure that they are hungry, willing to give the time, and willing to learn. Sound familiar?

As a manager, I always start by building the structure. Whether it was a smaller congressional race, Montana Senator Jon Tester's official Senate operation, or EMILY's List, my first step was creating a flowchart with the ideal sequence of jobs and job descriptions. If you come in with an operation already in place, you should start with this project. You've been asked to lead something, so you need to make sure that organization is built to achieve what you need to get done. That means taking the time to figure out the current structure, who's in it, and what their responsibilities are. Only then can you decide if you need to make changes.

Sometimes you'll find the right people are in the wrong roles. On several occasions, I've had to move people around so their responsibilities better fit their skills. Afterward, the campaign operated more smoothly and so did the staffers. I think if you asked most of them, they'd tell you they had a better experience after they got into the job that suited them. I'd made sure that they had what they needed to succeed.

Of course, the necessary fix is not always so painless. I've joined organizations with people who weren't supportive of changes in leadership or structure. After joining and assessing the existing structure, I've had to let people go who weren't right for the job or whose job was not needed at that time. Sometimes the organization needs a big shift. Those decisions are never easy, and they have real effects on people's lives. Decisions made in the best interest of the organization can cost individuals a lot, and thus should be made with careful thought and due respect.

When I started at EMILY's List, I was not just taking on the campaign manager role. For the first time in my career, I would truly be the leader of an organization. Knowing this was a step up from the responsibilities at my previous jobs, I talked to a lot of fellow CEOs and presidents of other progressive organizations, unions, and even a few friends in the private sector about how to provide a vision for an entire organization.

But I quickly realized that vision was not the problem at hand. There were external factors at play that needed my attention first. In 2010, EMILY's List was still trying to recover from the worst recession in decades—a recession that was still hampering the nation. We learned that when many of our donors lost money in the market, they cut their contributions dramatically. Though clearly the existing staffers and the organization itself were not at fault in this case, EMILY's List was in a financially challenging moment.

On top of that, the organization had also just suffered a loss in the special election of the Massachusetts Senate race. Looking back, that loss was the canary in the coal mine portending the massive Democratic losses to come later in 2010. At the time, though, we had no idea what was to come. Not only did it feel like EMILY's List was at fault for losing what we thought would be an easy election; many in the political world laid the blame at our feet and our candidate's.

However, stepping into my new role would have been challenging no matter the external circumstances. I was starting as only the second president ever for EMILY's List, following the founder, Ellen Malcolm, and walking into an existing structure with twenty-five years of history. Several positions, including executive director and communications director, were being held open for financial reasons, and also so I, the new president, would have the chance to hire my own people. The problem was that the organization was grinding to a halt because of the recession, so we needed to make some serious decisions. And we now found ourselves at the beginning of what was about to be the 2010 Democratic bloodbath. In short, money troubles, political troubles, and morale troubles were coming straight at me.

It was a huge management challenge and a huge leadership challenge, one that taught me some valuable lessons. I wish I could say I did it all correctly. But of course that's not how life goes. I made mistakes. I chose to stop the bleeding first, but that meant not taking time to build trust with the board and chair. That was a mistake I made. Leadership transitions are difficult for organizations even under the best of circumstances. Despite the mistakes, I'm proud to say that with the help of my incredible staff, EMILY's List righted the ship.

This experience confirmed my belief that people are the most important aspect of any endeavor. How they work, and particularly how they work together, makes all the difference between success and failure. I spent my time getting to know the staff to figure out who was in the right role and who needed to be shifted. We were in for a fight, so I needed to know who had it in them to rally after a tough season. Needing money and preparing to reorganize, I made the toughest decision I have had to make in a job yet. After the election, EMILY's List had to downsize. In one brutal day we let eighteen people go.

It was awful. But these are the moments when leaders have to step up. Making the hard decisions to not just survive but thrive is part of the job. From that day on, we started to rebuild. I began to get those who stayed on the support they needed to succeed—emotional support, more resources, technical assistance, and ultimately additional staff support. If you don't find a way to treat your people right, you are setting yourself and your organization up to fail.

By the way, at the end of 2010, EMILY's List had thirty-three staff and a $32 million budget for the election cycle. By the end of the 2018 cycle, we had more than one hundred staff and raised and spent $105 million over those two years to elect a historic number of women. And we are continuing to grow. Those hard decisions ten years ago made EMILY's List stronger, smarter, and more powerful than ever. Do what's right for the long term and do your best to take care of those you can't bring with you. It is hard to be at the top of any organization, but that can't stop you from making the tough calls.

There was one more big challenge EMILY's List faced when I took over as president. I quickly realized we had a significant technology deficit that had to be fixed before we could move forward. Just to give you a sense of where we were technologically, we didn't have a digital department *at all* in 2010. But what was amazing was that the best person to build that department was already there. There was clearly opportunity to grow online, and fast, but the then-one-person website staff, Emily Lockwood, was buried in the direct marketing department. They oversaw all the small-dollar donors, which, at the time, were mostly direct mail donors.

I wasn't sure what I was going to find when I went to speak with Emily (we have a lot of Emilys at EMILY's List—call it fate) for the first time, but I was open and optimistic to see the potential in people already working at EMILY's List. Long story short, she was a gem. I immediately promoted her and told her to start building a digital department. We have had many fabulous digital directors since Emily Lockwood, including our current rock star, Ben Dotson, but without those early decisions by Emily, I don't believe we would have taken EMILY's List from an online community of 180,000 to well over 5 million members today. When you step into a new leadership role, I urge you to look at the talent that is already there and take some risks. You might be surprised in the best ways.

FIND YOUR PARTNER

Now that you have your team, either one you've built from the ground up or one you've inherited, the next thing you'll need is your own partner in management. This is especially true in a campaign. The roles of candidate and campaign manager are different but both vital. As the president of EMILY's List, I am the public face of the organization, and so I do much of the fundraising and I'm often on the road. I needed to find an executive director who could manage the staff when I wasn't there and lead the team in ways that complemented my own skills. This is often a situation where opposites attract. In other words, don't hire another you. Hire someone who brings to the table things that you don't.

When you find that person, you need to build trust with them. The most important quality for them to have, whether they're a close friend or a new hire, is that they are comfortable telling you no. In the ten-plus years I have been president of EMILY's List, I have only had three executive directors, which is a great record in politics, where turnover is typically fast. The first two were recruited to be the CEO of the Democratic National Committee directly from our operation. Now I am holding on to the third one for dear life.

My first executive director was an old friend and colleague, Amy Dacey. She and I had worked together back in 2002 at the Democratic Senatorial Campaign Committee. We worked hard and we had fun on that committee, and built up a lot of trust and respect. We became very close friends, and she supported my move to the Howard Dean presidential campaign in 2003, even as she was a leader in John Kerry's presidential campaign. We cheered each other's careers on for years and saw each other when we could.

Eight years later, when I took this big new job, I knew I had to have her by my side. She was a woman whose work I knew and respected, and I knew she would be a partner whom I could trust to be honest with me. It took a little convincing on my part, but Amy finally said yes, and together we did some amazing early work. We made some hard changes at the beginning, including the massive downsizing to rebuild EMILY's List. I would have never survived the first few years of EMILY's List without Amy Dacey by my side. When President Obama called her to a meeting to recruit her to run the Democratic National Committee, I knew it was time for me to learn to survive without her. You just don't say no to an offer like that! So after three years of reorganization and growth, off she went.

My second executive director was also someone I had known and trusted since my days on the Dean campaign. It was 2013 and still early days for me at EMILY's List. Given the growing pains we were facing and the big challenges ahead—including likely having a woman at the top of the presidential ticket—I still felt like I had to have someone who knew me well and had my back in that role. Jess O'Connell was the person I needed. Jess had worked for Hillary's presidential campaign with me in 2008. I knew from working with her that she had great relationships in the political world and, more important, had serious skills managing a growing team.

Plus there was the added benefit that Jess O'Connell had done a stint at EMILY's List before I got there. In fact, she knew the organization so well, when I became president, Jess bought me a celebration/condolence drink. She was concerned about the future of EMILY's List and doubted whether I (or anyone) could succeed following the founder. During that drink, just like the Jess I had known on the Dean campaign, she was always willing to speak honestly, whether I wanted to hear it or not. She was straight with me about the changes she thought I could make as the new president and had advice on how to make progress for a cause she loved. She also told me it was going to be harder than I could imagine. She was right about that, too. She gave me a list of ten things I should consider doing. Ten years later, I still have that letter and have executed at least half of those suggestions.

Jess was a different kind of partner than Amy, but EMILY's List had already changed a lot under my leadership, and I needed a new kind of partner for this next chapter. She came on board in 2013 and guided us through the storm of 2016, but then the Democratic National Committee called again, and she, too, became the CEO, in 2017.

I was lucky to have two women I trusted from day one by my side in those early years. In a lot of cases, though, you'll need to build trust with your number two from scratch. Being president of EMILY's List was the first time I was in charge, but I had been the right-hand woman a few times in my career. And each time, I had to build trust from the ground up. That was what I had to do when I became finance director for Howard Dean, and later the campaign manager for Senate candidates Jon Tester and Al Franken. I didn't know those guys when they hired me, or at least not in a real or personal way. It takes time to build a relationship. But because of those experiences, I knew it could be done.

After hiring two close friends as executive directors one and two, EMILY's List and I were ready for a different type of executive director. It was 2017, and as an organization, we were also focused on figuring out what came next after Hillary Clinton's loss. I knew we needed a leader to come in with new energy. To be honest, I was dragging a bit after seven years in this tough but wonderful job. Cue Emily Cain.

Emily Cain was a legislator in Maine for ten years before she twice ran unsuccessfully for Congress with EMILY's List's support, most recently in 2016. When she called to apply for the job, I wasn't convinced she would be the perfect person for it. She was an unconventional choice, and being the candidate and being the person behind the scenes who makes sure the trains run on time are two completely different jobs. But though she didn't fit 100 percent of the job description, she had unique and impressive experience, she was passionate about EMILY's List and its mission, and most important, she was willing to learn the rest. It didn't hurt her case that she is a human ray of sunshine.

Emily and I didn't really know each other, so this was a first for me. I was the boss and I was bringing in a partner whom I knew only minimally. I took a risk on hiring her, but I felt in my gut that she was the right person at the right time. She is the definition of a joyful warrior, and that was what we needed in 2017.

But we had to build trust, and quickly, because we were beginning to lose staffers who were exhausted from the 2016 election and everything that came after. Even I was burned out, so first I needed Emily to learn the job quickly and without interference. So I put all my trust in her while I went for a five-week vacation to Europe just a few weeks after she started. I know she might have thought it was crazy, but it ended up working brilliantly. I knew she needed me out of the way so she could build trust with her direct reports. And by leaving and putting that trust in her to run the organization, I strengthened her confidence that she could do the job. It proved to us both that I believed in her.

I learned a long time ago how to delegate, and that is what I did. It wasn't for me to teach her how to be the executive director. I simply laid out the vision of where I wanted EMILY's List to go in 2018, the direction I wanted to see the staff start moving in, and the parameters of decision-making she could do with me and without me. Then I let her run. I knew things would be mostly fine, with a few hiccups here and there. And guess what? They were. Since then, we talk damn near daily and have become great friends. As you read earlier, she was my first call when I had my stroke, because I knew she would be there for me and keep EMILY's List going.

So that is how I built trust as a leader, by believing in the person I hired without knowing 100 percent that it was going to work. For me, that's been a really effective strategy, but I've been lucky to have worked with such capable women. There may be times when a new hire does need a bit more oversight from you. In those cases, you fix it by providing guidance, direction, and, when necessary, a second chance. If it still doesn't work, well, you may have to make a change. That's just the reality sometimes, and that is okay. I don't like letting people go, but if it isn't a good match, trust that your campaign or organization will benefit from decisive action. Knowing when things aren't working is part of leadership, too.

I've had ten years to learn my process on this. Campaigns are much quicker than that! So if you're the candidate, you won't have this much time for trust building. When you are building trust with a campaign manager or a second-in-command, I suggest being open to having a true professional partner, not a subordinate. So I recommend a couple of things. Try to get to know the person in a social setting fairly quickly. And in doing so, it's always nice to get to know their spouse and family, if possible. Leadership is hard and it can be lonely. Being a candidate is also really hard and lonely. It's important to have a true partner in this and not a "staffer." I am not suggesting you need to be best friends. But to work together effectively, trust is essential.

I know that some people prefer to maintain a separation of work life and personal life. But in order to build trust in a partnership, you need to know your partner, respect them, and understand how they tick. Liking them is a huge bonus. In return, you have to open up so they can learn about you, too. For those of us in campaigns or movement work, it's easy, since we start out on common ground. When we're all devoted to the same cause, we come in with a clear understanding of each other's motivations and the knowledge that we're both working to change the world in a similar way. But whether it's nonprofit work or corporate, building professional partnerships at the top is key to your success as a leader and the success of the organization. You cannot do this alone.

A real professional partnership is a very special relationship. If that relationship is working, the rest will be a lot easier. That's why we teach all of our campaign managers that a good working relationship with their candidate is the most important part of their job. In each of the races I ran, I made the rule that the last call of the day from each candidate was with me. I never cared how late it was. I just wanted to have that last gut check. Being able to share the experience and the pressure of leading a big operation with a specific and short-term goal is key to getting through it with your sanity intact.

I got to know the spouses and the kids. I included them in the plans I was making. I had some late-night cake with some candidates and late-night wine (or hard liquor, depending) with others. Changing the world is no small task. Having someone next to you in that fight with whom to vent, cheer, cry, laugh, and, most of all, think, is critical.

FIGURE OUT YOUR STYLE FOR DEALING WITH FUMBLES

Once you've found your work partner and figured out the right roles for your staff, then you have to figure out how you're going to lead and motivate your team. I spend a lot of time worrying about whether my team is clear on what they are doing. Luckily for me, EMILY's List has a mission that could not be clearer: elect pro-choice Democratic women. As their leader, I hope, through optimism and with this clear goal in mind, I can keep this team motivated and productive. You will have to take on that role, too, as a candidate, an elected official, or the leader of an organization.

Another part of maintaining morale and motivation is deciding how you're going to deal with it when your team screws up. The simple fact of the matter is, people make mistakes and things go wrong. And while every leader will develop her own ways of dealing with mistakes, I can tell you the philosophy that has served me well: I'd rather have people run as hard and as fast as they can, knowing they'll trip and fall sometimes, than have them walking on eggshells. From the get-go, I want everyone working for me to know that they can be honest with me when something goes wrong, and that I'm ready to help them get back up and keep moving. To me, tripping, even breaking things, is better than having people stand still to avoid missteps.

Put simply, risk-taking is crucial, so don't make a demand for perfection that will impede progress. It's not that details don't matter or that we don't want to do things well—good, clean work is vital in a well run organization. But I've watched too many organizations freeze up with indecision under the pressure of perfection. If you can instill in your team the idea that taking risks and moving forward is better than indecision, it's a win for everyone. Fostering an environment that rewards creative thinking and doesn't punish mistakes too harshly will serve you in the long run, whether you're leading a campaign, leading an organization, or involved in any other endeavor.

Studies have shown we view risk through a gendered lens. Women are perceived as being more risk-averse because they are statistically less likely to take certain kinds of risk. So, ladies, let me be especially clear on this: We need to take risks. We need to take chances. We need to foster environments that reward innovation and initiative. That's easier to do when you, like me, view smart risk-taking as the best kind of way to move forward. It is also easier when you have people around you whom you trust and you are okay with making a mistake once in a while, as long as you don't make the same mistake twice.

As a risk-taking candidate, leader, or manager, you'll make plenty of mistakes. As will your team. Your job is not to be perfect. It's to ensure that you don't make the same mistakes over and over, that you answer for the ones you and your team make (that's on you, by the way—the buck stops with the leader), and that you make sure the entire team learns from those mistakes. And then get back to moving forward as fast as you can.

LEARN HOW TO EARN LOYALTY AND BUILD STRENGTH
THROUGH A MILLION ACTS OF KINDNESS

As a leader, building loyalty is how you build power. Loyalty is the key marker of a strong relationship, but it only truly means anything when it goes both ways. I can look across the Democratic political spectrum and see where people I've managed have landed. Having even a tiny part in their getting there is the coolest thing I've ever done, and one of the things I'm most proud of in my career and at EMILY's List is helping people spread their wings. Too often, we hear about managers who try too hard to hold on to good people. While I'm sad when we lose great staffers, we don't demand loyalty when a superstar employee is thinking about leaving, and we certainly don't hold it against them after they're gone. The idea is that if you help people grow, they'll do just that, and someday they'll be ready to fly away. Hopefully they'll come back and visit once in a while. (You all know who you are—and I hope you all know I am always here for you!)

Your responsibilities as a manager don't end when someone's job with you ends. In fact, as you get to know your team and their motivations, it's also good to understand their long-term goals. We're no longer in a world where people stay in one job for fifty years and retire with a gold watch. That's especially true in the world of campaigns and politics, where jobs often end in a single election cycle. Unfortunately, those short-term goals mean that professional development is too often not a priority for the management of staff. The goal is to win the race, not make sure that your staff is ready to take the next step or get the next job.

That is systemic shortsightedness, and it is just a mistake for a leader. You get two important things when you invest in your people. One, you help people grow and expand their ability to change the world. Get to know your team and think about where their skills lie, as well as where they need to improve. Ask them where they want to end up next or in the long run. Offer them guidance based on your experience, think about who you can connect them with, and give them the feedback they need to get better. What skill (even if it's not one of your strengths) can you help them improve? Doing that helps you with the second thing: You grow your own network as those people move on and become increasingly powerful and effective.

Loyalty is not a one-way street. The best relationships are built on earned loyalty between both parties, rather than a series of quid pro quos. So I never demand loyalty, but I try to earn it every day. I feel this way with my girlfriends but also with my team. Our senior leaders know that I don't just want to know when someone on their staff is going through a family issue or has some good news, I want their phone number to call them myself and check in. I learned that from my mom's girlfriends in Butte, who took care of each other throughout their lives and careers. My mom kept up with all of the families in our neighborhood—Dad always called her the social director because she maintained all the relationships. I like to run my organization with that same mindset.

Good leadership is built on relationships, and those relationships are built brick by brick, not all at once. Speaker Nancy
Pelosi is the master of showing how the hundred little things
we do can add up to a truly meaningful relationship and help
strengthen loyalty. In the middle of the impeachment hearings,
with chaos swirling all around her, and with two of the people
closest to her very ill, she somehow heard I was dealing with a
health issue. She called me herself, giving me a (gentle) lecture
about taking care of myself. Then she and her team sent me
flowers (an orchid, of course—her signature). And when I
called her back to express my condolences after her brother and
her dear friend Representative Elijah Cummings passed away,
she picked up the phone. Then I sent her chocolates (her favorite) because that's what you do for those who matter to you. But
more important—not that I needed much more of a reason—I
would do anything for Speaker Pelosi. My loyalty to her will
last forever for a million different reasons. She clarified for me
a critical lesson—that loyalty is not demanded; it is earned by
the leader, and it is a two-way street.

Speaker Pelosi is an expert at maintaining hundreds of
close relationships and knows that each action builds a little
bit more loyalty. I look up to her immensely for that skill. Of
course, she would be the first to tell you that she has a process
and a team to help, especially with thoughtful gestures like
the orchid she sent me. She has been deliberate in setting up
that team, and in honing a process to make sure that her
friends feel the thoughtfulness and intentionality of her
attention. And look what has resulted from that: She's now

arguably the most powerful woman, and easily one of the most powerful people, in the world. Frankly, I owe a great deal to Speaker Pelosi for teaching me how to be a different kind of leader.

In recent years, I've learned that good leadership has both strength and softness. Both those characteristics build loyalty and a network for changing the world. My network is not just about me, nor is it about doing favors for someone solely so you can get something in return. It's about getting to know people, lifting them up because you value them and because you know it's good for the cause for them to keep working within the movement. There is a softness to leadership that I didn't recognize as power at first. Worrying about people's whole selves makes you a good leader, not a soft one. There is strength, not weakness, in valuing your team's personalities and their emotional intelligence. It's back to building trust as well. Trust and loyalty go together. Being nurturing is *smart*. It may seem like a very womanly way to run things, and perhaps it is. That's what's revolutionary: This so-called womanly way just might be the most effective way.

This isn't only my opinion. Decades of Gallup research show that people with women managers and leaders are more likely to report that a coworker has encouraged their development, talked to them about their progress, or recognized their good work. This is because women managers tend to foster this kind of behavior, or what the experts call "employee engagement."[2]

Finally, we get to the most important part of good management: building and valuing a diverse set of voices. This requires intentionality. You must be deliberate about it, by looking for people who represent diversity in gender, culture, race, sexual orientation, even age. We understand that lesson at EMILY's List—it's why we were started, after all, because we believed that Congress would work better if it better represented America. We have increased the diversity of our team, at all levels, but we're not done yet. We have more work to do. This is an effort that must be consistent, and it takes life learning and an ability to admit that you don't understand everything. You need to make a real effort to think through which voices your team is missing.

Lifting up underrepresented voices and ensuring diversity in your team and inclusive environments is not just the right thing to do, it is the smart thing to do. Research shows that it's the best thing for your organization. A variety of studies show that diverse organizations with inclusive policies and environments also do better at retaining employees, maximizing productivity, and creating better job satisfaction. Not surprisingly, operations with management diversity are more innovative. They have fewer instances of discrimination and less interpersonal aggression.[3]

A recent corporate study showed that companies in the top quarter on gender diversity in their executive ranks were 21 percent more likely to have above-average profitability, and those with the same rank on ethnic and cultural diversity were 33 percent more likely.[4]

THE SUPPORT SYSTEM

The campaign team (or internal office staff wherever you are) is critical, but you also need a team focused on your well-being, both physical and emotional. At EMILY's List, we know that behind every great and successful woman is a motivating text chain and a group of great women (and, yes, great men). As you head into a new job, a big project, or a major change, you need to think about who's going to have your back, who's going to challenge you when you need it, who's going to remind you there's life outside of work.

As with any major undertaking, from a big job, to a move, to a new project, your family is your first line of defense. Whether it's your spouse or partner and children, your parents, or the family you've made, you will need the support of the people closest to you as you launch this effort. For candidates, that means figuring out new schedules and responsibilities around the house. You won't be able to make everything at home the same priority as you do now. So you've got to figure out which are the most important priorities at home and work your campaign schedule around those. And perhaps most important, you'll have to prepare your family for the fact that campaigns involve personal attacks against the candidate. This is an ugly truth of modern politics, and it can be hardest on the people who love us the most.

Our candidates have leaned on their families in nearly every campaign we've run. Haley Stevens's and Gina Ortiz

Jones's mothers were their best volunteers and huge hits on the campaign trail, where they knocked on doors and talked up their daughters. We saw this during the presidential primary, too. Minnesota Senator Amy Klobuchar's daughter, Abigail, and New York Senator Kirsten Gillibrand's son Henry were both stars of popular videos for their moms' campaigns. And California Senator Kamala Harris's husband, Doug Emhoff, and Massachusetts Senator Elizabeth Warren's husband, Bruce Mann (and their pup, Bailey), have campaigned across the country for their wives.

Candidates' families play vital behind-the-scenes roles as well. Candidates—and any woman looking to get something big done—will need to work with their family on how best to divide work and responsibilities. There are only so many hours in the day, and life won't just go away because of this new, crazy undertaking.

Virginia Congresswoman Elaine Luria's husband was a fellow Navy veteran who gave up his post-military job to stay home with their eight-year-old when his wife decided to run for office. They both knew it would be too tough to keep up with everything on a campaign schedule.[5] Michigan Congresswoman Elissa Slotkin's husband is a retired army colonel who worked in the Pentagon but also found time to help out as his wife's sometime driver and aide, and on one memorable occasion "hot dog bun Sherpa" for an office party.[6]

Delaware Congresswoman Lisa Blunt Rochester came from a political family but hadn't considered running until the untimely death of her husband at age fifty-two. In the end, campaigning was something that brought her and her family together and allowed her to channel her grief. As her daughter pointed out, Lisa "picked the highest thing to reach for" when she was at her lowest point. Lisa especially leaned on her sisters, because they saw her strength even when she didn't. She noted, "My family name is Blunt! We are not afraid of discussion. We challenge each other."[7] Her extended family helped her through many tough times, and she even carried a piece of them and their history with her when she got sworn in. Lisa's sister found a voter registration card from their great-grandfather three times removed who couldn't write but signed an X to vote during Reconstruction. She had a scarf made for Lisa with that record printed on it, to remind her of the history and family behind her every step of the way.[8]

Of course, it's not just your family by blood. Your support network will include the family you create—the friends, coworkers, and, yes, family members who become your own network. I learned this firsthand when I had my stroke. I don't know how I would have gotten through it without Emily Cain, my right hand at EMILY's List, who didn't just keep things moving at work but joined me for dinner catch-ups and made sure I had all of the support I needed to heal properly. I got through that hard time with friends like Christa Jones, Amy Dacey, Dayna Swanson, Jon Haber, and Bonnie Levin, who each took on different roles depending on the day and what I needed at that moment.

Our founder and chair, Ellen Malcolm, and my dear friend and board member Donald Sussman played vital roles in my support network, as did my dad, who flew in from Kansas before I even knew what was wrong and reminded me that everything was going to be okay. He also flew back when I found out it was a stroke and was back in the hospital. I had a great doctor and even got advice from Washington Congresswoman (and doctor) Kim Schreier. And, to this day, when I talk to either Speaker Nancy Pelosi or Senate Minority Leader Chuck Schumer, they ask about my health first before we get down to business. These people, and many more, were my team of angels, helping me heal and get ready for everything that was coming in 2020. I hope you find your own team of angels—and that you make sure you're a part of one for the people in your life who may need it. We can't make change if we don't knit together a powerful community of people who will lift each other up and help us each take on the world.

SPECIFIC ROLES NEEDED IN YOUR SUPPORT SYSTEM

Let's talk about the specific roles you'll need filled in your support system. Think through your friends and mentors, and consider who can play these roles:

The One Who Will Tell You the Truth

Campaigns are full of people who will give you unsolicited advice, but you need someone who knows you best and gives you the advice you need. This is a friend, family member, or adviser who won't let you wear that unflattering outfit. They'll make sure you never sound like someone else or give up on your priorities. This is your human gut check. It's the person who knows you well enough to know when you're making a choice that goes against your values. And it's a person you know you'll trust when they bring something to your attention.

Notice that I said someone who will tell you the truth, not someone who will tell you the brutal truth. Some friends are just a little *too* honest. Those are the ones you need for other things, but the goal here is to get the facts, not crush your spirit. Choose this person carefully.

The One Who Will Tell You How Great You Look or How Well You Are Doing

Some days are tougher than others. Some days you'll have great events with big crowds and powerful interaction with the voters. And some days will feel like you're stuck on the wrong side of an Internet comments section. On days like that, you need to rely on your cheerleader. Think of them as the opposite of an online troll. They're the person who knows just what to say to lift your spirits and boost your confidence. You need to talk to them after a tough prep session before the debate or on days when you think you've done everything wrong. They'll make you remember that you can do this, no matter how hard it gets, because you are amazing. Full stop.

The One Who Will Listen to You Vent at the End of a Long Day

Sometimes on the tough days, you don't need a cheerleader. What you need is an outlet for venting. Campaigns require being "on" and keeping your cool the entire time you're around voters. That can be even tougher now, thanks to increasingly polarized politics. The public is learning to treat politicians as their enemies and not real people with real feelings. As a candidate, you'll constantly have to avoid angry voters, getting into arguments (even when provoked), and losing your temper. It's the political version of "the customer is always right." The voter, no matter how antagonistic, always deserves respectful interaction, even when they aren't affording you the same respect. I know from experience how frustrating it can be to bite your tongue.

So you need an outlet, a sympathetic ear who won't try to solve every problem but will listen to you, let you vent, and remind you that you're doing this for the right reasons. This person needs to be patient and capable of helping you carry some of the weight and stress of being "on" all the time.

The One Who Will Hold You Accountable

This is a key role for candidates and for women in general: the accountability partner.

For the EMILY's List team, some of our favorite moments

(beyond the wins, of course) are the ones when women find each other and create their own support system. Long live the sisterhood of women who have run for office. We've seen these relationships develop across the country, and we've even helped facilitate some of them. In our Run to Win program, EMILY's List staffers connected candidates as pen pals, giving them partners to run ideas by or to keep them motivated when things got tough.

Illinois Congresswoman Lauren Underwood found an accountability partner at an EMILY's List training, and they stayed in touch throughout her campaign. And many of our North Carolina legislative candidates are on a group text chain where they share ideas and frustrations, motivating each other and keeping each other moving toward their goals. Our private Run to Win Facebook community, where candidates running for the same kind of race or facing the same kinds of problems can find each other, has helped women connect across the country. They ask each other questions, give each other support, and check in on how the work is going. It's inspiring to our whole EMILY's List team, but it's also actually helpful for those candidates in a very practical way.

The Ones Who Will Run and Win with You

We've seen this more and more in recent years, when technology and groups like ours have helped connect women who are all going through the same thing.

In 2018, five amazing women—Jessie Danielson, Kerry Donovan, Brittany Pettersen, Tammy Story, and Faith Winter— all won Colorado state senate seats, flipping the Colorado senate blue for the first time in five years. They'd met years ago and supported each other through campaigns and attack ads; Winter was even a bridesmaid in Pettersen's 2017 wedding. They also supported each other when Winter came forward alleging a fellow legislator had sexually harassed her. "Our families are incredibly supportive," Winter noted, "but it's not their name on the thousands of pieces of mail going out or on the TV, so being able to talk to them, and they are going through the exact same thing, it was so supportive."[9]

Being a first can be daunting; this we've covered. But by banding together and being "firsts" who support each other along the way, these women candidates are making sure they are no longer alone. The first Native American women elected to Congress, Kansas Congresswoman Sharice Davids and New Mexico Congresswoman Deb Haaland, offered each other the same kind of support. When Sharice decided to run, Deb was one of her first calls. "Just hearing her on the other end in that first call, telling me, 'Yes, do this,' was the validation I needed," Sharice said.[10] We all got to see that friendship continue when, after they were sworn in together in 2019, Deb borrowed Sharice's scarf to wipe a tear away at the historic moment. There wasn't a dry eye in the house at EMILY's List when we watched that happen.

There's one more lesson in all this, as you work to build your own team, your support system, your squad, your own set of badasses: In addition to looking for all of these people, you should think about which of these people you are for the women in your life. We all need these relationships to sustain us, but we also need to *be* these women to sustain others. We didn't flip the House with one woman winning; it took twenty-four. The Women's March showed the power of women joining together, and it took all of those women standing in the cold, fighting for their rights, to illustrate just how strong we are together. The world may not have been made for us, but together, we can build a new and better system. Whose village are you in? How are you helping them make a difference, improve their lives, and change the world?

THE TOPLINES

No one should go it alone. Your village may come in a variety of forms, but you need to build it with care and intentionality. You need two types of teams, and they are both critical to any successful effort, from running for office to starting a business to changing the world.

First, there's your staff, whether paid or volunteer. No matter how small or large that team is, you will have certain roles to fill, including:

Leadership: Professional managing of the team and the process.

Strategy and messaging: Determine your platform and how you are different from the opposition.

Communicating with key audiences: How to use your paid, owned, and earned media to meet your goals, reach your audiences, and deliver your message.

Raising the necessary resources: Every big effort takes money, time, and work. Everyone does the work and helps to create the time needed to get things done, but someone has to focus on the money.

Building allies: Outside validators and allies are vital to successful campaigns of any kind. They can provide you with credibility, advice, and help in doing the work.

Convincing the voters: If you want to win a race, or just make a change, you have to convince someone else that you—your position, your effort—are the right thing to support.

Chairwoman of the Board: Remember what Harry Truman said: The buck stops with you. No matter how big or small your team, you are the leader, the inspiration, and the guiding force behind that team.

Then there's the team of outside support, starting with your family—by birth, by marriage, or by your own creation—which is key to your efforts. It also includes the people in your life who will:

- Keep you honest and tell you the truth (but not the bru-
  tal truth)
- Boost your spirits and remind you of how great you are
- Let you vent and keep you sane
- Hold you accountable
- Go through the same thing as you and share the experi-
  ence

Being a leader doesn't mean going it alone. How you
manage and lead is as important as who you have on your
team. Here are some lessons I've learned after years in politics:

- Your management style will help determine how effective a leader you are. Take the time and make the effort
  to be a good manager and, if you're a candidate, a good
  leader.
- If you are joining an existing team, take the time to figure out your team's individual skills and whether those
  skills are being put to the best use. Are your people in the
  right roles?
- Keep moving forward, and be willing to take smart risks.
  Remember that doing nothing is making a choice.
- Find your better half, your work partner who comple-
  ments your skills rather than duplicates them. Make that
  person a true partner, and make sure they are your last
  call of the night, either literally or metaphorically.
- Good management and leadership can be what we think
  of as soft *and* strong. Just as you bring all of yourself to

your leadership roles, get to know all of your team. You'll all be better off for it and you will build longtime loyalty.

- Loyalty cannot be demanded. Relationships should be knitted together, not a quid pro quo.
- It is critical that your team represents a diverse set of voices and that you encourage an inclusive environment. That requires constant and deliberate effort on your part and on the part of your whole staff.

CHAPTER 6

Learn How to Make the Ask

HERE'S A FUN fact about me: I loved being a Girl Scout. The leadership lessons, the sense of community, and the chance to learn and make friends in an environment that was totally pro girl power were so important to me as a kid. I loved that my mom was a Girl Scout troop leader one year. I loved that I got to earn badges, and if you looked in my dad's attic today, you would find that green sash I was so proud to wear. But what I loved most about being a Girl Scout was all the activities— community service, hiking, camping, and, yes, selling cookies. I never stopped spending a lot of time in nature, and in many ways, my future empowering women and raising money has merely been a continuation of the lessons I learned as a Girl Scout.

Think I'm exaggerating? Let me tell you about little Stephanie (yes, me!). When I joined the Girl Scouts, most cookies were sold door-to-door. We hadn't quite figured out the methods used by today's troops, like posting up in front of grocery stores and selling online. So I walked around my neighborhood and asked people to support our troop by buying some cookies. A classic win-win scenario, if you ask me!

But I felt I could be even more efficient, so I asked my dad if I could sell to his coworkers at the hospital where he worked as the lab director. He said I couldn't go to the hospital to sell because there was a no-solicitation rule, but he had another idea. He gave me a staff directory so I could make my pitch over the phone. That meant that in order to make sales, I had to work up the courage to call adults I hardly knew, introduce myself, and then make my ask. It was a daunting task, especially for a nine-year-old, but my dad encouraged me to be brave. And boy, did it pay off. Not only did I sell the most cookies but I also learned a valuable skill for my future career in politics and fundraising. I have to thank my dad for that, though my poor mom had to help me organize all those cookies for delivery!

Since then, I've raised hundreds of millions of dollars for the different campaigns and organizations that I've worked for and led. It makes me laugh to think it all started with a cookie.

Years later, when coaching candidates to do "call time" with donors across the country, I would tell this story to show I knew how they felt, and also to remind them that if a little kid could do it, they could, too.

The Girl Scouts are still training future fundraisers. In 2019, I dropped off some clothes at the dry cleaner's and ran into a young Girl Scout on a mission, selling cookies from a table in the store with her mom. When I told her I wanted to buy a box of Thin Mints (still my very favorite), she asked me how many boxes I wanted. Right away, instead of just one box, she had me in for at least two, because let's face it, a six-year-old selling cookies is too adorable to refuse.

And then when I pulled out my $20 bill, she turned to her mom and asked, "Mom, for twenty dollars, can she get five boxes?" And when her mom confirmed her math, she turned back to me with a determined look and informed me, "You could get *five* boxes with that. I would recommend the Thin Mints and the Tagalongs." Then this pint-sized saleswoman asked if I had tried the new S'mores cookies. After I expressed an interest, she noted that the S'mores cookies were $1 more. She upsold me, and I was appropriately impressed. I left that day with five boxes of cookies (most of which made it into EMILY's List for my team), having made a $21 donation and a promise to that Girl Scout and her mom that when she was ready to run for office, I would be the first to sign on.

Campaigning is all about asking for things. You ask for support, you ask for volunteer help, you ask for votes. And you spend a lot of time asking for money. Of all the things you have to learn as a candidate, that's the one most people find the toughest. This is my reminder that even if you never sold cookies door-to-door, you have spent your life asking for things—from your parents, friends, and colleagues. You can do this! Find that inner Girl Scout.

At EMILY's List, we've spent a lot of time teaching candidates how to do it, because when you can make the ask, you can get all kinds of things done. I understand why this is hard for people. As a society, we are told not to talk about money or politics. That is particularly true for women. Many of us grew up hearing that talking about money wasn't polite, or dignified, or ladylike. We are afraid to do it, because we've been taught that it's wrong and awkward. Asking for money is a social taboo that we're afraid of breaking.

And that challenge is coupled with the fact that as Democrats, we are working to *lessen* the impact of money in politics. Our candidates support campaign finance reform and efforts to make sure that the voices we value are those of the voters, not the major donors. We are proud of the rise in grassroots donations, and we believe that you shouldn't be able to buy access or policy change because you have more money. EMILY's List actively seeks candidates who will pass laws to take the money influence out of politics. But until we're able to pass those laws, we choose to play by the rules that currently exist. We won't leave our candidates at an unfair disadvantage while we are trying to make the rules better.

While I understand all of the concerns, being good at making the ask and fundraising will be a huge advantage to your campaign. And like telling your story, speech making, and interview giving, it's a skill you can learn through practice.

I didn't originally intend to go into fundraising. My first political job was as a scheduler with Mary Rieder's House campaign. I thought it was great and the perfect way to learn every aspect of the campaign. At twenty-three, with almost no

professional experience, I had no way of knowing that sched-
uling is perhaps the most complicated of all the jobs. Just ask
my director of the president's office at EMILY's List, Francie
Harris; she is in line for sainthood. But luckily for me, my
time as a scheduler was over before it began. When I arrived
in Rochester, Minnesota, for Mary's campaign in 1996, she
told me what she actually needed was someone to raise the
money so she could hire other positions.

I had student loans and rent to think about, and the fundraiser job paid a whole $100 more a month than that of sched-
uler, so I said yes. Let's be honest—I knew I could do it. I had
a solid foundation from my cookie-selling days, and more recently from a part-time job selling furniture that had helped
me pay my way through grad school. I had a knack for making
the ask, and I liked doing it. What I learned on that campaign
was that the people who raise the money are, by necessity,
usually the first ones hired and the last ones fired—and I am
nothing if not a pragmatist.

While I love that Girl Scout story, and while I love helping
candidates conquer this skill, this chapter is not just about
asking for money. Making the ask is so much more than just
fundraising. It's asking for what you deserve, whether that's a
job, a promotion, a raise, support for a big effort, or a little
help around the house. Life is about asking for what you need
and deserve—and for too many women, we're far more afraid
of making the ask than doing the work.

Everyone's got a hang-up about asking for certain things. I
can ask someone for a million dollars without batting an eye

(and often do). What I couldn't do for a long time was ask for a promotion. (I'm also not great at asking people out on dates—but that is a whole other book!) What I eventually learned through experience is that at the core, all asks are the same.

When I was the finance director on Howard Dean's presidential campaign starting in 2003, I knew that I did much more than oversee the fundraising. I had become a good manager and helped provide leadership and support for the entire campaign. There wasn't a day during that campaign when someone from another department—the communications director, the research director, the field director—wouldn't come into my office and ask for help thinking through some problem they were facing. I knew that I was ready to take on a bigger role and was already doing the work of a deputy campaign manager.

I may have had the confidence to do the job, but I lacked the guts to ask for it. And if you don't ask, you don't get. Without my pushing for it, no one in the leadership thought to move me out of the role I was doing, since I was doing a great job at it. I ended up doing a ton of work on that campaign, but without the title or recognition I deserved. I had no trouble making the case for Howard Dean to donors and voters across the country, but I couldn't make the case for Stephanie Schriock in the office.

For so many women, we assume that if we just keep working hard, put our head down, and do our best, we will be rewarded for good behavior. It's a nice thought, and it happens on occasion, but don't count on it. The truth is, as women, most of the time, we have to plant the seed that we are capable of something more or something different. It's rare to be considered for a promotion that you don't ask for yourself. The failure of leaders to see the potential in us can be disappointing, especially when we are working so hard and feel like our bosses shouldn't be able to help but notice. But when we're killing it at work, it's easy for the boss to settle into a happy and complacent place. The idea "Why change something that is working?" sneaks into the boss's mind, and often into ours. It feels good when things are working, and it can feel selfish to put that at risk to ask for more. I'm speaking completely from experience here!

It's ironic, isn't it? We work hard to succeed at our jobs, but then we let that success lock us into a role, when we are capable of so much more. As a manager, I believe hard work should pay off and be rewarded, and there is no shame in knowing your potential and asking for more responsibility or money, or a bigger title.

The first step is having confidence in yourself. I learned that lesson the hard way. I wanted a promotion, I knew I could do the job, and I still let fear stop me from asking. I thought if I just worked hard enough, the next step would follow naturally. And so I sat back and waited for things to change on their own. It was only later, in examining my role in the loss (something everyone in a senior position should do when a campaign is over), that I realized that my lack of self-confidence meant I didn't take a risk that could have been better for the campaign. I didn't just hurt myself; I hurt the entire team.

I learned my lesson. The next time I was looking for a job, I spoke up for myself. I knew I was ready to manage a Senate race, and I made the case to the people who could make it happen. They agreed and helped me land my next job. As a result, I went back to my home state of Montana and managed Jon Tester's winning Senate campaign in 2006. This was not an easy race. We beat the odds and defeated an eighteen-year Republican incumbent in a fairly red state. I took risks, showed leadership, and trusted my instincts. I applied my skills in making the ask to my own career and learned how to speak up for myself with confidence.

Yet, even having learned from my experience on the Howard Dean campaign, when it came time to build Jon Tester's first official Senate office staff, I still didn't initially think of throwing my hat in for chief of staff. Embarrassingly, it hadn't even crossed my mind until my campaign deputy Bill Lombardi suggested it. I was so good in my role as campaign manager that I forgot to look up and see myself as anything more, especially when I had not worked on Capitol Hill before.

As I thought about it, though, I knew that my knowledge of Jon, of politics, and of Montana made up for my lack of Hill experience. I realized I was perfect for the job. So I took a chance and went to Jon. As it turned out, he hadn't thought of it, either, but I made a strong case for myself and he took a chance on me. It was an important life lesson, that working hard and being successful alone wouldn't get me where I wanted to be. I had to have confidence in myself, I had to understand what I wanted and how to get there, and then I had to make the ask.

I've been a boss and I've been a staffer, and I know how easy it is to put people in a box and stop seeing their potential. Your job, no matter your position, is to make sure people know that you're ready to explore every opportunity. Sometimes it's making the ask outright, sometimes it's planting the seed, sometimes it's just asking the right question. That's what often happens when we first ask women to run for office. They may tell us no the first time, but we've found that if that seed gets a little water and a little sunlight, it just might take root and begin to grow, so by the third or fourth conversation, they're not questioning their abilities; they're asking us how to make a campaign work.

So let's assume that you've gotten over the initial concerns and built up your confidence, and you're ready to make a big ask. What do you need to know?

BUILD THE RIGHT ASK

Ask the Right People (All of Them)

You may know what you want, but now you have to know who the right person to ask is. That's an easy answer if you're after a promotion or a raise, because you know to go to your boss or manager. But if you're looking to raise funds, garner support for an idea, win votes in an election, or gain petition signatures, knowing who to ask is quite a bit more complicated.

To start, you need to map out everyone you know. We often call this Rolodexing, but since most people haven't seen a Rolodex in ages, let's make this simpler: You need to think through all of your contacts and figure out who can get you closer to your goal, and how.

Remember: If you're going to make something happen, you're going to need help, and lots of it. That means laying out everyone you know and figuring out what you can ask from them. When it comes to candidates, you'll ask for votes, support, money—and often more than one of these things. And you'll need to ask more than just the people you talk to regularly, like your neighbors or your coworkers. It's a comprehensive list that will include your college friends, your kids' friends' parents, your high school teachers. If you're bold, like Senator Amy Klobuchar, you can even ask your former boyfriends for their support. She raised $17,000 from ex-boyfriends in her first Senate race.[1] And beyond that, it means asking people you don't know but have a connection with, like members of your sorority, other alumnae from your alma mater, people you see at your place of worship, former coworkers, or people who share a specific interest (other military families, members of clubs you've joined, and so on). Your goal should be to have as many names on this initial list as possible. You'll constantly be working to expand your network even further. That's the name of the game.

Next, don't say no on somebody else's behalf. You should

never rule out anyone because you assume they don't agree with your platform or you think they don't have the resources to support you. Let every individual decide whether they want to invest in you. Give everyone in your network, no matter their party affiliation or wealth level, the opportunity to be part of your success. I have no plans to run for office right now (I'll never say never). But if I were to run, I would include everyone I know on that list. That includes my staunchly Republican family members. Our politics are different, but I am close to these uncles and aunts, and you know what? I would ask them all for their support. Your network, even your family, will include people across the political spectrum. Don't assume they won't show up for you. It is a kindness to include them and a kindness on their part to accept that invitation. Let them say no. Don't say no for them. I have to remind women of this all the time. Who are we to make assumptions about what another individual is going to do or care about?

Real and perceived notions about our networks are exactly what kept women, people of color, and working-class candidates from being backed by the political establishment for many years. It was even worse if the candidate fell into more than one of those categories. The conventional thinking was that people from those groups couldn't possibly have access to the same capital as the moneyed networks of older, wealthier lawyers and businessmen (yes, I said "businessmen" on purpose). Add to that the reality of pay gaps, systemic racism, and sexism, and it starts to feel true. But it's our mission at EMILY's List to fight this institutional, self-fulfilling bias.

We won't assume that candidates are less worthy of our support based on their gender, skin color, sexual orientation, or economic background. It is our promise to go further, to actively support candidates of color and from diverse backgrounds. I am so proud to head an organization that helps effect such positive, meaningful change.

EMILY's List was founded on the belief that the first step to bridging that gap is fundraising—"early money is like yeast," remember? I still think back to my favorite days on Mary Rieder's campaign, when a bundle of checks for all amounts from donors across the country would arrive in the mail from EMILY's List. They would show up with these little notes of encouragement. "Mary, you can do this." "Mary, we are so proud of you." "Thank you for running, Mary!" Those notes kept us going. That's the thing—at EMILY's List we've spent thirty-five years honing training programs to help women candidates learn how to build their own networks and make their own asks. But we also helped teach tens of thousands of women donors that their $100 contribution could make a real difference to the candidate they believed in—that small investments can add up to huge sums.

Every now and again I will meet an older EMILY's List member who tells me that she used to have to hide her donations to our candidates in the grocery checkbook, so her husband didn't know that she had made contributions to the pioneering women candidates of EMILY's List's early days. Those members now tell me with pride that not only do they no longer need to hide their donations; they're the ones in charge of the checkbooks and they're making more donations than ever. Women's donations to women candidates and to EMILY's List directly have increased over the years; it's just another way women are making their voices heard in politics. Asking women to give isn't just good for the candidate. Every time a woman donates to a campaign she believes in, she uses her voice and her power. That is how we ignite change.

Are you supporting a candidate without a big network of wealthy donors? One who has worked in worlds without lots of money, more focused on making their community better? Help them reach more people. Throw a little extra in the check you're writing. We all know our government is better when it looks like the people it represents. Let's all be a part of making that happen.

Do Your Research

Now that you've figured out *who* you're asking, you need to figure out what you're asking for. When it comes to asking for money, while it can be scary to ask for too much and risk turning off a donor completely, asking for too little is a more common, and potentially more costly, mistake. You need to find a balance between realism and optimism and do your research to figure out what the market will bear, so to speak. Even that six-year-old Girl Scout figured out I was a customer who could spend more than $4! This is true of everything from campaign donations to asking for a raise. No matter what you're asking for, try to know as much as you can about the market and about the person you're asking so you can make the most effective ask. You'll never know it all, but a little research increases your likelihood of success.

What we want to avoid is under-asking, or not asking for as much as a person can give. In our experience, women are more prone to this mistake than men. If you're asking for money, research whether your donor has given before and, if so, how much and to whom. If a donor has given $1,000 to several candidates, why would you ask for $100? Many women we coach on fundraising assume that when they don't know the person, they should lower the amount of their ask. They make the wrong assumption—that they are not worth it. We already face the donor version of a pink tax: Even some of our biggest donors at EMILY's List give us less than they give groups that don't focus solely on women. Don't make that worse for yourself by not asking for what you deserve.

Congresswoman Lois Frankel from Florida loves to help our EMILY's List candidates raise money, and she gives one of the best fundraising pep talks to candidates who are sheepish about making big asks. "Nobody ever died because you asked them for too much money!" she says. And she's absolutely right. I know a few candidates who have put those wise words on a sticky note in plain sight during call time. They can be a good reminder just before you take a deep breath and make a big ask. The worst thing that can happen is that they will say no flat out. But in a lot of cases, you'll be surprised with either a yes or a lower offer that makes sense for them.

Not asking for enough is a challenge in salary determinations as well. Managers and organizations frequently base an employee's salary or raise on their previous salary. The danger is in exacerbating the pay gap that women already face. When you've been consistently paid less than coworkers (or consistently failed to ask for what you deserve), you are just building on a salary that's lower than it should be in the first place. This is why some states and localities have instituted salary history bans—meaning employers can't ask what you earned in your last job—designed to end pay discrimination.[2]

The same advice goes for any kind of ask, no matter if you are asking for help, to take on new responsibilities, or for support of any kind. Ask for what you want, not just what you need, or you're leaving an opportunity on the table.

Doing good research also means paying attention while you have conversations—also known as listening—and keeping good notes. This goes for conversations you have with donors, supporters, volunteers, staff members, endorsers, and basically everyone you meet. Every conversation you have with a potential supporter reveals a little more about what matters to that person. And when you pay attention, they feel more connected to you. People's lives and circumstances change over time, for good and for bad. It's helpful to keep up with your supporters and what's happening in their lives. It's a big task, but it's one that makes you a better elected official or candidate—and maybe even a better person. The more you can show a person that you're paying attention and understand the things they're dealing with, the more likely you are to earn their support.

All that said, it *is* possible to ask for too much—but if you listen well and do your research, it will happen only rarely. If you know what you need and have formulated the right ask, you may ask someone for more than they were planning to donate but not more than they could reasonably give.

There's still plenty of room for mistakes, though. I ask for money all the time and I still don't always get this right. Not long ago, I was in California completely ready to ask a donor for an upgrade from $15,000 to $25,000. I felt good about it, the research was done, and this seemed like an appropriate amount. As I was gearing up to make the ask, the donor looked at me and asked what he did last cycle. I answered that he had done $15,000 and I was hoping— He interrupted me and said, "What? Is that all I did? I need to fix that. I am in for a hundred thousand dollars this year." I damn near fell off the chair and was grateful he preempted my under-ask, which would have cost the organization $75,000. There is a lot of art in this asking business.

Make the Ask About Them, Not You

If you want to gain voters' support, you have to convince people that you're the right candidate for the job and that you can win the election. If you want to make change, you're going to have to get people to join your cause. To get people to join your cause, you're going to have to ask them to be a part of your team. And in order to convince them to join your team, you need to make that ask more about them than you. In short, you need to win people over. That means helping them connect with your story. It means having a conversation about things that matter to their families and communities, to learn about the issues that keep them up at night.

I didn't use the word *conversation* by accident there. We should all work more to ask questions and, in turn, listen to the responses. Too often, as leaders or candidates, we've convinced ourselves that we have all the answers and all we need is the support (the money, the vote, the help). But we are better at what we do—better members of a community, better colleagues, and better candidates—when we are paying careful attention to the person across the table. If you've heard their needs and concerns, you can better answer their tough questions. You can anticipate what they'll worry about and think through the best way to approach them.

The best asks are based on shared interests and values. They give you the opportunity to find and build on common ground. And by doing that, you are making it about the person you are asking, not about you.

Now, I raise organizational money, so my job is to build long-term relationships with donors. All that research, all those conversations, all that seeking of common ground—it means that I often become friends with the EMILY's List donors, making my job incredibly fun. It helps to remember that donors are individuals who seek out your organization for personal reasons. EMILY's List has a dear donor now who initially reached out because he had heard I grew up in Butte, Montana, and he, too, was originally from Montana. I started getting to know him over the phone, beginning with our shared Montana ties and then our shared desire for good government, and then eventually moving to our shared belief that women leaders are key to America's next phase of governance.

He is strategic, pragmatic, and a very good businessman with a huge heart. I started by asking him for $50,000, which he gave years ago. Now he gives EMILY's List hundreds of thousands of dollars a year to elect women across the country. I still love talking to him, and I learn something from him every time. He is one of dozens of donors who have become part of my own kitchen cabinet.

Find the Right Approach for You and the Person You're Asking

You've asked, you've listened, you've found the places where interests align, and you're ready to make your case. Great; content matters. The last piece is your approach. You're trying to win someone over and convince them to give you something you need. You have to figure out how best to convey your message.

I find that I have four general themes in my asks. Consider them to help you understand how best to frame an ask, especially as you're starting out.

- Enthusiasm: "I'm really excited about this ask, I think you will be, too, and I hope you'll join me." Excitement can be contagious. This ask is about hope and progress, and as a progressive Democrat, I've found this to be the most effective way of energizing other progressive Democrats.

- Fear of Failure: "If you don't support this ask, we will not be able to do X or hire X staff or finish X program." In the Trump years, I've found that this method has gotten even more dramatic. I often remind voters, volunteers, and donors that our very democracy is at stake—and, sadly, that hasn't been just a hyperbolic talking point. I really mean it.

- Guilt: "I have nowhere else to turn." "If not you, who?" Here's where you get to go back to your childhood days of trying to guilt Mom or Dad into something, letting them know how much you really need their help. As with anything, this doesn't work on every donor or voter, but this is another approach that has resonated more since Donald Trump got elected. More and more people do believe they have a responsibility to do more, to take up the mantle of impacting change—and if your ask gives them a way and a reason to do that, you can be incredibly effective.

- All Business: "I know you care about climate change. I am a candidate who shares that concern and will fight climate change in office." "You care about Congress's better representing all of us—join me in helping elect more women and making Congress more diverse." And so on. This one is about aligned interests, not emotion. It is, in a sense, transactional and more businesslike. That said, this is not the kind of transaction that promises a vote or establishes any kind of quid pro quo. It's important to make clear that this is about shared interests, not a promise that someone's support will mean influence over your interests in the future. That is exactly the type of politics we are working to end.

You may find other ways of making your ask work for you. There is no one right or wrong way to do it, and the effectiveness of an ask depends on the preferences of both the asker and the person being asked. Think about what's most comfortable for you, do your best to figure out what the most compelling argument will be to the person you're asking, then try to find the best way to marry the two.

Getting Through the Awkward Parts

If you're going to change the world, you will need to have patience and persistence. If you're a candidate, much of your fundraising will be on the phone, so you're going to spend a lot of time making calls. You'll leave a lot of messages. You may go entire hours without anyone's actually answering the phone. And when you're not talking to people, it can be boring. Really boring.

You may be reading this and thinking, Great, Stephanie,

but I'm not going to be a candidate. My ask will be for something else—to recruit people to a cause, to ask for support for something, to build my skills, and so on. That's fine. There are parts of every important task you do or goal you have that are just plain boring. Door-knocking for campaigns can be really fun when you talk to voters at every house, but when you're getting a lot of empty houses, the experience can be disheartening. Whether you're doing data entry, phone banking, or even organizing your accomplishments in order to ask for a raise, sometimes the most vital work we do is also the least exciting. Even in our dream jobs, not every moment will be full of excitement. That shouldn't stop you from giving it your all. Sometimes you have to do the grunt work. Because the grunt work is the foundation for everything you're fighting for.

So when you've left dozens of messages and not talked to a soul, my best advice is to keep smiling. Because that next call could be the magic call, the person who is grateful for the outreach and happy to connect. The one who will answer the ask in a way you couldn't have imagined. Keep smiling, because I swear the person on the other side of the phone line knows if you are. It comes out in the tone of your voice. Just like your mom or dad can tell when something isn't right with you on the phone, so can the potential donor. So make yourself smile, even if you aren't happy. They might be your hundredth call of the day, but you're their first.

In addition to smiling (really—it's the best example of faking it until you make it), you should also keep yourself occupied through the grunt work. Women who want to change the world tend to be high-energy and often have difficulty sitting still through the more mundane times. My first candidate, Mary Rieder, couldn't stand doing nothing while we made phone calls, so she started knitting. It was perfect, and as long as we made sure we gave her enough yarn, we had a happy candidate. Plus I got a killer hat out of it.

I've got another knitter in my life now: Judy Lichtman, one of the founders of EMILY's List, a senior adviser to the National Partnership for Women and Families, and the woman largely credited with getting the Family and Medical Leave Act passed. Judy is on our EMILY's List board, and she often knits all the way through the meetings. In the beginning, I wondered if she was actually paying attention, until one time she threw a detailed legal question at me in the middle of knitting a scarf. I knew then that Judy, like Mary, was just putting her hands to good use while her brain focused.

Maine Congresswoman Chellie Pingree has another method: She bakes pies during call time. Of course, this tactic is a little risky for the less advanced bakers or for anyone prone to klutziness. But it worked really well for Chellie and her campaign team. I still remember her mixed-berry pie. Magical.

Next, you need to get over any concern about the awkwardness of asking for money. A bit of awkwardness is natural on these calls. Particularly when you feel like the ask is about you, not about a charity, your child's school, or your church, asking for money is difficult. That feels odd for many candidates.

My advice is to remember that even when you're asking

someone to support your campaign, you're not actually asking for you, after all. Just like you are not running for you or looking to change the world for just your benefit. You are looking to make change for your community, for your company, or even for your family. Your ask is not only about yourself. You're asking for support on behalf of everyone and everything you are working for. As Texas House candidate Gina Ortiz Jones reminds herself, she is asking on behalf of her community. The struggles her constituents face are worth a few awkward moments. Gina's right—you can do anything if you remember who you're doing it for.

Here's the bottom line for every ask, and a great way to get over the inherent awkwardness: You have to let them answer! Silence has a way of changing conversations, and by getting comfortable with silence, you put pressure on the other person. Reporters use this tactic. They ask a question and then stop talking. Silence is uncomfortable, and it is human nature to want to fill it pretty quickly. We want to have normal conversations, without those awkward pauses, so we keep talking to fill the space. I've found silence to be a powerful negotiation tool.

You can see how silence can be intimidating and put pressure on the prospective donor. Use it to your benefit. Make an ask, stop talking, and let the other person answer. It's not just in fundraising. I've had friends who've talked themselves out of the salary they wanted by following up a fair request with "but I'm really excited about this job and money's not going to be a sticking point."

The only answer is to own the silence and let it work for you. On this score, there are two reliable tips we give our candidates. The one I use is simply to count to seven after you make the ask. Just count (in your head, obviously). I love it, but it is awkward and harder than it sounds, so it will take some practice. If that is too hard for you as you're getting started, then make the ask, take a sip of water, and swallow. When you do that, you force yourself to shift the burden of the silence to the person you just asked, and I guarantee, most of the time they will come your way.

LET GO OF BAD ASSUMPTIONS

When it comes to making the ask, the most important thing you can do is let go of some bad assumptions and stereotypes. We all make these kinds of judgments in our everyday lives. Hopefully we try not to let them get the better of us, take over our thinking, or impact how we view people we've never met. But that doesn't mean these assumptions don't exist or that these implicit biases aren't powerful deterrents. For example, the assumption that a woman couldn't lead (particularly if she still had children at home) kept many out of politics for decades.

Emily Cain, our EMILY's List executive director, saw this firsthand during her first campaign for the Maine legislature. Emily was twenty-four, had just graduated with her master's degree in 2004, and was about to get married when she ran her first campaign. Clearly she's not one for the easy path! When she knocked on doors, she heard doubts about her age, questions about whether her husband would be supportive (he definitely was, but since he wasn't the one running, she rightly found this question to be irrelevant), and concerns about her timeline for having children if she was in elected office. Yes, people can get very intrusive when you're running for office and especially scrutinize young women. Now that we've seen more young women run for office, these questions are losing their power, but in 2004, Emily was far from the norm.

Luckily, Emily is always willing to try to win anyone over. She didn't give up or get mad when faced with these awkward questions. In fact, she welcomed the conversation. Emily realized that, in most cases, the people asking these questions weren't sexist or hateful; they just had never met anyone like her running for office. They had made their own assumptions about what a young woman could do. An open conversation about shared values turned those assumptions into an opportunity for Emily and her constituents to learn about one another. The best part is, this open dialogue usually led to votes and supporters. That approach is how Emily became a Maine house member, a state senator, and a leader in her caucus.

All this comes with an important disclaimer: Some people are actually sexist or racist or hateful. And if you feel unsafe, you need to trust your gut and move along to the next door or conversation. Even Emily has some of those stories, and in order to stay safe, she moved along to the next new person to meet.

But for the most part, you'll be surprised how open-minded people can be if you take the time to engage them. You won't win every person to your cause, but you might just shift their thinking a tiny bit. Even that is a victory in our eyes! Letting go of bad assumptions and faulty narratives can be hard, but it's a key to success. Here are a few that you should drop from your thinking.

Assumption 1: People Will Give (or Vote) Without a Specific Ask

When it comes to campaigns, or anything important in your life, you cannot afford to assume anything. You especially cannot afford to think that other people will take action without a specific ask.

In politics, there's a story about legendary US House Speaker Tip O'Neill, in which a neighbor of his, Mrs. O'Brien, told him that she'd voted for him even though he hadn't asked her to. Tip responded, "I've lived across the street from you for eighteen years. I cut your grass in the summer and shovel your walk in the winter. I didn't think I had to ask for your vote." And Mrs. O'Brien reminded him, "People like to be asked."[3]

If you want people to do anything, you have to ask them to do it. Period. Full stop. I know that seems obvious, but you don't want to learn this the hard way. Even your closest friends most likely will not give you money or support unless you ask, very specifically, for what you need. Your friends, family, and neighbors want you to succeed, and likely they will surpass your expectations when you do reach out, but they need some direction. You're going to spend time on the front end thinking about who you know and what you can ask from them. Don't forget to actually make that ask.

Assumption 2: Only Rich People Give Money

If at this point in the book you believe this one, you haven't been paying close attention. EMILY's List was founded on the principle that there is power in numbers and enormous value in small-dollar and grassroots donors. I saw it firsthand on my first campaign. When my candidate, Mary Rieder, was endorsed by EMILY's List, opening the mail became a very exciting office chore. Suddenly we were inundated with these checks, in large and small amounts, from people around the country. These were people whom we didn't know and we wouldn't have known how to reach. Plus those little notes I mentioned earlier—well-wishes and cheerful affirmations from strangers in every state—made our day.

Later, thanks to the Internet, we would have ways to connect interested voters around the country to candidates within moments, where they could give however much—or little— they wanted. It's not just that those donations add up (and they do—take a look at Elizabeth Warren's 2020 presidential fundraising if you still doubt it); it's that we have put the power back in the hands of all voters, not just the wealthy ones.

Now, I am not saying you aren't going to ask wealthy individuals for contributions as well. You are going to call them and ask for big amounts, which you'll know is appropriate based on your research about their giving abilities. The harder part of the job is learning how to ask someone living paycheck to paycheck to give some of their hard-earned money to you, especially for an effort that might not be successful.

I know that it's hard. But I urge you to consider the fact that the person who is living paycheck to paycheck is probably the one who needs change the most. They are the ones who need the best, most understanding leaders in office. They need strong women who are driven to help families make ends meet—women who know how hard some people have it. Trust that hardworking individuals may be willing to give a little bit every month to help you, a person committed to fighting for them. Don't say no for them. Give them the opportunity to be a part of your campaign. Ask and you may be surprised how many will give something because they want to invest in the values that you are advocating for.

We don't decide how people are going to spend their money. Many people might consider running but decide it's not the right time for them. They want to get involved, maybe knock on some doors or make some calls, but they don't have the time. So the one world-changing thing they might be able to do right now is to spend their money on the campaigns that resonate with them—and your race (or your effort) just might be the best way for them to get involved and act on their convictions.

Assumption 3: Fundraising Should Be Centered Around a Big Event or News

You can make asks around big events or moments. There's a reason many organizations hold annual dinners or galas. At EMILY's List, our We Are EMILY dinner is one of my favorite nights each year. But if you assume that everything will happen around one big event or one moment—and if that assumption means you're not working at your goal all year long—then you are not working to your full potential. And while you need to be able to capitalize on that big moment if and when it comes (for example, both Elizabeth Warren and Amy Klobuchar saw huge spikes in donations after having decisive wins in debates), you also can't count on it and build your budget around one big moment, because those moments are the exception and not the rule.

You have to raise money like it is part of every activity. You need to be ready to make the ask whenever the opportunity presents itself or actively create opportunity if you don't see one coming.

One of my favorite parts of my job is getting to call the candidates who are getting an EMILY's List endorsement. In 2018, I called Washington congressional candidate Carolyn Long and caught her doing her grocery shopping. When I told her we were endorsing her, she was so excited she screamed out loud in the grocery store. We talked briefly about the details of the public press rollout, and then, without missing a beat, she said, "Thank you—and since I'm getting the endorsement, can I also get a PAC check before the end of the quarter?"

Well done, Carolyn, well done!

I've called hundreds of candidates, and not many of them make an ask while I'm on that first phone call. But whether it's having their name included in a mailing or asking that I write a check, plan an event, or make a phone call for them, I'm always impressed when our candidates make the ask of me while they have the opportunity. They probably won't get an answer from me on the spot, but I always note it positively in the call report.

Because, after all, you've got nothing to lose. The worst that can happen from a well-researched, well-thought-out ask is that you get a no. When you ask for a well-earned promotion or a raise, your boss isn't going to fire you just because they aren't able to give you what you asked for. When you ask a donor for money, they might say no, but they're not going to stop supporting you because you asked them.

You have a lot of money to raise. You will do fundraising calls every day. You will send out emails. Some of you will send out mail through the post office. Others will text. The truth is, you will need to do it all: make calls and mail letters and send emails and do house parties and a million other things to get as many asks out there as possible. Just maybe you'll get lucky and something unexpected will happen— you'll run into an old friend in the grocery store or connect with someone at a wedding. I have asked for EMILY's List in both these settings successfully, by the way, with no planning ahead. The point is that when an opportunity—big or small—arises, you must be bold enough to take it.

Now, you heard me earlier call this fly-fishing fundraising, because you just keep casting over and over again. Another way of thinking about it is the famous Wayne Gretzky quote: "You miss one hundred percent of the shots you don't take." That's absolutely true, but I'd love to point you to the wise words of a strong woman, world champion gymnast and Olympic gold medalist Simone Biles, who said, "I'd rather regret the risks that didn't work out than the chances I didn't take at all."[4]

Assumption 4: The First Answer Is the Final Answer—or an Answer at All

One vital tip to making an ask is to actually get an answer. It seems obvious, I know, but too often we take the first words out of someone's mouth as the end of the conversation. Instead, you need to make sure you keep trying until you get a definite yes or no. "I need to check with my spouse" is not an answer. Neither is "Let me think about it." You may need to ask more than once, but you should get either a yes, or a no, or a counteroffer. Just like patience, persistence is key to getting you what you want.

And even when you get a no, chin up. To a true fundraiser, a hard no sounds only like "no for now." If your campaign's circumstances change—let's say you go up in the polls, your opponent falters, or you get a big endorsement—it's worth starting back at the top of your call list. After a big change, return to your nos and give them another opportunity to invest. They might surprise you.

WHEN TO STOP ASKING

As important as it is to be able to make the ask, it's also vital to know when you do actually need to walk away from one. I first learned this lesson when I worked for my friend Shari Yost Gold at the Democratic Senatorial Campaign Committee. As the Southern regional finance staffer, I enjoyed working with a variety of donors. But one man, a midlevel donor who had been giving to the committee for a while, was particularly needy. He demanded information and lots of my time on the phone. Then he started demanding more time in person. As my work continued, I became increasingly uncomfortable with the way he was behaving toward me and I started to feel unsafe around him. And yet, I didn't think I could do anything about it because I was a young staffer and he was a donor.

At some point, I got overwhelmed enough to talk to my boss, Shari. I explained the situation and told her I wasn't sure what I was doing wrong. That's when she taught me one of the most valuable lessons I've learned in two decades of fundraising: You should never feel uncomfortable in a fundraising situation, and if you do, it's okay to walk away.

That's one thing that people—and particularly women—in

campaigns forget. It doesn't happen often, but there might be times when you need to fire a donor. Or a volunteer. There's a tendency to believe that if someone wants to help, especially for free, you must accept that help. That's just not true.

Shari and the whole organization backed me when we told the donor that we were no longer going to work with him. He was angry and didn't understand how we could not want his money, but we knew it was the right thing to do. Shari raised another key point: The cost of the time I would waste, the emotional energy I would spend, the angst—all of that was not worth whatever the donor might give.

I remained grateful for that lesson and for the freedom to say no when a person's behavior crossed a line. Someone on my team on the Dean campaign approached me about a donor who had made repeated advances at her, despite her making it clear that she didn't want a personal relationship. Plain and simple, dealing with inappropriate advances should not be part of any job, though women have long been made to believe it is. As her manager, it was my responsibility to end the relationship with the donor. Which, of course, I did.

You also don't need to put up with abuse just to raise money—or ask for votes, or get support for your effort, and so on. Shortly after I started at EMILY's List, I was with one of our development staffers en route to touch base with a six figure donor. We were running a few minutes late, and when she called to give him a heads-up, he lit into her with a furious tirade that was completely unacceptable. She was clearly shaken (I would have been, too), and I decided in that moment we were done with him and he would no longer be affiliated with EMILY's List. Was it a hit to the organization to lose his money? Maybe. But just in the short term. When I think about the staff time and mental energy lost on people like him, I know we more than made up for it. We are an organization built on high ideals, and I think it's fair to hold our donors to the same high standards I expect of our staff and candidates.

When you make an ask of someone and then accept their help, you are welcoming them into your organization or your campaign. You are associating yourself with them. Make sure they are a good fit and, most important, that you and your team don't have to bargain away your values in order to work with them. There is no donation worth it.

THE TOPLINES

Making an ask is a skill. It takes practice. But asking successfully for what you want and need is the critical ingredient to your campaign's success.

There are a few key steps to making a successful ask.

- Do your research. Find out what the market will bear and ask for the top end of that range. If it's a donation, ask for the highest end of your targeted range. If you're talking to a voter, ask them to vote *and* volunteer. If you're talking to your boss, ask for a title change *and* a raise.

- Find the right approach for your ask, one that allows you to make the best case and will be effective for you and the person you're asking.

  - Enthusiasm: *I'm excited about something, and I'd love to bring you along with me.*
  - Fear: *Without you, we will miss a deadline, fail to hit a goal, not be able to meet the needs of our community.*
  - Guilt: *If not you, who? I have nowhere else to turn.*
  - All business: *We share values and goals. With your help, I can get it done.*

- Find your own way through the awkward moments.

  - Occupy your time in a way that works for you—doing puzzles, baking pies, knitting.
  - Count to seven, or take a big drink of water, after you make the ask, to ensure you don't talk yourself out of a good answer.
  - Remember that you are asking on behalf of a community, not yourself.

- Let go of bad assumptions: Too many of our thoughts around making asks, particularly asking for money, are based on flawed assumptions, like the ones below. You know what they say about when we assume . . .

  - People will give without an ask: You can't assume people will help. You have to ask them to do it, no matter how close you are.

+ Only rich people give money: In recent years, we've seen the rise of grassroots fundraising, and more and more, Americans are giving their time and money, even when they don't have much of either. People recognize the importance of changing the world and want to get involved—don't exclude them just because they can't give as much as others.

+ Asks should happen around big events: Use any opportunity you can.

+ The first answer is the final answer: Keep asking until you get an actual answer, yes or no.

▪ There are times when you should stop asking. If a donor, volunteer, or supporter is making you or your team uncomfortable or is being abusive in any way, you do not need their help. You will likely make up whatever you would have lost in time, emotional energy, and team well-being by not having to deal with a problematic supporter.

★★★

CHAPTER 7

Grow a Thicker Skin

THEY SAY POLITICS is a contact sport. While I used to think that was a colorful exaggeration, turn on your TV in the last weeks of an election and you'll see how true it's become. In fact, it's not just politics. In a world with social media, anonymous online reviews, and any number of ways to criticize people, *life* can feel like a contact sport.

I sometimes think how hard and awkward being a teenager was in the 1980s. I never was the popular kid, but still, I had good friends. I was a mix of athletic and nerdy, was super tall, and never felt quite like I fit in. It was hard at the time. But goodness, at least I didn't have to worry about Instagram, seeing photos of other girls in bikinis or posing with some cute boy I would never be brave enough to talk to.

I bring this up because those of you my age and older didn't grow up worrying about how many likes a photo had or what the cool kid said about you online. This is all new to us still, and it is changing everything, not just for kids but in all industries and aspects of business. Those younger than the Gen Xers have a better handle on this world. On the other hand, they have way more of their lives already made public. And since campaigns are often about making your opponent look bad, living your life online means there's a lot more material to mine for missteps and indiscretions. And all of that material can be amplified in a post or tweet. It is only getting more intense.

Campaigning is hard. You have to learn to live with attacks and judgments. You will have people who don't like you, even when they don't know you and never will. There are people who will hate you just because of the party you belong to. People will make assumptions and attack because of where you're from, who you support, your gender, your age, and so on. That's just the way it is.

Don't quit yet! There are far more people open to getting to know you.

So, we need to toughen you up! When we work with candidates, we tell them they don't have to start with thick skin, but they have to be willing to learn how to grow some. Frankly, with the world we are in, thick skin is helpful no matter what—especially when you are a woman trying to change the world.

You get to offer your point of view and put your best self out there, but that's the only thing you control. You can't control how your opponents will portray you. No matter how much you might want to, you can't control what people think or say about you. They might be with you, against you, or undecided about you, or simply not care at all. And the more you let what others think about you dictate your feelings or your reactions, the further you move away from what you came here to do.

DON'T TAKE IT PERSONALLY

"Don't take it personally" is advice we've given to countless candidates over the years. It's good advice. But much like "Use your diaphragm," though it's easy to say, I'm not always exactly sure what it means. Every time someone tells me not to take something personally, I think back to the great movie *You've Got Mail*. Meg Ryan, put out of business by Tom Hanks, whom (spoiler alert!) she falls for anyway, wonders what he means by "It's not personal." She asks, "What is that supposed to mean? I am so sick of that. All that means is that it wasn't personal to you. But it was personal to me. It's personal to a lot of people. And what's so wrong with being personal, anyway?"[1]

Someone's snarky remark on Twitter, their letter to the editor, or their comment on your Facebook wall may have meant nothing to them. They don't know you and they likely never will. But of course it's personal for you. I'm not saying you must shut down your feelings or ignore insults. Even if that were possible, I don't think it'd be the right way to handle unfair, often mean-spirited criticism. We're human, after all.

Here at EMILY's List, we get hit a lot in very gendered terms because folks don't like that we are supporting women in primaries or that we are fighting for reproductive justice. To put it lightly, these folks can get nasty. And I can handle it when people disagree with me or something EMILY's List has done. I have a tougher time when the attacks are personal.

It used to be the attacks on my appearance that hurt me the most. I have battled my weight for as long as I can remember. I have been up and down in weight over the years, and when I'm attacked online about a political action, my weight gets dragged into it. I know this sounds minor, but I remember early on when I first became the president of EMILY's List, I was anonymously told that I needed to get a makeover, join a gym, and get a personal trainer if I was ever going to "look the part" of the leader of the organization. That hit me hard, because it spoke to an insecurity I already held. I learned quickly that by stepping into a public role, I was opening myself up to unfair attacks from Internet commentators. And this is nothing compared to what our candidates go through from anonymous trolls who think threats of violence and rape, and comments about women's bodies, are appropriate and effective in a policy debate. Those are the comments that come at women all day long. I just don't see the same toward male politicians.

My advice is to do your best not to dwell on the hate. Take it in, take a deep breath, remember who and what you are fighting for in this battle, and get back to work. For me, I know I've got a million other things to worry about, so I do my best to let go of insults and personal attacks and keep focused on the things that fuel my work. If that doesn't help, I pound it out on a hike or long walk blasting nineties music or some Kasey Chambers. But that's just me. Find your own outlet, and let that be the place to remember what is important not just to you but to the work you are committing to do. As time goes on, I promise, the skin thickens. The good overtakes the bad.

The truth is, it doesn't matter what arena you're in once you enter the public sphere. Be honest with yourself: Have you ever made a snarky remark about a celebrity? Told a joke about a politician? Those comments are likely not based on a personal understanding of that figure. It's the same for the strangers coming at you. People are judging an idea of who you are, not the real you.

But sometimes, for the sake of your campaign, you have to make a tough decision about responding to critics. Whether or not you let an insult hurt you personally, you must consider how it might hurt your campaign efforts. It's a particularly challenging question for women, who are judged more harshly when they push back on attacks and especially when they call out sexism. For decades, both in and out of politics, calling something sexist would have been dismissed outright or considered overly sensitive.

Thankfully, times are changing and more women—in politics, in workplaces, in the media—have decided to call out misogyny where they see it. In 2018, we saw senators, congresswomen, and candidates note when their experience was diminished or when they received a proverbial (and dismissive) pat on the head from their male opponents. For example, in her 2018 race for US Senate, Jacky Rosen faced attacks from her opponent, incumbent Nevada Senator Dean Heller, who erroneously claimed that Rosen had made up her experience in technology and that she had no computer degree. Rosen showed reporters her diploma and was backed up by the school she attended. She proved Heller wrong, though she shouldn't have had to.[2]

Women are diminished in public spaces in other ways, too. Often, they are objectified and assigned different expectations than their male counterparts. We've seen women judged for their hair or their clothing (still rare with male candidates) or described in terms of physical appearance (as I have been many times), as if that's part of their qualifications. For example, in 2018, in a single news story, Virginia Congresswoman Abigail Spanberger was described as "willowy" with "blond good looks," and her opponent was allowed to attack her service while understating the number of years she served in the CIA.[3] Here's where I note that Abigail is a mom, a Virginia native, a former CIA officer. She is far more than her appearance, clearly.

Sometimes candidates choose to call out efforts to objectify them or reduce them to their physical appearance. Other times, it's not worth the effort. New York Congresswoman Alexandria Ocasio-Cortez once tweeted, "I don't owe a response to unsolicited requests from men with bad intentions . . . And also, like catcalling, for some reason they feel entitled to one."[4]

When the attacks are simply untrue, it's easy for a candidate to ignore them. But racist or homophobic comments get deeper under the skin and might require a response. Kansas Representative Sharice Davids is a Native American who grew up in Kansas, went to Leavenworth High School in Kansas, and attended Johnson County Community College—in Kansas! After graduating from Cornell Law School and serving as a White House fellow, she brought her skills and education back to her home state of Kansas. As an editorial from *The Kansas City Star* put it, "So, yes, she is from around here."[5]

And yet despite all that, a local GOP official called for Sharice to be "sent back packing to the reservation."[6]

Sharice kept on going through these offensive attacks, reminding people that not only was she "from around here," but she was running precisely because she wanted to take care of the issues facing the community she knew and loved so well. She knew that she couldn't control what her opponent and his, frankly, ignorant supporters said about her, but she could work hard enough to beat them. And come Election Day November 2018, she did just that.

Political attacks are nothing new, but the volume and the vitriol of these attacks seem to have grown since Donald Trump's election. It's not a huge surprise given that so much of his political reputation was built on questioning President Obama's status as an American, part of the blatantly racist birther movement that demanded to see the president's birth certificate to prove his citizenship. Since that indicatory debut, Trump has spent years weaponizing social media against people he doesn't like, mobilizing a base with fear and xenophobia.

In his campaign, Trump spent time attacking Mexicans and continued his attacks throughout the campaign on entire nations, a religion, the women who have accused him of sexual assault, a Gold Star family who lost their soldier son overseas, Megyn Kelly, Rosie O'Donnell, the media, a disabled reporter. In January 2016, *The New York Times* made a list of the people and groups Trump had insulted just since launching his presidential campaign in 2015, and it reached 598.[7] That was several years ago.

Those hundreds (or by now, surely, thousands) of people have all figured out their own way to handle personal attacks from the most powerful person in the world. Their variety of responses can offer some ideas about the many ways you can grow your own thick skin.

Let's look at two examples from the same month, December 2019. First, after then-sixteen-year-old Greta Thunberg was named *Time* magazine's Person of the Year in 2019, Trump tweeted, "Greta must work on her Anger Management problem, then go to a good old fashioned movie with a friend! Chill Greta, Chill!" It was a petty, although no longer surprising, attack from a world leader against a teenager just trying to make the world a better place. But Greta Thunberg dealt with it the way only a savvy social media native could: with a little bit of shade. Greta kept up her work and changed her Twitter profile so it read "A teenager working on her anger management problem. Currently chilling and watching a good old fashioned movie with a friend." It was so brilliantly simple. And it exposed Trump's attack for what it was: utterly ridiculous.

Then, later that month, on the day President Trump became the third president to be impeached, he attacked Michigan Representative Debbie Dingell and her husband, John, who had passed away earlier that year. John Dingell was a legend in the US House; he served for fifty-nine years and had been instrumental in protecting the auto industry. He helped to pass bills like the Medicare Act, the Clean Water Act, the Affordable Care Act, and the Civil Rights Act. For nearly six decades, his work made the lives of his constituents measurably better. In short, he was a man worth honoring. Instead, Trump implied he had gone to hell, wondering aloud to an audience, "Maybe he's looking up, I don't know."[8]

Representative Dingell responded directly to the president, tweeting about the pain he caused, "Mr. President, let's set politics aside. My husband earned all his accolades after a lifetime of service. I'm preparing for the first holiday season without the man I love. You brought me down in a way you can never imagine and your hurtful words just made my healing much harder."[9]

Both Greta and Representative Dingell responded perfectly, in ways that fit their positions, the moments in time, and the attacks they had suffered. There is no one right response to an insult or a criticism. The goal is to identify the most effective course of action that will allow you to keep doing the job you're trying to do.

DON'T READ THE COMMENTS

If I have said this once, I have said it a thousand times to candidates and their loved ones: Don't go looking for people who are attacking you. That means avoid the comments on stories about you, and it definitely means avoid the replies on Twitter and Facebook. You can have your team take a look periodically so they can flag the responses that are real questions or comments worth reading. But spending your time reading snarky or negative spiels isn't helpful.

This advice isn't just for candidates. It's good advice for anyone at any age, and if you're raising teenagers, I hope you'll pass this advice on to them. Stop reading the comments! Rest assured, you'll still hear feedback of all kinds, especially if you're running for office. But anonymous voices online shouldn't hold any power over you, your message, or your mission. Protect your psyche and your productivity by denying them daylight.

Once, when I was a campaign manager, my candidate couldn't take the negative comments anymore, particularly in the last few weeks of the campaign when things really got hateful. It felt like the negative ads were everywhere. We sat down together over a glass of whiskey to commiserate about the nastiness, and I reminded him that he needed to build up some armor around him. He decided with as much as he had to do—talking to voters and the press, smiling the whole way, and so on—he didn't want to see any of it anymore. No more ads, no more news clips, no more content. It seems drastic—and maybe it was—but we decided to figure out how to make it happen.

I took on the responsibility of monitoring the ads, and the campaign made the decisions on how best to respond to them, if at all. All the candidate needed to do was focus on convincing as many people as he could that they should vote for him. In the end, he did his job, I did mine, and he won.

There's no easy way to grow a thicker skin, but in the hardest times, a fail-safe option is to tap into your passion for the cause. You'll feel stronger right away. For me, I am so proud every day about working to elect Democratic women to office. I love it, I am thrilled by it, and I find it endlessly exciting. So if someone wants to attack me or EMILY's List, I push it aside, and I spend time reflecting on how much that mission means to me. Changing the world keeps me busy and doesn't leave time to deal with trolls.

That doesn't mean I won't listen to legitimate criticism, of course. But it does mean I have made the decision that I'm not going to let unfair or personal attacks stop me from doing work that matters to me. And that's the best advice I can give you. Find the thing that matters to you more than those attacks, and you'll find a way to ignore them and refocus your energy on your true goal. If you're doing the right work on the right issue, you will likely be so busy doing the thing you actually need to be doing, you won't have time to get distracted by small and demeaning comments from small and demeaning people.

DON'T SURROUND YOURSELF WITH YES MEN AND WOMEN

Growing your thick skin doesn't mean surrounding yourself with yes-men and -women who tell you what you want to hear. You need staff, friends, and family who are honest with you. When they have honest criticisms, which they will, you need to be open to those constructive conversations. They should be allowed to share their thoughts freely, and often, though not always, they will be right. Being willing to have these conversations will mean having the confidence to face potentially tough changes and to not worry that you're not perfect.

I find these conversations incredibly useful. Basically, I have a lot of ideas. Some of them are brilliant (I believe). Some are really important. But others are too expensive to execute. Or have political ramifications that I don't see. Or just don't make sense. I want (and I have) people around me who tell me when they think one of my ideas is bad. They are not always right and sometimes we fight it out. And yet sometimes they are spot-on, and I stand down.

This is all a balance, and I have learned that in growing my thick skin, it's for the best that I don't always get my way. I don't get my way when we can't afford it or when it is not the right thing to do at that time. I will admit, sometimes it pisses me off. But then I remember that I hired really smart people to tell me what they think and to keep us out of trouble. Be strong enough to fight for what you believe in. Be strong enough to listen when someone tells you you're wrong. Hope you have the wisdom and experience to decipher the right path forward. Some days you have to stand down. Other days you have to stand tall. Your job is a lot easier if you trust the people you're surrounded by.

The process of being in the public eye, leading an organization or a campaign, makes you stronger and smarter. You'll learn to be better at dealing with people and better at having really hard conversations. And that, my friend, will help with every Thanksgiving dinner you'll have in the future. It's a win for life.

PLAN FOR THE WORST

Some people would tell you that there are no more silver bullets on the campaign trail. That no one issue or incident can end or save a run for office. The goalposts have been moving over time, allowing for different behavior from people in public life than in years past. Celebrities involved in scandals have found paths to redemption. A man credibly accused of sexual assault and who bankrupted several businesses was elected president on the platform of making America great. And so on.

So maybe we've entered an era in which one brutal attack can't end a campaign by itself. But don't kid yourself: How you, the candidate, handle that attack will determine how well your campaign withstands it. In fact, while one attack may not kill you, a bad response to that attack can be deadly. That's why you *must* prepare for the worst.

Step One: Know Your Own Vulnerabilities

You may have heard about opposition research—trying to find "dirt" on your opponent. In campaigns, you start with knowing all the dirt on *you*. We call learning about your own vulnerabilities "self-research." It's digging into all of the publicly available information in your record, from your voting history, to your financial and real estate information, to your social media accounts and public comments. It's standard for campaigns, but this is good advice for all of us who foster ambitions in organizations, corporations, and movements. If you are facing a fight against any opponent, you need to be armed with at least as much information as the other side. You need to prep, ideally learning as much as you can about your own potential trouble spots, by researching what can be found publicly about you, well before the fight gets under way. As my cowriter, Christina, who was a rapid response director for President Obama and Hillary Clinton, would note, the best protection against a vulnerability is preparation.

Presidential campaigns will have large research teams doing this work. Federal campaigns will have smaller teams or maybe a research consultant. At other levels, you may be relying on volunteer help. Regardless of what your team looks like, you will need to look into your own record, ideally as early as possible. You don't need to be a private investigator (or to hire one). You need to look at what others can find out about you and what's publicly available: your voting record, your property tax record, your social media, things you've written, and so on.

We live in a world where it's increasingly popular to share our lives online. It's good in some ways and challenging in others, but above all, it represents a shift in behavior. Social media has made it possible for us to know more about the people we follow, date, hire, elect, and so on. So, if you're running for office or applying for a job, make especially sure your social media reflects what you want it to. No matter your privacy settings, there's always some chance that your posts will become public, so you should review it all and make sure there's nothing you are uncomfortable sharing.

Step Two: Be Prepared to Address Each of Your Vulnerabilities If Necessary

Once you figure out your biggest vulnerabilities and brainstorm the most likely attacks, you can begin to formulate effective and appropriate responses so you're ready if—or more likely when they come up. Remember that preparation is your key to success. In some cases, where there are policy details or key facts that can be useful to your response, your team needs to gather helpful, complete background informa tion or line up experts who can argue your point.

In scenarios with smaller vulnerabilities, it will be possible to make an easy fix as soon as you're made aware of an issue. That way, you've already addressed the issue even before the attack comes. At other times, on issues that don't have an obvious or easy fix, it will be better to just draft your statement now, knowing that you'll likely need to tweak it depending on how the attack is delivered, and think through who might be a good validator or supporter when the time comes for a defense, apology, or explanation.

The reason to go through this process is obviously to make sure you aren't paralyzed by an attack. But it is also part of growing that thicker skin. If you know what your vulnerabilities are and you know how you are going to respond, you won't be as surprised when the attack comes. You will have already gone through some of the emotion of an attack without having to do it in public. It will help keep you calmer (not necessarily calm, but calmer!).

Attacks on the candidate are to be expected. Modern politics is a contact sport, remember? But attacks on a public figure's family can be harder to swallow and trickier to prepare for. The gut reaction is often outrage. You've heard this before: "How dare you go after my [wife, child, etc.]? I am the one in the public eye; leave them out of it." That's a fair response and can be effective. But bear in mind, lines that were once clearly defined have become blurry. If a candidate uses her children as part of her story, it's hard to argue that the children should be off-limits to opponents or the press. Many voters also believe that adult children and spouses are fair game in a campaign, particularly if their work has anything to do with the candidate's (for example, Ivanka Trump and her husband working in her father's White House, or a spouse or child who works in a business that gains from the actions of an elected official).

You have prepared for your family to be a part of your race and the story you are telling to the public. So prepare them also for the most likely attacks, so that from the beginning, you can make a plan together to deal with them. What will your family want to hear from you (rather than having to see something in the press or hear about it from a staffer), and how much will they want to be engaged in the process? You don't want to figure this out on the spot. Say it with me: Preparation is key!

Step Three: Ensure That Your Supporters Hear Your Response and Are Ready to Rally Around You

Consider in advance who your supporters are. Who will have your back no matter what? Who might be concerned about a particular issue, personal or policy related, that is vulnerable to attack from your opponent? And how can you tailor your responses to reinforce their faith in you as a candidate when attacks, valid or otherwise, come at you? If you have built a strong relationship with a group or voter block and understand what is important to them, then you'll know the right messaging to counter your opponent's attacks.

Like nearly anything in life, politics is built around relationships. Who you know, who will give you the benefit of the doubt when things go wrong, who will introduce you to the right people—these connections all matter. That can be tough for women candidates in a political system that has been led by men for generations. Even the socializing in politics is driven by more traditionally masculine activities, such as playing basketball or golf, chatting about last night's football game, and so on. Men do this *a lot*. It's not just politics; it's any big industry where money and power come together.

My long-term solution is to elect more women who will smash the patriarchy. But for now my best piece of advice is that we must work a bit harder to build and maintain real relationships with our political partners. That means everyone from fellow elected officials to union, church, environmental, and all sorts of movement leaders. That's the basics of politics: relationships. It is so much easier to weather a storm if your "political friends" are by your side. They won't always agree on your policies, but they will trust in your integrity and commitment and offer a political support system when the attacks feel especially hard to weather.

RAPID RESPONSE 101: THE FUNDAMENTALS

Rapid response is a vital part of successful campaigns. National campaigns often have multiple people who work on nothing but responding to crises (my cowriter, Christina, has led those teams more than once). You may have heard of campaigns or even some government operations setting up "war rooms" to prepare for political fights. It all sounds very dramatic—but at times these situations can be. So much of campaigns, business, and everyday life is just putting out small fires. Below are the key steps to rapid response, a process we've honed over years of doing this work.

- **Create a process for response before you need it.** When the proverbial shit hits the proverbial fan, you need to be able to act fast. That means you need to know exactly *how* you're going to get a response written and disseminated. You need to figure out who will be a part of the decision-making process, who will actually do the work, who will need to sign off on the response once it's drafted and researched, and so on. You'll need to let all of those people know their roles and get buy-in from the candidate and any senior people as to how it will work. Everyone should agree on the process or you'll spend time you don't have in a crisis debating each of these issues rather than getting a response out quickly and cleanly.

- **Decide whether you are going to respond.** Not responding to something is making a decision like any other. Make sure you are making a conscious choice on what you want to do rather than letting time or inertia decide for you. It's also important to make sure your response doesn't make a situation worse. There are times when the response makes an attack more interesting or more newsworthy than it was to begin with. Make sure you're not adding oxygen to a fire that would have died out on its own.

- **And if so, how you'll do it.** If you do decide to respond, your delivery will be the next important decision. In general, you don't want to go bigger than the original attack. If someone tweets at you, you likely don't want to respond with a TV ad. An attack from an anonymous online troll probably doesn't deserve your candidate's time and voice in response. On the flip side, if something has spread far and wide via the Internet, just putting out a press statement may not reach all of the people who have engaged with the harmful rumor. You may need to push something via social media or put some advertising behind it, depending on how widely it's been spread.

- **Make your response fast, accurate, and thoughtful.** Each one of these requirements is equally important— and your process will need to balance all three. You need to be fast, because otherwise the news will move on without you and your response. And yet you shouldn't sacrifice accuracy for speed. Ensuring that something is accurate can certainly slow you down, but you don't want to have to correct a mistake or fact down the road, as it will discredit your response. Last, you need to consider how the response will be taken by voters. Your goal as a campaign should be to know as much as you can know within a certain amount of time and then make an appropriate response that will satisfy your voters. You need to think through who will be impacted or affected by the attack and how they may view your response.

- **Assign clear roles and deadlines for next steps.** Once you've decided that you're going to respond, you need to figure out who is going to do what and by when. You'll have determined at least part of this process before the crisis strikes, but in the moment, you need to tailor clear and explicit assignments and deadlines that respond appropriately to the attack. You need a person responsible for drafting the statement. They will send it around for approval, and all feedback must be given quickly. This staffer is responsible for turning that statement into talking points for volunteers, or for posting it on social media, and ensuring it gets into the hands of all allies so they can speak on your behalf. Make sure everyone on the team knows their individual assignments and their deadlines. This will prevent mission creep (people crossing lanes or duplicating efforts unnecessarily) and confusion. Duplication of work wastes time and makes you look unorganized, something you can't afford in a crisis.
- **Think about your audiences.** Anytime you're going to communicate, you need to think about your audiences: Who are they, how do you reach them, will they care about this attack or this issue, what do they need to hear from you? Keep in mind, not everyone is your audience. It's not that you'll use fundamentally different messaging for your response for each group, since you don't want to change your answer or look like you're telling people whatever they want to hear. But the format and

delivery may change. Think about which of your supporters, donors, and so on might actually care about and
have heard the attack, and who needs to hear the response. Remember that you don't want to draw unnecessary attention to something negative if it might go away
on its own.

■ **Monitor and recalibrate accordingly.** In every political
attack, our goal is to create the kind of response that
shuts it down altogether, never to return. Sadly, even the
best response rarely pulls an attack out by the roots. The
news media or your opponents might find a new angle—
or they might go after your response itself, no matter
how carefully constructed. It's important to continue to
monitor the press, social media, and even what your volunteers are hearing at the doors or on the phones. Keeping your ear to the ground, so to speak, will let you know
if or how the story has shifted and whether you need to
update or add to your response.

These are the basics for rapid response, and they've served
me well throughout years of campaigns, but they are useful
beyond the political world. Each situation is different, but a
solid process that works through the steps is like a how-to
guide and a security blanket rolled into one. It will provide
you an actionable to-do list, so in the moment when you're at
your lowest, you don't have to think about anything but the
matter at hand.

TURN THOSE WEAKNESSES INTO STRENGTHS

No elected official is perfect. Politicians are people, after all. And yet too many women assume they must be perfect in order to run for office. Perfection is an impossible standard, but more important, it's an inappropriate one. Shouldn't we want people representing us and fighting for us who have lived lives and actually understand the challenges we face?

It's with this idea in mind that candidates in recent years have turned their vulnerabilities into strengths on the campaign trail. For example, when Georgia Democratic gubernatorial candidate Stacey Abrams released her personal financial disclosure, she faced questions about being over $200,000 in debt. But Stacey flipped the script and used those questions as a way to tell her own story. As one of six children, she graduated from college and then an Ivy League law school with a good salary but extensive student loan and credit card debt. She later extended that debt helping out her parents through illness and their own financial issues. Stacey used her debt to talk about the role race and gender can play in economic inequality and what financial disadvantages women may face, including gender wage gaps, legacy barriers, and systemic biases. Stacey left voters—particularly those with their own debt challenges—with an inspiring message: "Yes, we all still make money mistakes—but they don't have to be fatal to our dreams."[10]

Virginia Delegate Hala Ayala was one of the first Latinas elected to the Virginia legislature. At the time of her election she was a mom and a cybersecurity specialist with security clearance, but earlier in her life, she had worked at a gas station and relied on Medicaid for health care. In her reelection campaign, Hala didn't try to hide any part of her biography. In fact, she talked regularly about what that first job and the public assistance she had relied on meant to her, and how it inspired her to fight for others who need help.[11]

As with all of the lessons in this book, this advice doesn't just apply to candidates. We all have weaknesses and vulnerabilities. By acknowledging what you've learned from past mistakes or experiences that feel somehow shameful, you can find ways of weaving stories out of those moments. You take power from your detractors when you learn to get in front of vulnerabilities such as these. When you're applying for a new position, you may know you had an issue with a past job or past boss that you need to address. That conversation could be a chance to show how you made it through a challenging situation and what you learned from it.

If you are a candidate, your so-called weaknesses make you relatable to people who aren't used to seeing a person running for office with flaws just like theirs. If you are a leader in an arena other than politics, acknowledging your weaknesses can help inspire your team to continue to improve their own job performance and show them a path forward. What some people might consider a vulnerability can be the thing that helps others understand and relate to you, so don't be afraid of owning those traits.

Sometimes my favorite defense tactic, humor, can defuse a

serious attack. In 1984, when critics believed President Reagan's age was going to be a concern for voters, Reagan took on the issue with both a wink and a smile, noting in a debate with his younger opponent, Walter Mondale, "I will not make age an issue of this campaign. I am not going to exploit, for political purposes, my opponent's youth and inexperience."[12] In doing so, Reagan was acknowledging the attack while simultaneously showing that he had a sense of humor about it, thus making it seem less important.

Sometimes humor can highlight how ridiculous an attack is. In 2019, when conservative gadfly Jacob Wohl held a press conference in which a twenty-five-year-old man claimed he'd been hired by Elizabeth Warren as an escort several times, the backdrop for his ridiculous press conference was a banner asking, "Elizabeth Warren Cougar?" Elizabeth took the absurd lies in stride, responding with a tweet that found a good use for her alma mater's mascot. Warren tweeted, "It's always a good day to be reminded that I got where I am because a great education was available for $50 a semester at the University of Houston (go Cougars!). We need to cancel student debt and make college free for everyone who wants it."[13] She used humor to dismiss an attack *and* talk about policy. Elizabeth really does have a plan for everything.

Humor can be an effective tool, but it must be used judiciously. A joke actually has to be funny for it to work. If it's too hard to understand or is delivered poorly, it will fall flat. As with any response, it should be appropriate and proportional to the attack. Some comments or questions call for a serious response, meaning a joke will seem tone-deaf and make the situation worse. Delivery is important as well. There's a fine line between wit and sarcasm, and sarcasm can read as caustic, especially from women. If you're going to try making a joke, test it out on some friends or trusted supporters to make sure it doesn't go too far or feel inappropriate.

When all else fails, remember the strategy of Hillary Clinton, a groundbreaking woman who was attacked for many different things: "If I want to knock a story off the front page, I just change my hairstyle."[14] Distraction is a good tactic in an emergency, and the media just can't seem to stop itself from reporting on women candidates' haircuts!

REMEMBER, NOTHING LASTS FOREVER, EVEN THE WORST ATTACKS

We've all faced challenges, some larger than others. But what about when the attacks just keep coming? Or what about the ones that feel particularly disheartening or damaging? Hopefully this chapter has given you some tactical advice on how your candidacy can survive attacks. Now I also want to address the personal and emotional side.

I understand that you might feel overwhelmed at times when you're being criticized or attacked. Whether it's a public critique of your job performance or some attack on your efforts to change the world, you're not weak for feeling wounded by something that's meant to wound you. Every woman, no matter how strong or how self-confident, gets low and feels unworthy sometimes. We all have moments when we wonder if we're up to the task or why we're even trying.

I can't tell you it's easy to dismiss something that hurts you. I know it's not. But I can remind you that the feeling will pass. What you're facing represents a moment in time, and it's fleeting. The public, the press, the voters, your coworkers—anyone thinking or saying the worst will move on eventually. And in our world of increasingly short attention spans, "eventually" will be here before you know it.

Take care of yourself as you're going through the difficult spells. That means taking the time to remind yourself why you're doing what you're doing. For women running for office, sometimes that's talking to volunteers or supporters, or doing community outreach and engagement. For others, this is a great time to buckle down on work as a means of productive distraction. If a rolling stone gathers no moss, a busy woman gathers no insults . . . or something like that.

This could also mean enjoying comfort food, getting in a good workout, having a massage, or escaping into some good bad TV (Bachelor Nation, stand up!). Allowing yourself a short break to buck up your spirits is not admitting defeat.

Now's the time to make use of that support system we mentioned in chapter 5, particularly the people who are on your side no matter what, or who know just how to distract you from a bad day or an abusive tweet. It's not just that supportive friends make you feel better. Someone with more distance from the situation can give you the clear-eyed outside perspective you might be missing. That's not to dismiss what you're going through. But it's a good reminder that the rest of the world isn't as focused on this issue as you are.

Keep in mind that others have been through tough times in the public eye and have come out of it just fine in the end. I can't count the number of men who have come back from major controversies and attacks. We've watched celebrities come back from scandals. Monica Lewinsky turned her role in the middle of an impeachment fight and an infamous White House scandal into a lesson in bullying and owning your power.[15] Keep an eye on how the candidates and public figures you love deal with attacks, and try to learn from them.

Finally, always remember, the fight goes on and you are an important part of it. Former California Congresswoman Katie Hill went through hell and back less than a year after being sworn into office. Katie was going through a difficult divorce, which ultimately led to cyber exploitation and the release of nude photos. She had to own her mistake of having a relationship with a campaign staffer, and Katie decided to resign from Congress in late 2019. In a powerful *New York Times* column, Katie laid out how dark things got and the night when she contemplated suicide.

But she also told the story of a party her roommate, Representative Lauren Underwood, threw for her, with other congresswomen offering their support. She talked about how Speaker Nancy Pelosi treated her with love and respect, and how many of her constituents and donors had reached out to voice their support. Katie noted, "I don't know exactly what's ahead for me, and I know there's a lot more pain ahead. But I'm in the fight and I'm glad it's not all over after all."[16]

THE TOPLINES

Successful women aren't perfect. No one is. One of the keys to success is not failing to make mistakes or draw attacks; it's figuring out how to grow a thick enough skin to roll with the punches and learn from them.

Don't read the comments: You only have a certain amount of time and energy every day. Why waste any of it on people who just want to make you feel bad?

Know your vulnerabilities: No matter what you're doing or how you're trying to change the world, someone out there is going to hate you for it. Figure out what they can find out about you and how they might use it to undermine your work and your credibility.

Plan for the worst: Failing to plan is planning to fail. Now that you know what might be coming (assuming you did your homework in the last point), it's time to think about how you'll deal with that incoming attack and how you'll move forward from it.

Learn the fundamentals: The best way to grow thicker skin is to build a process and a plan to deal with the arrows that might break through.

- Create a process before you need it
- Determine whether and how you will respond
- Assign clear roles and deadlines for next steps
- Make your response fast, accurate, and thoughtful
- Think about your audiences
- Monitor and calibrate accordingly

Turn your weaknesses into strengths: Being able to talk about what you've been through, and most important, what you've learned from hardships and mistakes, makes you a compelling leader. When you can, do that with humor.

Remember that the bad times don't last forever: Remind yourself why you're working to change the world. Lean on your support system. And remember that this attack and this moment will pass.

★★★

CHAPTER 8

Get Back Up. A Loss Is Just a Part of Your Journey.

HERE'S THE THING: Not all you do, no matter how well planned or oft practiced, is going to go perfectly. Maybe you'll be the lucky one who wins every race you enter, gets every job you apply for, and succeeds at everything you try. But for the rest of us, that's just not how life works.

Luckily, a loss is not the end; it's just one step on your journey. That's something we believe very firmly here at EMILY's List. I try to remember it in everything I do.

This is, perhaps, a lesson you've been taught before. You might not know that Barack Obama lost his first race for federal office or that Michael Jordan got cut from his high school basketball team before becoming the greatest men's basketball player of all time.* But what about women? Can we bounce back from a loss the same way?

---

*I am writing this book with a University of North Carolina Tar Heel, so I have to say this. Please take your debates about LeBron James or any other basketball players up with my cowriter, Christina.

We know that more is demanded of us. For women in public life, we are expected to bring nothing less than perfection. And it's easy to feel like one misstep might cost the whole game. But while that might feel true, I promise it's not. I'm here to tell you that not only can women come back from a loss, but at EMILY's List, we think learning from a loss, especially a hard one, makes women stronger as candidates and as advocates.

That applies to everything from a tough debate, to a harmful campaign attack, to actually losing the race. Winning is great—don't get me wrong. Winning is good. Ultimately, that's how you change the world. But coming back from a failure or even a loss is nothing to be afraid of. It's just another skill to learn. And it's one I learned the hard way.

From what you know about me already, you might not be surprised to learn that I *hate* losing. I know, no one loves it. But let's just say there's a reason I went into a field that involves campaigns, election days, races, and victory speeches. I'm competitive, plain and simple.

In high school in Montana, I was a competitive swimmer. I was even pretty good. Definitely above average, though admittedly not the best. That didn't stop me from wanting to be the state champion. I worked and trained and practiced, even after it became clear I wasn't going to make that goal. It truly bothered me that despite having a clear goal and putting in the effort, I just couldn't get to that level.

One season, that effort was producing some positive

momentum and I set my sights on the regional swim meet in California. And yet, in swim competitions all summer long, I kept falling just short of the qualifying time I needed to hit in order to make the cut. I was having a good season and working hard, but I was just a little bit off the mark. Still, I kept training until the final meet of the season, which was in my hometown. I felt like if I could just swim fast enough that night, it would be a perfect storybook ending for my high school swimming career.

Instead, I got to the swim meet and completely choked. I had one of my worst swims of the season and was completely devastated. Thankfully, my coach believed in me. The state swimming association decided to offer one more qualifying opportunity for those of us who had come close to qualifying. But this final meet would be in Bozeman, a seventy-mile drive each way. And it was on a weeknight. I was a nervous wreck the whole way there. I felt an intense responsibility to my coach and the people who had put so much faith in me, and on top of that I felt terrible that my dad had taken nearly three hours on a work night just so I could make this swim.

A girlfriend and competitor of mine knew that swimming this on my own might be too much for my nerves, so she came and swam next to me, giving the push I needed to fight harder and swim faster. With all that support and that fight back in me, I got into the water, took a big breath, and kicked off. I hadn't given up and I hadn't let a setback stop me, and neither did the people around me. And because of that, I didn't just make the meet; I beat my best time by nearly two full seconds. It's a lesson I've never forgotten.

LEARNING LESSONS FROM A LOSS

We've just spent the last chapter talking about growing a thicker skin and preparing for the hard times. Now it's time to put that thick skin to the test. You need to learn from what happened and move forward stronger and better.

I saw this in my first professional campaign, Mary Rieder's race for the US House in 1996. Mary was hitting her stride at just the right time (toward the end of the campaign), and we felt the momentum was moving in our direction. Unfortunately, Republican presidential nominee and Kansas Senator Bob Dole realized that he couldn't defeat President Bill Clinton and changed his schedule in the last two weeks to doing events focused on keeping the GOP control of the House. I wasn't a supporter of Senator Bob Dole, but even I admit that this was a pretty honorable thing to do for his party. Dole came into Minnesota and campaigned for our opponent, and it worked. Mary's momentum slowed at the most crucial moment. Vote counting went long into the night, but eventually Mary lost.

I was heartbroken, but as the finance director, my job was not over. Everyone had to be thanked, and we had debts that would need to be paid. So the next day I went into work with a big cup of coffee and my old glasses on, because my eyes were swollen from crying and I couldn't be bothered with contacts. Mary saw me that morning and hugged me, and assured me that this loss was not going to take her down. She said she had put her contacts in that morning to prove that she was still standing.

It was a little thing, but it has stuck with me. For Mary, that one act of putting in her contacts like she did every day wasn't going to change just because she had faced a big loss. I remember being so impressed that though she was the one who had lost, she was picking all of us up. And I also learned that some days you just need to put on the good clothes (or the contacts) of a survivor and push yourself through.

Mary and I sat there that day after the election, and for many days after that, calling her supporters and thanking them. After years in the business and plenty of calls made after disappointing losses, I can tell you, they never get any easier. You will always feel like you let these people down. They counted on you, gave their time, money, and effort, and you didn't win.

But the other thing I learned from Mary is that no matter how hard these calls are, your supporters deserve that time and effort from you. Mary handled the time after her loss with the grace that I had come to expect of her, and I am lucky to have been by her side through both her victories and her defeats. Mary has since passed away after a battle with cancer, but I remain grateful for her kindness and the many lessons she taught me.

Here's yet another piece of advice that is easy to say and

much harder to do: Take one step at a time and just keep going. It's hard, but it's totally the right thing to do.

When you go into politics, you are asking for a life of professional wins and losses. The wins are amazing, but it's brutal to spend months, even years, working with a candidate and have them ultimately lose. And then, almost immediately, to have to pick yourself up and start all over again. Luckily, campaigns build camaraderie—sometimes that's even truer in losing campaigns than in winning ones. Your saving grace will be the relationships you build and the people you're with in the trenches. Chances are, you'll work with them again.

When I was a staffer on my first presidential campaign, Howard Dean for America, I learned plenty of hard lessons. It wasn't always easy in Burlington in the fall of 2003. First off, it gets cold in Vermont, and fast (yes, even for a Montanan who went to college and worked in Minnesota). It also gets dark early. When things started going badly with the race, honestly, it was sort of miserable.

Joe Trippi was managing the campaign and brought in some truly great talent to try to right the ship. One of those men (and most of them were men) was Mike Ford, whose job was to help manage and rally the troops. He had been the deputy campaign manager for Walter Mondale's presidential campaign in 1984 and deserves a lot of the credit for getting Geraldine Ferraro on the ticket—the first woman ever to be on a major-party presidential ticket.

And in Burlington, in 2003, Mike gave me a piece of advice I've never forgotten since. He looked me dead in the eyes and told me that campaigns are war. Campaigning is how we change our government. We don't take up arms to incite change in the United States, but elections are battles nonetheless. And in battle, the thing that matters most is the people fighting beside you. He told me that when I look to the left in the foxhole and then to the right, it is those folks that I will never forget.

He was totally right. I think about it all the time.

Politics is a tough business, but you are surrounded by people throwing their whole heart into the work, just like you are. Those people understand the challenges you face better than anyone, and you'll form friendships and bonds with these people that will last for a very, very long time.

A HOW-TO GUIDE FOR MOVING ON AFTER LOSING

So what do you do when you've been dealt a loss? I've talked to many EMILY's List candidates the day after they've lost an election, and the reactions vary greatly. Some of them are angry, some are sad, and most of them are worried about having let their supporters down. There are the candidates who want to file their paperwork to run again that day and the ones who swear they are done with electoral politics forever. I tell them all the same thing: Before you do anything, get a little rest and don't make any rash decisions. And then when you're ready, there are a few things that need taking care of.

First, the wallowing. That's okay. You can be sad—you fought hard for something you believed in and it didn't go your way. You are, in a way, grieving. Whether you're a candidate or a campaign staffer, for the last few months you have devoted all your time and energy to a cause you believed in. When you put your heart into something, you don't get it back quickly or easily. If you were the one on the ballot, you are surely battling a sense of failure, and even loneliness. If you were a staffer, you might feel disheartened or aimless. It is a lot to take on, and I respect that.

Get yourself a pedicure (because if you've been on a campaign, you probably haven't had time to do that). Spend time with your family, read a book, be like Hillary Clinton and go for some nice walks in the woods with your dogs. Whether you want to eat a pizza by yourself or you want to get back to the gym for the first time in ages, go do it. Know the whole time that the inner strength that got you to run (or launch your effort to change the world, or even apply for that job) is still there in you. In fact, it's probably even stronger because of what you've been through.

The thing about a loss is that it gives you time to reflect and improve. When you win a campaign, you have immediate work to do. You have to start planning your office and your move and so on, so you have no time to think about how and why it all worked. That's why you should take advantage of the downtime after a loss, because you have a fact-finding mission ahead of you. It's best to do it when things are still fresh in people's minds. You'll want to gather together your campaign leadership, your consultants, the people whose opinions you value, party activists, community leaders, even some voices from outside your campaign who paid attention to what was happening. If you're the candidate, make sure you're a part of the conversation, but this time as a listener and a student, not as the leader. Too often, either the candidate drives the whole conversation and fails to get an open and honest take, or the candidate isn't there at all and therefore doesn't learn from others' experience of the loss. This is how you turn defeat into a learning experience.

I do this myself at both the start and the end of every election cycle. I gather up smart people, consultants, political staff, and so on, and I sit down with them, sometimes one-on-one, sometimes in small groups. Beforehand, I ask them what they're expecting, who they think will decide the election, how the voters are feeling, what obstacles we will face, and so on. After the election, I ask them what the mood of the electorate was. Who ended up deciding the election? What was the most effective use of our resources or our candidate's time? What did we miss or what didn't we see coming? What was new in this election—was there a tool or trend we saw for the first time ever?

You should do this, too. Sit down and talk about the key questions, seeking both the positives and negatives in your campaign. And remember through this process that it's just as important to learn what worked as what didn't. No campaign or effort is a *total* disaster, just like no winning campaign is perfect. You must have gotten something right along the way, so don't be afraid to recognize and celebrate the victories in your defeat.

It's easy to understand how this could happen. You get caught up in the daily grind of "How am I doing?" and "Am I doing this right?" and you completely miss the fact that you've made huge steps forward. It's worth finding a video of one of your early speeches or interviews and comparing it with one at the end of the campaign. Watch it and be surprised at how good you got over time. You are not the same candidate who started the race. You'll take that knowledge and growth into your next campaign. I've done my own version of this. Looking back at when I gave my first big speech, at EMILY's List's twenty-fifth anniversary gala, I can't believe how far I've come. It's a good exercise for your confidence, I promise!

A campaign loss feels like the end. But we do these exercises to make sure we're being realistic about why we lost. We tend to blame ourselves and assume we did everything wrong. But oftentimes, the political or economic environment was working against you. Or you were facing an outside force (voter suppression, Russia, James Comey, a sudden influx of outside ads running against you—did I mention voter suppression?). Sometimes you lose even though you did nearly everything right.

So instead of dwelling on the things you could never have fixed, focus on the things that were in your control. What areas have growth potential for your next run? Consider these possibilities.

Maybe you were never able to draw the attention of the right donors. Maybe you hired the wrong team—or set them up in a way that didn't work for your district. Maybe you were the wrong candidate profile for the time (you worked for an industry that's unpopular in your area, you supported or even worked for a candidate who has since become unpopular, you're on record having taken an unpopular position in the past). These are all things to consider. Now ask yourself, how would you have done things differently to get ahead of these problems? More important, how would you change things moving forward?

This process has applications across the board. You didn't get the job? Think about how you prepared, which of your skills you highlighted for the people doing the hiring. Did you have the right mix of references? How was your cover letter or writing sample? Do you know someone involved in the hiring well enough to ask for some insight? Get people you trust to review your résumé and make sure it's saying what you want it to, and so on. And if you didn't get the promotion: How was your argument framed? Do you have a clear set of accomplishments in your current job and did you make successful arguments as to how you meet the next job description? What does the person who got the job or promotion have that you don't? Can you get that skill, experience, etc.? These questions can be uncomfortable, especially when you're down. But answering them is critical to your growth as a candidate.

If you're an activist or organizer who didn't get enough signatures for a petition or enough public support to pass a bill, think back to your action plan. Did you have the right number of people involved? Were you engaging in the right areas and aiming at the right audiences? How was your messaging? Did it make the most effective points and was it delivered well? Did you use enough technology? Or perhaps too much?

This kind of postmortem can be tough. Getting people to be honest and let go of any defensiveness they may feel about their own role is not easy—especially for the person at the center of the action. But it's a worthwhile exercise whenever you've failed to reach a goal, and one that has the added bonus of keeping you busy rather than letting you dwell on the loss.

Sometimes you do the analysis and acknowledge your own mistakes but realize that mostly you were the right candidate in the wrong race, or were in the right district in the wrong election cycle. In cases like these, it's worth figuring out if there are ways to change what's wrong. Let's take a look at how you can deal with scenarios where the deck is stacked against you.

Should you run for a different office? Sometimes you're facing an incumbent who is too tough to beat or a field that's just too large. Sometimes you realize there's a better opportunity in a different race. Still other times, you recognize that you might actually want a different job where you can do more to fight the battle you care about. Whatever the reason, you could be part of a long history of candidates who've lost one race and then gone on to win a different seat. It is a time-tested tradition that has worked for a number of our candidates.

Wendy Carrillo is a former labor activist and journalist who moved to California from El Salvador as a child, becoming a citizen in her twenties. Like so many of us, Wendy was motivated to run after getting involved in political activism (for her, the Dakota Access Pipeline protests) and seeing the polarization after the 2016 election.[1] When Xavier Becerra vacated his US House seat to become California's attorney general, Wendy jumped at the chance to run in that 2017 special election. While she ran a good race (even though it was only her first race), there were nearly two dozen candidates and she ended up losing to an incumbent member of the California State Assembly. Instead of making that loss the end of her political journey, Wendy turned right around and ran for the then-open seat in the California assembly later that same year. EMILY's List was proud to stand with her in her campaign and even prouder when she won.[2] Wendy is a powerful advocate for her community in the assembly and she's got a bright future in politics ahead of her. That's why we named her our 2019 Gabrielle Giffords Rising Star Award winner.

Should you try again in another cycle? Minnesota Congresswoman Angie Craig lost by fewer than two points in 2016. When she decided to run again in 2018, she was following a long line of candidates who won in their second attempt— or in the case of many of her Minnesota colleagues, third or fourth attempt. Apparently, Minnesota candidates are made of tougher stuff. One of Craig's Republican predecessors in Minnesota's Second District was John Kline, who won the seat after three tries. Why do these candidates keep running for the same seat? As Kline put it, "For the same reason you run in the first place: You want to change things and you think you can make a difference." Angie was the same way: She ran to make a difference for families like hers, and though she lost the first race, she wasn't ready to throw in the towel.[3]

For our candidates, there are big advantages in trying for a win the second time around. Every candidate gets better over the course of a campaign, so automatically they start off that second campaign at a higher level than they did the first time. Those candidates have already done hard work. They've built a network of supporters, volunteers, and donors, so now they can focus on growing those networks, rather than starting from scratch. Reconnecting is an easier task than connecting. They have experience running against the incumbent already, and they start with some built-in name identification. They have also had an entire campaign's worth of public speaking, interviews, and debates, getting better each time. It is just really practice.

There are advantages for all of us in trying again after we've failed. There's a risk in it, too, of course. We can handle one loss, but too many of us believe that failing twice would make us failures. Or perhaps we don't want to be seen as trying too hard. I know this is a challenge for women, who are sometimes punished in the public eye for seeming too ambitious. For whatever reason, trying that second time can seem much harder, when in fact, it will be much easier. We all know we get better the more we do things. It's a lesson we teach our children and remind ourselves of when we're trying something new. Simply put, "If at first you don't succeed, try, try again."

LET THE LOSS INSPIRE YOU TO FIND A NEW WAY TO SERVE

When I say you should keep going, that doesn't have to mean that you do exactly the same thing again. Sometimes a loss can push you in an equally rewarding but different direction. Several of our EMILY's List candidates have used a lost election to launch onto a new path.

Tammy Duckworth first ran for a US House seat in Illinois in 2006. She lost in a tough race but didn't stay out of the fight for long. Within a few weeks, the Illinois governor appointed her to serve as the director of the Illinois Department of Veterans' Affairs. In 2009, she was nominated and confirmed as an assistant secretary in the US Department of Veterans Affairs under President Obama, a position she held until 2011, when she resigned to run for the House again.[4]

No matter how carefully you plan your life, things will rarely go as you expect them to. As these women and so many others like them prove, the path to your destination isn't always straight and clear. And sometimes those swerves and stops can change your whole trajectory in the best possible way. Often, when I speak to young people just getting started in campaigns, they ask about the path that got me to where I am. They want to take the same route I did. Well, if you've paid attention so far, you know the truth. I didn't plan for this. I took jobs and joined campaigns that I believed in. I found mentors who taught me valuable lessons and challenging work that allowed me to learn and grow. I worked for people I admired and I fought hard for them. And when one fight was over, I looked immediately to the next.

That doesn't mean I don't think actively about my career development or spend time considering what I'd like to do or learn next. I think about those things all the time, as a matter of fact. But if you try to create an exact map of your career when you're just getting started, how will you react to your first big bump in the road? What happens to your path when you don't land the job you planned to get or you discover that you like another job better?

We make a lot of plans. And then we grow and change and discover new things about ourselves, and the plan falls apart. Our wishes and desires change as we get older. Family factors in along the way, and unexpected personal things just happen. That's life. So plan, sure. Then adjust. Then make a new plan. And adjust again. You need to remember that when your heart is set on something and you're just positive it's going to happen, sometimes you're right. And sometimes you're wrong. As with any good heartbreak, you eat some ice cream (metaphorically or literally) and move on.

Your success—and, I believe, your happiness—will depend on your ability to deal with those bumps.

Sometimes a loss means the end of this chapter and the start of a very different one. The next step in your journey could be in a new field or involve making your voice heard in a different way. We see this all the time—and for some of these women, their second (or third or fourth) career is the one for which they'll be remembered. It's a good reminder that we are not defined by one loss, one win, or any one anything. We can make our own legacy—and then remake it again and again.

Former Missouri Senator Claire McCaskill is exemplary in so many ways. After serving as a member of the Missouri house of representatives and a Jackson County prosecutor, and while serving as the Missouri state auditor, Claire ran for governor in 2004, beating an incumbent in the primary but losing in the general election. All of those years in politics had helped Claire grow the thick skin she needed, and she bounced back from that loss by running for US Senate in 2006. Missouri was a state trending red, but Claire pulled out a victory in 2006 and won reelection in 2012. She was a great senator and is one of the best political minds I know, but sadly she lost her election in 2018. She could have retired from the public eye, but instead she decided to keep sharing her hard-earned political expertise as an analyst on NBC, where you likely saw her throughout the 2020 election cycle.

Or consider Montana's own Nancy Keenan, another woman who found a new way to use her voice and pivot her career. She was a special education teacher who entered politics first as a member of the Montana house of representatives, then as the statewide superintendent of the Montana Office of Public Instruction (a.k.a. the lead education official in the state). Nancy ran for the US House in 2000 (another statewide position in Montana, due to the small size of the state's population) and lost. Nancy could have left politics then with her head held high, having devoted nearly two decades to state government.

Instead, her activism took her to Washington, DC, where she became the head of NARAL Pro-Choice America. Nancy served there for eight years, where she was a passionate leader and a fantastic mentor and partner to me as I started at EMILY's List.

Nancy already had a powerful legacy by the time she left NARAL in 2013, but she still felt she had work to do. She moved back to Montana and served for four years as the executive director of the Montana Democratic Party. Nancy didn't go back to be a figurehead or to take on a more honorary position earned through a long and successful career. She chose instead to be the staffer in charge.[5] So very Nancy. As of this writing, she has retired . . . although she's still advising Democratic women. I wouldn't be surprised to hear that she's picked up a new project or made her voice heard in some other way. Some people never stop giving back, and Nancy is definitely one of those.

The lessons that you learn from your losses can lead you to build something new. Stacey Abrams decided to do something about the voter suppression she'd seen in her failed run for governor in Georgia and created Fair Fight.[6] And because Stacey knows that part of getting fair representation means a fair census, she started Fair Count, a nonprofit designed to strengthen civic participation and ensure a fair and accurate count of everyone in the 2020 census by partnering with hard-to-count communities.[7] I can't wait to see Stacey on the ticket again, but boy am I proud of the work she's doing for voters everywhere in the meantime!

LET'S TALK ABOUT LOSING AND HOW WE RECOVER

We spend a lot of time celebrating victories, sharing good news, and so on. I get it. We live in a world in which we put a nice filter on our life to post online while keeping the bad news—the messes, the accidents, the failures—in the shadows, hoping no one will ever see them.

I think we're doing ourselves a disservice by not talking about the losses and the mistakes. Everyone loses. If you look at campaigns, in each election, there's one winner and at least one loser. With primaries, and third parties, there could be many more than that. The math is clear. In politics, there are far more losers than winners. And in life, it's no different. We all face setbacks. We've all had a bad interview, a job we didn't get, a flight we've missed, a relationship that fell apart, a client we didn't land, and so on. We've already talked about Michael Jordan's and Barack Obama's losing early on, but even Beyoncé lost *Star Search* before she took over the world.[8]

Losing can be many things. It can be disappointing, or even heartbreaking, but it is not something to be ashamed of. It is (say it with me now) just a part of the process, a step in your journey. If we destigmatize losing by being open about it, we can reframe the conversation to talk about what we've gained instead of what we've lost. What have you learned? What new experience have you had? What do you understand better now? It's a much more constructive way of thinking. Pretending we are perfect doesn't make it true, so how about

291

we all agree to put down our filters and our unrealistic expectations and acknowledge what's really there?

I've tried to lead by example. If you've read this far, you know I'm not afraid to talk about my own losses or mistakes— or to put them in a book for anyone to read. It wasn't a tough decision, because it's all part of my story and because I think there are valuable lessons in my setbacks. I'm happy if even one person can learn from my openness. And frankly, my years in politics have taught me that most of us don't judge people for their losses; we judge them for how they react in the face of defeat. And I have always been willing to pick myself back up, dust myself off, and keep moving.

THE TOPLINES

The lesson here is easy: A loss isn't the end; it's just another step in the journey. Period.

When you face an obstacle or a loss, you can grieve or wallow for a little while. Take care of yourself first. And then, once you're ready, prepare to take action. Thank the people who contributed to your campaign or cause. Reflect on your loss for yourself, and ask others to help you think through the big questions: What worked, what didn't, what could you have done better, and in what ways did you improve?

There are a variety of ways to respond to and learn from a loss:

- **Try again:** In campaigns, this means running again in the following cycle. This could mean asking for the pro motion again, trying to organize for a cause a second time, and so on.

- **Try again on a different stage:** This could involve running for a different office or finding a non-electoral way to make the change you want to make. It means just shifting your time frame or scope while working toward the same goals.

- **Find other ways to use your voice:** Remember that there are many ways to make a difference. Starting something new, finding a new path to your goals, and even changing your goals and plans are all ways of moving forward. Service comes in many forms. Be open to something totally new

And finally, let's all agree not to hide from our losses. Setbacks are something we all face, and they're made easier by knowing we're not alone and by learning from each other's losses. Let's talk about it as we move through it.

CHAPTER 9

Campaign Joyfully. Show Gratitude Deliberately. Celebrate Liberally.

SO NOW THAT I've spent an entire book telling you how hard it is to run for office, we finally get to the fun part. You know well enough by now that fun doesn't always equal easy. But if you've trusted me this far, I hope you'll trust me on these last lessons.

Campaign joyfully. Show gratitude deliberately. Celebrate liberally.

Let me acknowledge how daunting those final three tasks might seem. Believe me, there are days when positivity seems out of reach. How can you fight this hard, work with integrity, have a thick skin, respect your team, connect with your voters, and so much more, and still have the energy for joy? I hear you. But I'm here to tell you that joy, gratitude, and celebration are the only things that sustain this work in the long term. Holding on to that truth is the best way to be successful at it.

Let's be clear: This doesn't mean that you have to pretend

it's all easy and fun. There's very little worth doing that isn't hard work, and changing the world is no exception. You can and should acknowledge the effort you're making. To pretend that things come easily undersells the work you're doing and does a disservice to others in the field.

We've all seen those workplaces. The places where the employees are just running out the clock, waiting for the end of the day. Some offices are too quiet, which is deadly for collaboration and is typically a clear indication that the organization is headed toward a loss. In others, you can cut the tension between management and employees with a knife. The emotions associated with these offices are bad ones: stress, frustration, hot tempers, and so on. In business, these environments stifle creativity and decrease profits. In nonprofits and campaigns, where folks are getting paid less than they could get in the private sector, this negative energy is a surefire way to drive away volunteers and supporters, and, yes, ultimately voters.

I suspect most of us have joined a club or an organization because we liked its mission, only to discover oppressive rules, demanding leaders, or unnecessary and frustrating challenges. We've all had a friend who made fun activities feel like work or a boss who sucked the little pleasures out of even the small moments.

We've all seen it happen. You are out on the town getting ready to go to the club (okay, I haven't done this in years, but work with me here). You have put on the best outfit you have, and your hair looks great. You and your girlfriends are ready, but there is the one friend who just thinks she looks fat, is mad at her boyfriend, hates the music, and doesn't want to stay, and inevitably, within a few hours, everyone is ready to go home. A bad attitude is contagious and can ruin an office environment just as fast as it can ruin your night out. It's especially true when the person with the bad attitude is the one in charge.

Put more simply: In your office, your attitude will speak volumes about who you are and what type of leadership you bring to the table. Good or bad, it will influence your team and impact the work they do. Putting forth joyful, positive, and open energy is crucial to promoting a workplace that people will *want* to contribute to.

First and foremost, you want your team to say that people are treated with respect. That is the bare minimum we owe our coworkers and those giving their time for us. But you also want people to say that they liked being there, doing the work, and getting to know you.

This next point is important, and it's something I have come to appreciate after over a decade of being the boss. When you are in charge, everyone who works for you watches you closely. It's not just what you say but how you stand, what your face says, what your body language is conveying. That sets the mood more than anything else, and your team will take their cues from you. Let me give you an example.

When I was the campaign manager for Al Franken for Senate in 2008, we were under immense stress during the recount in November and December. We had believed that, win or lose, after Election Day, our jobs would be done. Instead, because of the recount, we had to immediately double the size of the organization and get folks motivated for a whole different type of fight. Quite frankly, it was exhausting, and more than a little emotionally painful. But it was what had to be done.

Fortunately, I had fabulous folks working with me on that team. Dan Cramer may be one of the most joyful warriors I have ever known, and even though he was getting tired, he helped everyone keep their energy up. And we had reinforcements of fired-up and energized attorneys like Marc Elias and Kevin Hamilton, which helped to infuse new life into the team. Nevertheless, it was a trying time, bringing all these new folks into an existing and exhausted organization. I knew I had to remain focused and calm. It was my job to work the problem and be the centering force throughout the chaos. Until, one day, I lost it.

And I didn't lose it privately. I lost it in the office. I always try to stay calm in the worst of moments, a lesson my dad taught me long ago. But I also have a really terrible toddler inside me that sometimes wants to come out raging. I bet some of you know what I mean. Well, that day, that toddler got its way. I flew off the handle, yelling at the lawyers, slamming doors, and storming out of the office in front of everyone. It was totally unprofessional and embarrassing. It also scared much of the staff, who needed reassurance that things were going to be all right. I screwed up. I knew it as soon as I got into my car. At a time when my team needed leadership the most, I had left them more uncertain than when they'd started their day.

I gave it a night, calmed down, and walked into the office the next day. I gathered everyone and apologized for the way I'd behaved. It didn't excuse what I'd done, but taking ownership and saying I was sorry was a good first step at earning back the trust of my team. We all have bad moments; that's human and it's okay. We're not asking for perfection, remember? But when you are the leader, a single moment of anger can deeply affect the staff who depend on your strength. I won't say I have been perfect since that moment, but I certainly try to keep myself in check better and find other, more productive ways to handle that kind of negative energy.

You have so much more power than you think you do as a manager and a leader. People are looking up to you and expect you to earn their respect daily. That power is even greater when you are running for office, because what your staff sees is often what voters see, too. It's part you, part your message, and part something greater than both of those things. Voters want to be excited and feel connected to something.

And that means bringing some joy into everything you are doing.

FIND YOUR JOY

I love Lucinda Williams. In my down moments, I think of her song "Joy." She sings, "You got no right to take my joy." I cling to those words when I feel a loss, an individual, or just a bad day threatening to bring me down. Losing joy in those situations just makes them that much harder.

The 2020 Democratic presidential primary was historic for many reasons, particularly because it was the first with half a dozen women running for the nomination. After so many years watching qualified women get overlooked by the establishment, it was absolutely thrilling to see those women up on a debate stage, proving centuries of bad assumptions wrong. They were the top-tier candidates, and two of them were endorsed by *The New York Times*. They proved that there is no one lane for women and that there is no one model for an acceptable woman candidate. They shared some things in common: their integrity, their drive to change the world for the better, and more. They also faced some of the same challenges based on their gender, like the unfair electability debate, ridiculously bad questions and commentary about everything from their appearance to how they were going to raise their children or why they didn't have children, unrealistic expectations from the media on how they should campaign or wear their emotions, and so on. But to me, it was their individuality that was most striking and the biggest marker of the progress we've made. These women ran their own races that played to their personal strengths and their unique visions for the country's best path forward.

That was particularly clear in the way they managed their campaigns. I know these women—they are tough, smart, experienced, and also *fun*. They knew that campaigning could be hard, and they had to make sure it wasn't a slog, both for their own sanity and for their supporters. But each found her own way to find excitement and joy on the campaign trail.

To sustain her joy, Elizabeth Warren met her supporters in selfie lines after her events. She knows that there's nothing quite as energizing as meeting the people who believe in you and want to see you succeed. She made the little girls at her events pinky promise to remember that running for president is something girls do. (And thank you for that candidate recruitment, Elizabeth, on behalf of the EMILY's List team of a few decades from now.)

Kamala Harris literally danced her way through the campaign, one time joining in with a drum line as she entered the South Carolina Democratic convention,[1] and another time taking a Cardi B break during speech prep.[2] For Amy Klobuchar, it's her midwestern sense of humor: Amy loves telling jokes and used them to have some fun in debates, on late-night shows, and all across the country.[3] And for Kirsten Gillibrand, it was finding new ways to meet supporters and have fun on the trail. She hung out with drag queens at the oldest gay bar in Des Moines, swapping dresses and taking a turn bartending.[4] She and her team even went sledding together in New Hampshire.[5] If that's not joyful, nothing is.

These women have a tough job. Beyond the fact that presidential campaigns are like no other political activity in the country, research shows that women who run for office have the added challenge of balancing their perceived likability with their qualifications.[6] So these four women had to thread the needle between being taken seriously and not being seen as severe or joyless. And not only did they do it—they made me wish I was out on the campaign trail with them. I love sledding!

It's amazing how simple it is. Just a few fun, lighthearted activities can change the entire way you and your supporters feel. And you'll be amazed how quickly your mood, and your team's morale, will be boosted. Sometimes a few moments of pure silliness are all you need.

REMIND YOUR TEAM OF THE GOOD THINGS

The people who work for you, with you, and around you need to be able to find their joy as well. Now that you know how to find yours, you can help them find theirs. We know that changing the world can be disheartening work. Progress can feel slow, like for every step forward, you take ten steps back. Whether you face funding or staffing challenges, if you're having trouble breaking through on an important issue or there are tough circumstances outside your control, making real change is not easy and you will face stumbling blocks along the way. (See chapters 1 through 8.)

Your team is feeling that strain just like you. So make sure they know their value and find joy in what they do. There are many ways to do that. I know campaign leaders who make "One Up, One Down" a part of their team meetings. That's an

exercise in which people have to say one positive and one negative thing they're facing. Most meetings are about negative
things, the stuff we need to fix, the ways our jobs have been
hard. This practice makes sure that you are actually talking
about the good things, sharing them and reminding one another of all your amazing accomplishments.

Happiness at work doesn't just make you feel good; it has
measurable benefits for the whole team. According to neuro-
science and academic research, people work harder and smarter
when they are happy and engaged at work.[7] Science tells us
what we already know: that there are clear links between our
feelings and our actions, so when we are frustrated or chroni-
cally stressed, our work suffers, as we don't think as creatively
or process information as well.[8]

One of my favorite ways to build staff morale at EMILY's
List is to invite our candidates in to rally the troops. Our office
hosts a continuous stream of high-powered and motivational
women. Our candidates and elected officials come in frequently for meetings. So I figure, why not take advantage of
that incredible human resource? If ever they have a little extra
time, we gather our staff together in the middle of the office
and ask that visiting member of Congress, mayor, or future
senator to share a few words with our team. We always hear
great and moving stories, but perhaps most important, we
hear how the work of EMILY's List has an impact on campaigns. It's a powerful motivator and a great reminder of why
we do what we do. For me personally, those little speeches lift
my mood no matter what kind of day I'm having, and I can

see on the faces of our staff members it does the same for them, too. Think about the resources your own organization has at its fingertips, and make sure your team is reminded often of the impact of their work.

Make moments your team can rally around. It might be celebrating when you hit a milestone with volunteers, donors, or doors knocked, even if that celebration is simply ringing a bell or having an office cheer or just noting it in a meeting. It might be a great debate, a new poll, or a big endorsement. Some offices will do a secret gift exchange during the holidays. Some offices dress up for Halloween. My cowriter, Christina, worked on a campaign going through a frustrating few weeks when one of her coworkers declared it "Sheet Cake Tuesday" and brought in a grocery store sheet cake for an impromptu celebration. It became a tradition during tough weeks throughout the campaign. Ben Dotson, our vice president of digital, recognizes Pi Day every year with his team. Yes, math nerds, March 14 is of course celebrated by eating pie! There are a million thoughtful ways, and goofy ways, to make your team feel excited and appreciated. And when things are low, a little love (or a lot of cake) can go a long way.

At EMILY's List, we have ABIOs. They started as FABIOs—Friday Afternoon Beers in the Office—a tradition I borrowed from former Montana Senator Max Baucus's office. Since we don't always do them on Fridays, we had to adjust the name to be a bit more comprehensive. And it's definitely a tradition that has evolved over time. Our first few ABIOs at EMILY's List had just pretzels and cheap beer. Now we have a monthly rotating schedule. Each department takes a turn to plan it, picking a theme for the decorations, food, and drink. Our teams go all out; whatever day of the week the ABIO happens, it's always fun and creative, celebrating everything from Shark Week to *Star Wars*.

I hope you're seeing that you can find your own path here. Maybe it's a team activity (I've heard of everything from bowling night to cooking classes to softball teams to book clubs). But a little fun goes a long way.

And don't forget, this all starts with you. There is a lot of pressure on you to lead by example and try to carry yourself the best you can.

We all have our ups and downs. Relationships that fail. Sick kids. Water in the basement. Broken-down cars. Life happens every day. So, what do I do when things get too heavy? Sometimes, when it's really bad, I may have a few tears at night. Then I try to get a good night's sleep. I drive into work, listening to really loud, happy music—anything will do, from country to hip-hop and everything in between. And then I sit in the parking garage and give myself a pep talk.

I know that when I walk into that office, it must be with a true smile of joy. I need to mean it when I wish people a good morning. I need to be able to tease and joke around like I would on my best day. At first it feels totally fake. But I start to feel better almost right away. And I'm reminded immediately of how much my candidates, my colleagues, my staff, and my interns deserve it. They work so hard every day. I fill with pride when I see them, and I want to do right by each one of those committed, passionate team members. I remember not to make it about me. Instead I make it about them and our shared mission of changing the world.

Changing the world with hope is so much longer lasting than changing the world with fear. And hope is fed by joy. So find your joy. It's as simple as that.

EXPRESS GRATITUDE DELIBERATELY

You need to do more than just help your team find their joy. You need to also make sure that you are telling them thank you, honestly, regularly, and deliberately. It's the simplest thing, and yet it goes a long way.

You've built your team, whether that's your support system or your campaign team or just the people in your personal life you know you can count on. That team is working hard for you, sometimes in public ways, sometimes in ways that you may not even notice. On campaigns, it's the people stuffing envelopes in the back room or driving long distances for rallies, the ones who stay in the office late and show up early without anyone's asking or noticing. Your role as a leader is to show gratitude for that work and make sure that no task is thankless. It's that foundation of small tasks that supports a strong, winning organization.

I may sound serious, and I am, but let's be clear: This is not a hard part of your job. It doesn't have to take a lot of time. Sometimes this can be as simple as an email to the whole team, stopping by someone's desk before you leave for the day, showing up with many boxes of donuts and coffee the morning after a long night, or sending a handwritten note that says, "Thanks for your hard work." It's acknowledging, to the person and to the group, that their work is important, their sacrifices are noticed, and they are valued.

Expressing gratitude isn't hard, but it easily slips away when you are stressed or just too busy to think about it. We assume people who work for us and with us know we value them, so we don't say it out loud. But like everything we do, deliberately thinking about interactions with people—staff, friends, family, voters—matters a lot. You are the leader, so when things go right you get the credit, and when they go wrong you get the blame, publicly. That can create a mindset that you are the person carrying all the weight. Remember to share the credit when things are going well, and accept with humility your portion of the responsibility when you or your team makes a mistake.

A few tips from me, the president of the best team in politics (something I truly believe and tell my team regularly).

First, thanking the whole group matters. Whether it's at a staff meeting, on a team call, or at an event with supporters, taking a minute to acknowledge the team that supports you and the work of your organization makes a difference. It sets the tone that you are, in fact, a team, and that the success or opportunity you have created is the result of the group effort.

When thanking the group, take the opportunity to high-light a few individual members for contributions that went beyond the norm. This is especially effective for younger staff or newer members of the team. It shows you notice them and their hard work. My goal (and hopefully yours) is for so many people to be doing so many good things that it is hard to single out just a few.

Another way to accomplish this is by writing a quick note to a person or small group of people. You can also get them some chocolates or a bottle of wine or something little as a token of gratitude. I try to keep some nice gifts like that handy in my office so that when I think of it, I can just do it.

There is also the "pull them into your office for a quick talk" approach. It's nice to get some one-on-one time with people and to remind them that these kinds of talks are not just used when something is wrong. I sit the person down, assure them they're not in trouble, and then offer a big personal thank-you to them for making something happen. I always feel sneaky and fun when I take this approach and love to have a chance to really connect over something positive.

Work, especially political and campaign work, can be tedious and trying. Don't underestimate the power of a little pat on the back to remind your supporters that their work is seen. I would be nowhere without the team around me. They work behind the scenes to make me look good. I know that my life doesn't work without Joanna Knight, my speechwriter, or Francie Harris, who somehow manages my schedule, or Ray Keating, who has kept the tech equipment working for me and the whole building for fifteen years. And I know that our office doesn't work without Callie Fines, who has kept us legal and compliant for the last twenty years, or Denelle Robinson, who gets every new person through our hiring and onboarding process, or Angie Cohen ("Miss Angie," as she's known in the building), who greets every visitor, candidate, and staffer with a smile while she keeps our DC office running. I could do this all day—every staffer at EMILY's List plays a vital role in making our work happen. Empower your team to do their work, help them find their joy, and keep them motivated with gratitude.

That's how you win—and have something to celebrate.

CELEBRATE LIBERALLY

For years, women have been taught that they can't show too much ambition, that it's problematic to be more successful than our male partners, friends, or coworkers. Celebrating too much was considered unseemly, unladylike. I remember when the amazing Brandi Chastain scored on the penalty kick that made the US Women's National Team winners of the 1999 World Cup over China. Brandi whipped off her shirt and slid across the field, cheering in her sports bra, an image that became both iconic and controversial. Some believed it was too much, too over-the-top, unsportsmanlike.[9] At the time, a woman celebrating so liberally made some viewers uncomfortable.

To some extent, that bias still exists. Twenty years later, the 2019 World Cup–winning US women's soccer team was criticized for, if you can believe it, scoring too much.[10] But this time around, there were far more of us who called out that kind of negative, sexist thinking. And if you followed the team, you knew that they paid no mind to their critics. They knew they had done a phenomenal job and they knew that they deserved to celebrate and be celebrated for their athletic feat. And they were exactly right.

Everyone, and women in particular, can find a million reasons not to celebrate wins. We're worried about what others will say or how it will look. We are too busy. We have already moved on to the next task on the list or how we'll deal with what this victory means. We move right into the execution phase (or the part where we set up an office to begin governing or start a new job) and skip the victory celebration. That's true of accomplishments big and small. "I got a job offer, but I'm worried about the move, or the commute, or that I'll be making more money than my husband," or "I got two job offers and I'm so stressed out trying to make the right decision between the two." Why not "Holy shit, I have two job offers. How cool is that?!"

To be fair, I am terrible at this part myself. As an extremely goal-oriented person, my instinct is to immediately move on to the next task. But, as with all things, I've gotten better with practice. I have found that celebrating liberally is really fun and fulfilling. So I'm here to ask you to take a beat or two to celebrate your victories. You've earned it.

From winning the election to getting the job to managing a challenge that's been bugging you, there are all kinds of victories, and they all deserve their due. At the very least, you need to take a moment to be proud of yourself and what you've done.

I'm not going to tell you how to celebrate. Find the best way to pause and think about what you've done and how you've done it. Pat yourself on the back—privately, with friends, or with all your supporters over champagne. The victory party is one of the great moments in campaigns—when you allow yourself to remember all that you've accomplished, acknowledge that it was hard but so very worth it, and revel in the win together.

We live in a world that has erased women's work for years. It has happened throughout history and it continues today. Corey Cogdell-Unrein is a three-time Olympian who has won two bronze medals in trapshooting. But when she won her second medal, the *Chicago Tribune* celebrated in a tweet that noted, "Wife of a Bears' lineman wins a bronze medal today in Rio Olympics." Apparently, her name was less important than her husband's job.[11] In 2017, married couple Emily V. Gordon and Kumail Nanjiani wrote and produced a hit film called *The Big Sick,* about their relationship growing while she was facing a potentially deadly illness. The film was a hit and they were both nominated for Oscars for writing it, but too many headlines described the couple as "Kumail Nanjiani and wife."[12] The world isn't going to celebrate for you.

When women own and celebrate their accomplishments, they remind the world how much women can do. They help all women get the credit and attention they deserve. And don't we all owe that to ourselves and to each other?

AND THEN, SHOW THEM WHAT YOU CAN DO:
GET TO WORK—WITH JOY

You've worked hard (with joy!), you've celebrated your win, and now what? Now, my friends, the celebration continues in your work. That's right, a part of celebrating liberally is using your victory to get things done. Take your momentum into everything you do, moving the ball forward and making your mark. This is where you get to make changes in the world.

Redirect the same determination that got you into office (I was there! I know how hard you worked!), and put it into action for your constituents. Let your success help improve the lives of the people you represent.

In 2019, after EMILY's List women won enough seats to flip the US House and make Nancy Pelosi Speaker once again, the members in the House of Representatives got right to work. They passed H.R. 1, a far-reaching pro-democracy reform and anticorruption package, as well as bills to lower prescription drug costs, protect people with preexisting conditions, save net neutrality, and expand background checks for guns. That all feels pretty good. Each passage of bills like these is a reason to celebrate.

It wasn't a total victory, however. The Senate majority

leader, Republican Mitch McConnell of Kentucky, blocked Senate passage of those bills. And yet still, I could not be prouder of those amazing women for fighting to address all of the issues they had campaigned on. They each showed what can be done with the right leader in both chambers. Those folks laid out a vision through those bills that the American people could see—a vision that I believe will be a reality in the years to come.

And those aren't the only women to get things done.

On her very first day in office in 2019, Maine Governor Janet Mills signed an executive order that allowed the state to move forward on the Medicaid expansion that voters had passed a year before but the Republican former governor had blocked. That one action gave seventy thousand people in Maine access to health care.[13] New Mexico Governor Michelle Lujan Grisham used her first year in office to fill the many long-standing vacancies in the state government in order to better serve New Mexicans. She also launched a pilot program meant to boost mental health services in the state.[14] And when women helped flip both houses of the Virginia legislature, one of their first actions was to pass the Equal Rights Amendment, making Virginia the thirty-eighth state to ratify it.[15]

Your work will vary, and your actions may not be on a national scale, but if you're making progress, your work matters. Don't downplay your accomplishments. Acknowledge them, and then build on them. That's the best way to ensure you'll have lots more victories to celebrate along the way.

So celebrate, liberally and with joy, getting things done and making people's lives better around you. No matter the scale, that's changing the world for good.

THE TOPLINES

This chapter has the simplest instructions, but they might still be the most important ones in this book. Though we rarely have to convince women that they'll have to work hard, telling them that they must actually enjoy that work always takes a bit more effort. My hope is that you find ways to do the following:

Campaign Joyfully

- Find joy in what you do. That simple attitude shift will make you and your team happier and more productive.
- Remember that that joy attracts more supporters and help and makes those people feel more motivated and ready to be there.
- Staff, volunteers, employees, and voters are looking to you for nonverbal clues about how things are going. Some days that will be easier than others, but you owe it to them and to yourself to put a joyful game face on.
- A little fun goes a long way.

Show Gratitude Deliberately

■ Your team works hard. Thank them often and sincerely. It's that simple.

Celebrate Liberally

■ Your wins and accomplishments are important. Make sure you take some time to enjoy them.
■ Be proud of what you've done. Society has spent long enough ignoring the accomplishments of women. Let's all help each other out by demanding to be seen.
■ Now that you've won and acknowledged the win, go earn the next one by getting back to work. Let's see how far you can carry the joy and momentum. That next victory is right around the corner.

Conclusion

WHEN I DECIDED to write this book, EMILY's List was coming off the huge history making wins of 2018. Democrats had flipped the House, and we'd seen tens of thousands of American women step up to run for office and win. My cowriter, Christina, and I have worked in Democratic politics for years and have learned so many lessons in that time about the value of women and the differences they make as candidates, staffers, and volunteers. I knew I had something to share that could help all women take on the world and change it in big and small ways.

In this book, Christina and I have shared a lot of stories about women overcoming challenges and growing into great leaders. As we were writing, I hoped that hearing how other women had conquered their own challenges would inspire you the way it's always inspired me and that those stories would help you, our readers, understand that changing the world is completely within your grasp.

What I didn't realize was that I'd face some big challenges of my own in the middle of writing this book. In addition to having a stroke, there were constant disruptions in politics, from shifting leaders in the Democratic primary to Trump's impeachment.

And then we faced a global pandemic resulting in total economic upheaval, which meant figuring out how to keep EMILY's List running while making sure my staff and our candidates stayed safe and healthy. We started by shutting down our office for four weeks, and then eventually for months. As our team adjusted to working from home and Zoom calls, we worked with our candidates, who were doing the same. Both our staff and our candidates had to learn how to balance child care and homeschooling their children while also working and campaigning. Just like our candidates, we had to learn how to raise money when we could no longer do events (I'll confess, it was a sad day when we had to cancel our annual gala, which would have celebrated thirty-five years of EMILY's List).

While we were fortunate to be able to protect every job at EMILY's List, we all had family, friends, and people in our communities who lost their jobs or their businesses. We had staff who battled COVID-19 and staff who lost family and friends to the virus. We dealt with anxiety, about our own health, our economy, even how we would keep our families safe and sane.

We also watched as the nation rose up in protest of police

killings of Black Americans and the systemic racism that has been a part of this country for far too long. In our families and at work, many of us had tough conversations and worked through how we could deal with our own privilege and be better antiracist allies. In what President Obama called a "great awakening," we had hope for a transformational moment in our nation. And through it all, at EMILY's List, we kept being productive and focused on the November elections, while we watched the complete failure of leadership from the White House on these issues and many others, as more and more Americans got sick, died, or lost their jobs.

That's one of the things I love about EMILY's List: No matter what happens, our mission is clear and our work follows that. I am always motivated by that simple goal, but I was even more driven after watching our amazing women leaders, in particular the governors and mayors around the country who led their states and cities when the Trump administration failed. From San Francisco Mayor London Breed, whose quick, decisive action while her city was an early hotspot helped manage the outbreak, to Michigan Governor Gretchen Whitmer, who fought for her state while under repeated attack from the White House, to Washington Congresswoman Kim Schrier, a pediatrician who hosted a Facebook Live town hall with kids to help them understand COVID-19, these women inspired me every day.

We adjusted our work to help our candidates adapt to the pandemic. We created new trainings on raising money and doing events online, updated our training center with new materials, found new ways to help our candidates, and, yes, did countless Zoom calls to get it all done.

If you've read this far, you've figured out that not every lesson in this book is applicable in every single situation you'll face. But I hope you'll find, as we did during the pandemic, that there are universal truths and valuable tools in here as you tackle your goals.

So what did I learn?

I learned that you need to have motivation and a support system to get you through the tough times. That being able to deal with tough times and come back from a loss is vital. And that after you've fought through those challenges, you need to take a minute and celebrate. I also learned that even when you think you know how things are going to go, the world can turn upside down.

I have dedicated the last twenty-five years to Democratic politics because I believe in people and I believe in the power of American democracy. We've got differences, sure, but I believe we can keep striving to make that perfect union. We're not there yet, but we keep moving toward that dream. It will not be easy. We have shared a lot of tactics to help build campaigns and movements. We have shared ideas and stories of how to build winning plans. But at the end of the day, all of this is about people—and how we can work together to make people's lives better. What calling could be higher?

Over those years, I have worked for good men and good women. But let me make this crystal clear: We need more women in office. We need more women leaders in every aspect of our society. There is no reason that 50 percent or far more of every leadership role in our nation shouldn't be filled by women. True change will happen in the world when women and men stand together as equals in equal numbers making decisions for our future. Or, maybe better yet, when women outnumber men. When asked when there will be enough women on the Supreme Court, Justice Ruth Bader Ginsburg said, "When there are nine."

So now, I want to ask you something I've been hinting at throughout this book: Will you run for office? You know you want to make change, you know you care about what happens in the world, and you now have the tools to make an impact. So will you consider doing the bravest thing I can imagine—putting your name on the ballot and breaking the patriarchy from within? At the very least, I beg each of you reading this to consider public service—whether you hold elected office or not, if we want the world to be a better place, we all have to do our part, no matter what our careers are, where we are with family, whether we're in school or retired. We all have a role. Yours could be a leading one.

Women, we have a ton of power. How are you going to use it?

Acknowledgments

Acknowledgments from Stephanie Schriock:

Every step of my life's journey is full of individuals who have made me who I am today. Though there are too many to mention here, I am grateful for all of the people who have been a part of each job and experience I've had along the way. Each one of them led to the stories you will read here, and many other stories that may never find their way to the pages of any book.

None of what I have done could have happened without the endless support of my family. I have many blessings to count but none are bigger than family. My dad, Jim, has been my hero since I can remember. He and my mom, Janet, raised a stubborn, smart woman, which surely was not always easy when I was a child. My brothers, Charlie and Jonathan, had to (and still have to) put up with a bossy older sister who probably mothers them more than I should, even before we lost Mom. And though my mom slipped away too early from breast cancer, I think she would have really enjoyed watching my journey at EMILY's List and the rising power of women all across the country.

Just in case my parents weren't on top of it, I was graced with two grandmothers, Grace Schriock and Nancy Fairbanks, both stubborn midwestern women in their own way. I also had the backup of unconditional love from my mom's sisters—Sue, Jean, and Laura—all very independent women in their own right. Without my Mankato, Minnesota, family, Stan and Linda Schriock, I'm not sure I would have ever eaten in college or had any clean clothes. They put up with all my politics and student activities, often at their house. I have always been very lucky with all my family supporting my activism even when it wasn't their political persuasion.

No book and no life are complete without the family you make. I talk in the book about the stroke I had in the fall of 2019 and the team around me, a team that is family. No one is more important to me than my dear friend and sister of twenty-five years, Christa Jones, who has laughed, cried, and often just tolerated all my life choices without judgment. She has been and always will be there for me, and I for her, and that is just the way it is. So has the whole Jones family, who have taken me in as one of their own, thank goodness. Over all those years, I have also had Tom Russell, who is still one of my dearest friends. We have both made a lot of good and bad decisions along the way and yet still try to do good work. He got smarter than me at some point and moved to Wisconsin with his beautiful family, and I miss him. Amy Dacey stood by me at EMILY's List as my first executive director and while I battled recovering from the stroke, perhaps not surprising since our whole friendship started with her taking care of me during another health scare back in 2002. Even when working on opposing campaigns, we have maintained our loyalty to each other. Also with me for years even while we are always miles away are Dayna Swanson and now her partner, Denise Juneau, who have been beautifully and brutally honest with me, and always my moral compasses.

I have Jon Haber, Bonnie Levin, and their badass daughters, Erin and Alix, who have all brought me into their family and even let me stay at their house a few times. New friends like Laura and Jon Lewis and their three kids remind me all the time why I do the work I do—for them. You can't do these types of projects or this kind of work without a lot of people keeping you grounded. One can easily lose one's head.

For over seven of the ten years I have been at EMILY's List, Joe Fox had been by my side. I am grateful to have had someone for much of that time and still have a friend. His late parents, John and Gretchen Fox, became family and I still miss them. They were good progressives and loved the work EMILY's List was doing to change the world. They almost saw the 2018 election of a historic number of women. They were surely cheering us on.

My many campaigns and jobs prior to EMILY's List had so many staff I can't even attempt to list them, though I am incredibly grateful for every single one of them. I really have been lucky to work with and for truly passionate people, including the brave ones who place their names on the ballot. So, for the candidates who were willing to hire me and give me a shot along the way—the late Mary Rieder, former Congressman Bill Luther, former Governor Howard Dean, Senator Jon Tester, and former Senator Al Franken—thank you for trusting me. I know I didn't get it all right, but we all had a hell of a ride.

Speaking of taking a chance on a naïve fundraiser, a big thank-you to Shari Yost Gold, who hired and promoted me at the Democratic Senatorial Campaign Committee years ago. She was the first to really start mentoring me on the strange wonders of politics and political fundraising, and she single-handedly made me the fundraiser I am today. Shari also built a team of mostly women whom I still consider friends after twenty years: Jennifer Yocham-Poersch, Nicole Runge D'Ercole, Diana Rogalle, Colleen Brown, Allison Griner, Amalia Stott, Andrea Dew Steele (the founder of Emerge America), Chad Fitzgerald (we had to have one good guy), and Angelique Cannon, who is back with me today at EMILY's List after serving on Senator Kamala Harris's presidential campaign. There were also the guys who kept pushing me to take the next risk: Jim Jordan, Andy Grossman, Joe Hansen, and Cornell Belcher. Those four years were pivotal to all I did after.

The Dean for America campaign was a whole other adventure that needs its own book. I want to thank Howard for letting me build the team I needed, Joe Trippi, who allowed for creativity every step of the way, and Rick Ridder, who hired me in Burlington. My team needed two great leaders, Linnea Dyer Hegarty and Larry Biddle, whom I hired to run the whole show if I had to leave to take care of my then very sick mom. Mom made it through that campaign, though we, the campaign staff, barely did. We did make fundraising history, however, with the help of many talented staff like Nicco Mele, who has remained a trusted adviser to this day.

The Montana crowd is a whole other world, and after growing up there, it is great to have a whole Montana family that I can turn to for anything. In fact, my ten years at EMILY's List may be what I needed to balance my years of Montana men, starting with my boss, Senator Jon Tester, and, of course, Senator Max Baucus and Governors Brian Schweitzer and Steve Bullock. I am still trying to get some women elected in my home state in 2020.

I remain devoted to my Montana political family, starting with Jim Messina, a mentor and a friend who will always take my call to talk out a complicated situation. As will Matt McKenna, who finally said yes to me as I begged him to be Tester's first communications director in 2006. We wouldn't have won in 2006 without him and he is just one of the best. For all the great men I worked with in Montana—Bill Lombardi, Barrett Kaiser, David Hunter, Tom Kimmell, Rob Hill, Preston Elliott, Steve Doherty, Tom Rodgers, Jamie Wise, and so many more—there were the Power Women: Dayna Swanson, Nancy Keenan, Shannon Finley, Jan Lombardi, Tracy Stone-Manning, Diane Hamwi, Kendra-Sue Derby, Stacey Parenteau, Bridget Walsh, Susan Cierlitsky, Trecia McEvoy, the late

Holly Luck, Mel Haines, and so many others. One in particular saved me numerous times—Rachel Barinbaum. Nothing was better than our lonely women moments on the campaign when we blasted Wilson Phillips's "Hold On" to get through another day. Wonder Women—all in the land not always friendly to women.

Two years later, I was off to Minnesota to pull together what was thought to be a ragtag team of campaign staff for Al Franken, only to find some of the brightest rising stars in the party. Andy Barr, David Benson, Jon-David Schlough, Jess McIntosh, and James Haggar with the financial support of Finance Director Dinah Dale were holding together a campaign that hit some challenges. Thanks to their talent and the addition of a few more hands like Eric Schultz, the commitment of Bill Lofy, and, in particular, long-serving Executive Director J.B. Poersch of the Democratic Senatorial Campaign Committee, we had the team we needed. Well, a team and a passionate candidate and his wife, Al and Franni Franken, whose commitment to serving the state resulted in a hard-fought win. I love that team still. When on election night we had to double the size of the staff for the recount and the trial to follow, under the leadership of Dan Cramer, one of my dearest friends today, we did just that. Then Marc Elias brought in his power team of Perkins Coie lawyers, including Kevin Hamilton and some great Minnesota lawyers, like now Justice David Lillehaug, and my true education on how to expand an organization fast and learn election law like I never even imagined began. Thank goodness we had the best.

In my ten years at EMILY's List, we have had some amazing staff walk through our halls igniting change and following the lead of the twenty-five years of staff whose shoulders we all stand on to do this work. Without the vision and leadership of Ellen Malcolm for those years, there is no growth in the number of women in the Congress—the proof is in the lack of growth on the Republican side. It took grit to make this work. Fight to tear down the mindset of the Democratic establishment. Bravery to stand up for what she believed. Tens of thousands of donors backing her up, and then me. Ellen is a shero and an American stateswoman as far as I am concerned.

Ellen Malcolm, thank you for giving me this opportunity and letting me run with it. I don't know what else to say. You let your baby grow up and hang out with me. EMILY sure turned out to be a powerful, strategic, badass woman! Thank you to the founding mothers who still hold us accountable, as they should. Thank you to our board of directors that has had my back through thick and thin. Thank you to Donald Sussman for his organizational commitment and his personal friendship, particularly in the last year when I needed help the most. Thank you to our Wonder Woman, Karla Jurvetson, who has single-handedly changed our ability to win more races and elect more women, particularly women of color across this country.

As the president of EMILY's List, I have the honor to work with such committed progressive leaders, and none more important and inspiring than Speaker Nancy Pelosi. Just watching how she works will teach you new leadership skills every day. Leader Chuck Schumer continues to be a supporter of our work and to adding women to the United States Senate. He is a good partner to have. The partners in the choice movement are fighting every day for the rights of women, and for me, having the ability to call my friends Ilyse Hogue and Alexis McGill Johnson to figure out how to save our rights. They are such strong, strategic leaders. I also have great partners to call for counsel who are leading big organizations in their own right, including Guy Cecil, who has been by my side one way or another since 2006 in Montana. I am so impressed with the leaders in the progressive movement today who will guide this nation to a more diverse, inclusive, just country. From the civil rights and #BlackLivesMatter movement to labor and conservation, we are all living in the middle of a historic moment.

To the hundreds of EMILY's List staff who have worked for me in the last decade, thank you for your passion, energy, and commitment to change. You have all been part of making history and still are, no matter what you are doing. Three extraordinary executive directors made this all possible, Amy Dacey, Jess O'Connell, and now Emily Cain.

A huge thank-you to the Senior Leadership Team of EMILY's List over the last couple of years, who not only had to give Christina Reynolds and me time to write this book, but also give me time to heal. You didn't miss a beat. Not one. Thank you to those who have served on the team during that time: Madhur Bansal, Stefanie Brown James, Angelique Cannon, Sarah Curmi, Karen Defilippi, Ben Dotson, Louisa Farley, Callie Fines, Lucinda Guinn, Jenna Kruse, Geri Prado, Christina

Reynolds, Denelle Robinson, Mike Sager, Johanna Silva Waki, Muthoni Wambu Kraal, and Melissa Williams.

Then, there is only one reason this book became a reality, and that is my cowriter, Christina Reynolds. She rocked it. I never could have done this without her, which feels like most days at EMILY's List anyway. Christina is such a talented writer and it's her energy you feel throughout these pages. With an inspiring foreword written by Senator Kamala Harris, backup from Emily Cain, and additional help from Stefanie Brown James, I hope we have put something together to help every woman find her path to leadership in whatever field she is in. Let's face it, it is our time. We just have to grab it.

In grabbing it, many of you have to run for office. We need your leadership. So, a huge thank-you to all the women who have already run for office and to those who will. It takes courage to place your name on the ballot, but in doing so, you will change your life and your community. Just run to win. Always.

Acknowledgments from Christina Reynolds:

All of my life, I've wanted to be a writer. I've continued that practice through UNC's journalism school (Go Heels!) and in my career, but this book was really the culmination of a life-long dream. Thanks to Stephanie Schriock and Emily Cain for making this happen, and for trusting me to work on this and continue working toward our mission. I couldn't ask for a better partner than Stephanie or a better support system in this process than Emily.

This book wouldn't have been possible without the guidance of our editor, Cassidy Sachs, who has been helpful, thoughtful, and beyond patient with two first-time authors with full-time jobs. Thank you for your guidance and your belief in electing and inspiring women. Matt Latimer and Keith Urbahn are great agents and helpful guides in thinking through what the book could be and where it should go. To you three and the whole Dutton team, thank you for your faith in us. EMILY's List alumnae Kristen Bartoloni and Alex Platkin of Silver Street research firm did a diligent and thorough job fact-checking this book, and any errors are mine alone. Thanks also to the authors who gave me guidance throughout this process, great women and great writers, like Jo Piazza, Lauren Collins Peterson, Amanda Litman, and Kate Stayman-London.

My friends—from my Hillary, Obama, and Edwards campaign families to Team Elizabeth to my childhood friends, former roommates, officemates, and more—keep me sane and make my life interesting. Glad to know all of you and have you in my life. I'm especially grateful for my Jens (Bluestein, O'Malley Dillon, and Palmieri), who are the people you want by your side during the tough times and the good ones. I am lucky to have you, and your fantastic husbands and children, in my corner.

I am also so fortunate to have an amazing and supportive extended family. My parents, Mac and Cathy Reynolds, taught me that women can do anything, a lesson my mom has continued to prove through the challenges life has thrown at her lately. My sister and brother-in-law, Sara and David Kirk, are raising their kids, Maggie and Ian, with those same values, and I couldn't love all of them more. Thank you for the unconditional support you've shown me all my life.

Ultimately, this book is about women changing the world, which is also our goal at EMILY's List. I feel grateful to get to do this work each day for two reasons: the amazing women we work for and the phenomenal people I work with. That's true of the whole organization, and certainly of the senior team since I've been there—Madhur Bansal, Stefanie Brown James, Angelique Cannon, Sarah Curmi, Karen Defilippi, Ben Dotson, Callie Fines, Louisa Farley, Lucinda Guinn, Jenna Kruse, Geri Prado, Denelle Robinson, Mike Sager, Johanna Silva Waki, Muthoni Wambu Kraal, and Melissa Williams—people who work every day to make the world a bit better.

The EMILY's List communications team (past and present) already knows I can be a bit sappy, so it won't surprise them when I say that talking to them is my favorite part of every day. I am lucky, as are our candidates, that they have devoted their talents and time to this effort. Thanks for everything, Adonna Biel, Vanessa Cardenas, Miriam Cash, Jenn Medeiros Charin, Lauren Chou, Maeve Coyle, Lindsay Crete, Alex De Luca, Nanci Flores, Kristen Hernandez, Joanna Knight, Bryan Lesswing, Mairead Lynn, Julie McClain Downey, Ianthe Metzger, Ben Ray, Suzy Vazquez, John Weber, and Tonya Williams. You really are the best.

And to the women who have raised their hands to run for office: Thank you for the ways you inspire us and the ways you are changing the world.

Notes

INTRODUCTION

1. "Current Numbers," Center for American Women and Politics, Eagleton Institute of Politics, Rutgers University, accessed March 16, 2020, www .cawp.rutgers.edu/current-numbers.
2. "Women in Congress, 1917–2020: Service Dates and Committee Assignments by Member, and Lists by State and Congress," Congressional Research Service, June 20, 2020, crsreports.congress .gov/product/pdf/RL/RL30261.
3. "Grey's Anatomy," IMDb, accessed March 27, 2005, www.imdb.com /title/tt0413573/.
4. Deb DeHaas et al., *Missing Pieces Report: The 2018 Board Diversity Census of Women and Minorities on Fortune 500 Boards,* February 5, 2019, accessed March 25, 2020, corpgov.law.harvard.edu/2019/02/05 /missing-pieces-report-the-2018-board-diversity-census-of-women-and minorities-on-fortune-500-boards/
5. "The Data on Women Leaders," Pew Research Center, September 13, 2018, www.pewsocialtrends.org/fact-sheet/the-data-on-women -leaders/.
6. National Association for Law Placement, "2019 Report on Diversity in US Law Firms," https://www.nalp.org/uploads/2019_DiversityReport.pdf
7. Judith Warner, Nora Ellmann, and Diana Boesch, "The Women's Leadership Gap," Center for American Progress, November 20, 2018,

www.americanprogress.org/issucs/women/reports/2018/11/20/461273
/womens-leadership-gap-2/.

8. "Women of Color in the United States: Quick Take," *Catalyst,* March 19, 2020, accessed March 26, 2020, www.catalyst.org/research/women -of-color-in-the-united-states/.

9. "Women Who Have Chaired Committees in the US House, 1923–Present," History, Art & Archives: US House of Representatives, accessed March 26, 2020, history.house.gov/Exhibitions-and-Publications /WIC/Historical-Data/Women-Chairs-of-Congressional-Committees/.

CHAPTER I: GETTING STARTED

1. "History of Women in the US Congress," Center for American Women and Politics, Eagleton Institute of Politics, Rutgers University, January 6, 2020, accessed March 26, 2020, www.cawp.rutgers.edu/history -women-us-congress.

2. "Barbara A. Mikulski," National Democratic Institute, November 2, 2017, accessed March 26, 2020, www.ndi.org/people/barbara -mikulski.

3. Matt Vasilogambros, "What Stops Political Campaigns from Forging Signatures? Not Much," *Pew Charitable Trusts*, May 3, 2018, www .pewtrusts.org/en/research-and-analysis/blogs/stateline/2018/05/03 /what-stops-political-campaigns-from-forging-signatures-not -much.

4. Jaimee Swift, "Jordan Davis' Mother, Lucia McBath, Speaks on Gun Reform and Jordan's Legacy," *Huffington Post*, June 12, 2017.

5. John Verhovek and Meg Cunningham, "Lucy McBath Wins Seat in Congress, Was Inspired to Run in the Wake of Parkland and After Losing Son to Gun Violence," ABC News, November 8, 2018, abcnews .go.com/Politics/losing-son-gun-violence-wake-parkland-lucy-mcbath /story?id=58966402.

6. "About Patty," Murray.Senate.gov, accessed March 26, 2020, www .murray.senate.gov/public/index.cfm/mobile/biography.

7. Timothy Egan, "Another Win by a Woman, This One 'Mom,'" *New York Times,* June 17, 1992, 16.

8. Caitlin Moscatello, "When You're Not the 'Pick of the Establishment,'" Cut, August 27, 2019, www.thecut.com/amp/2019/08/8-women-on -what-its-really-like-to-run-for-office.html.

CHAPTER 2: ASK YOURSELF THE RIGHT QUESTIONS.
BE HONEST ABOUT THE ANSWERS.

1. Ken Rudin, "On This Day in 1991: House Members March to Senate in Thomas Protest," NPR, October 8, 2010, www.npr.org/sections /itsallpolitics/2010/10/07/130415738/on-this-day-in-1991-female -house-members-march-to-senate-in-thomas-protest.
2. "The Year of the Woman, 1992," History, Art & Archives: United States House of Representatives, accessed March 26, 2020, history.house.gov /Exhibitions-and-Publications/WIC/Historical-Essays/Assembling -Amplifying-Ascending/Women-Decade/.
3. "MOSELEY BRAUN, Carol," History, Art & Archives: United States House of Representatives, accessed March 26, 2020, history.house.gov /People/Listing/M/MOSELEY-BRAUN,-Carol-(M001025)/.
4. Ron Cassie, "Barbara Mikulski Finds Ford's Testimony 'Very Credible' in Kavanaugh Hearings," *Baltimore,* October 1, 2018, www .baltimoremagazine.com/2018/10/1/barbara-mikulski-finds-ford -testimony-very-credible-kavanaugh-hearings.
5. "'Year of the Woman,'" United States Senate, December 30, 2019, accessed March 26, 2020, www.senate.gov/artandhistory/history /minute/year_of_the_woman.htm.
6. "The Minuteman Missile," National Park Service, U.S. Department of the Interior, www.nps.gov/articles/minuteman-ichm.htm.
7. Tara Sophia Mohr, "Why Women Don't Apply for Jobs Unless They're 100% Qualified," *Harvard Business Review,* August 25, 2014, hbr.org /2014/08/why-women-dont-apply-for-jobs-unless-theyre-100-qualified.
8. "Expansion of Rights and Liberties: The Right of Suffrage," Charters of Freedom, accessed March 26, 2020, web.archive.org/web/20160706144856 /www.archives.gov/exhibits/charters/charters_of_freedom_13.html.
9. "About Me," Jayapal.House.gov, accessed March 26, 2020, jayapal.house .gov/about-me/.
10. Chris Jenkins, "Marshall Admits No Doubts About Marriage," *Washington Post,* November 4, 2006, www.washingtonpost.com /wp-dyn/content/article/2006/11/03/AR2006110301580.html?tid=a_inl _manual.

CHAPTER 3: BREAK THE RULES, BREAK OUT OF THE BOX

1. Ritu Prasad, "Eight Ways the World Is Not Designed for Women," BBC News, June 5, 2019, www.bbc.com/news/world-us-canada-47725946.

2. Katherine Ellen Foley, "25 Years of Women Being Underrepresented in Medical Research, in Charts," Quartz, July 3, 2019, qz.com/1657408 /why-are-women-still-underrepresented-in-clinical-research/.

3. Casey Bond, "7 Weird Examples of How Women Pay More Than Men for the Same Products," *Huffington Post*, July 10, 2019, www.huffpost.com /entry/pink-tax-examples_l_5d24da77e4b0583e482850f0.

4. Lyn Mettler, "Rep. Debra Haaland Wears Traditional Native American Dress to Swearing-in Ceremony," *Today,* January 4, 2019, www.today .com/style/rep-debra-haaland-wears-traditional-native-american-dress -swearing-t146280.

5. Brianna Holt, "The Glass-Shattering Power of Seeing Pregnant Women in the Workplace," Quartz, September 19, 2019, qz.com/1712336/why -audrey-gelmans-magazine-cover-is-important-for-working-women/.

6. Claire Cain Miller, "The Motherhood Penalty vs. the Fatherhood Bonus," *New York Times,* September 7, 2014, 6, www.nytimes.com/2014/09/07 /upshot/a-child-helps-your-career-if-youre-a-man.html.

7. Rachel Lubitz, "This Tatted-Up Texas Democrat Is Using Her Ink to Spread a Strong Message," Refinery29, September 6, 2018, www .refinery29.com/en-us/2018/09/209033/mj-hegar-tattoos-texas -congress.

8. Eleanor Van Buren, "Member Lapel Pins out, Necklaces in, Say Women in Congress," *Roll Call,* September 20, 2019, www.rollcall.com/2019/09 /20/member-lapel-pins-out-necklaces-in-say-women-in-congress/.

9. Jie Chen et al., "Research: When Women Are on Boards, Male CEOs Are Less Overconfident," *Harvard Business Review,* September 12, 2019, hbr .org/2019/09/research-when-women-are-on-boards-male-ceos-are-less -overconfident.

10. Darren Sands, "Stacey Abrams Wants to Be the First Black Woman Governor. But First She Has to Win the Nomination," BuzzFeed News, March 17, 2017, www.buzzfeednews.com/article/darrensands/stacey -abrams-wants-to-be-the-first-black-woman-governor.

11. Taylor Welk, "Stephanie Murphy Went from Vietnam War Refugee to Member of Congress," NBC News, December 26, 2016, www.nbcnews .com/news/asian-america/stephanie-murphy-went-vietnam-war -refugee-member-congress-n700181.

12. "Tammy Duckworth," Biography.com, A&E Networks Television, July 23, 2019, www.biography.com/political-figure/tammy-duckworth.

13. Savannah Behrmann, "'We Persist': Elizabeth Warren Says a Woman Will Eventually Become President," *USA Today,* March 6, 2020, www .usatoday.com/story/news/politics/elections/2020/03/05/elizabeth

-warren-we-persist-woman-becoming-president-maddow-interview
/4970767002/.

14. Donna Owens, "Sen. Kamala Harris, Daughter of Howard University,
Comes Home," NBC News, May 13, 2017, www.nbcnews.com/news
/nbcblk/sen-kamala-harris-daughter-howard-university-comes-home
-n758946.

15. "Transcript: The Third Democratic Debate," *Washington Post*, September
12, 2019, www.washingtonpost.com/politics/2019/09/13/transcript
-third-democratic-debate/.

16. "Harriet Tubman," Biography.com, A&E Networks Television, January
16, 2020, www.biography.com/activist/harriet-tubman.

17. "Her Life: The Woman Behind the New Deal," Frances Perkins Center,
accessed March 26, 2020, francesperkinscenter.org/life-new.

18. "Biography," RosaParks.org, accessed March 26, 2020, www.rosaparks
.org/biography/.

19. Emma Hinchliffe, "Every 2018 Female Congressional Candidate with
Kids Under 2 Lost. This PAC Aims to Help Moms Win," *Fortune*,
January 16, 2016, fortune.com/2019/01/16/vote-mama-liuba-grechen
-shirley/

20. Audrey Goodson Kingo, "The Number of Working Moms in Congress
Will Double in 2019," *Working Mother*, November 7, 2018, www
.workingmother.com/number-working-moms-in-congress-will
-double-in-2019.

21. Rebecca Lake, "The Hidden Penalty of Motherhood," Balance, October 3,
2019, www.thebalance.com/how-the-hidden-penalty-of-motherhood
-affects-women-careers-4164215; Gretchen Livingston and Kim Parker,
"8 Facts About American Dads," Pew Research Center Fact Tank, June
12, 2019, www.pewresearch.org/fact-tank/2019/06/12/fathers-day-facts/.

22. Maegan Vazquez, "FEC Approves NY Candidate's Request to Use
Campaign Funds for Childcare," CNN, May 10, 2018, www.cnn.com
/2018/05/10/politics/federal-election-commission-liuba-grechen-shirley
-childcare/index.html.

23. Sheryl Gay Stolberg, "'It's About Time': A Baby Comes to the Senate
Floor," *New York Times*, April 20, 2018, 14, www.nytimes.com/2018/04
/19/us/politics/baby-duckworth-senate-floor.html.

24. Rachel Bade, "'Congress Wasn't Built for Members Like Me,'" Politico,
November 26, 2018, www.politico.com/story/2018/11/26/congress
-new-members-women-1014696.

25. Jennifer Gerson Uffalussy, "'There Is Now a Nursing Mothers' Room in
the Maine State House—Thanks to Women in Leadership," Yahoo! Life,

January 16, 2018, www.yahoo.com/lifestyle/now-nursing-mothers-room
-maine-state-house-thanks-women-leadership-170045047.html.

26. Oriana Pawlyk, "MJ Hegar Sued the Pentagon and Won. Now She's
Running for Congress," Military.com, August 8, 2018, www.military
.com/daily-news/2018/08/08/mj-hegar-sued-pentagon-and-won-now
-shes-running-congress.html.

27. James Dao, "Servicewomen File Suit over Direct Combat Ban," *New York
Times,* November 28, 2012, 18.

28. Bill Barrow, "Inside Stacey Abrams' Strategy to Mobilize Georgia
Voters," Associated Press, October 12, 2018, www.apnews.com
/71c1ea8b3f0e4b6aabe1dc26f37a6171.

CHAPTER 4: KNOW YOUR STORY, LEARN HOW TO TELL IT

1. Theresa Avila, "18 Quotes About Political Action That Will Fire You Up
to Vote," Girlboss, November 2, 2018, www.girlboss.com/identity
/political-quotes-women.

2. "Transcript: The Third Democratic Debate," *Washington Post,* September
12, 2019, www.washingtonpost.com/politics/2019/09/13/transcript
-third-democratic-debate/.

3. Adam Herbets, "22-Year-Old High School English Teacher in Las Vegas
Runs for State Assembly," KVVU Fox 5, February 20, 2018, www
.fox5vegas.com/news/local/year-old-high-school-english-teacher-in-las
-vegas-runs/article_ef277fbe-738d-55a3-ace2-60b681f86f89.html.

4. "Elect Julie von Haefen for NC House 36," JulieforNC.com, accessed
March 26, 2020, www.juliefornc.com/about.

5. "Congresswoman Lucy McBath Delivers Weekly Democratic Address,"
Speaker.gov, February 22, 2019, accessed March 26, 2020, www.speaker
.gov/newsroom/22219.

6. Kate Abbey-Lambertz, "Lawmaker Bravely Reveals She Was Victim of
Rape in Emotional 'Abortion Insurance' Debate," *Huffington Post,*
December 12, 2013, www.huffpost.com/entry/gretchen-whitmer-rape
_n_4432203.

7. Jennifer Rainey Marquez, "Georgia Senator Jen Jordan on Her HB 481
Speech: 'The Least That Women Should Be Given Is the Ability to
Control Our Bodies,'" *Atlanta,* May 6, 2019, www.atlantamagazine.com
/news-culture-articles/georgia-senator-jen-jordan-on-her-hb-481-speech
-the-least-that-women-should-be-given-is-the-ability-to-control-our
-bodies/.

8. Pramila Jayapal, "Rep. Pramila Jayapal: The Story of My Abortion," *New York Times,* June 13, 2019, www.nytimes.com/2019/06/13/opinion /pramila-jayapal-abortion.html.

9. Carey Goldberg, "A Pregnant Candidate Discovers She's an Issue," *New York Times,* May 15, 1998, 14, www.nytimes.com/1998/05/15/us /a-pregnant-candidate-discovers-she-s-an-issue.html.

10. Lisa Fritscher, "Glossophobia or the Fear of Public Speaking," Verywell Mind, April 25, 2019, www.verywellmind.com/glossophobia-2671860.

11. Leslie Larson, "The Brevity of Abraham Lincoln's Gettysburg Address Continues to Inspire on 150th Anniversary," *Daily News* (New York), November 19, 2013, www.nydailynews.com/news/politics/length -lincoln-gettysburg-address-continues-inspire-150th-anniversary -article-1.1522370.

12. "Hillary Clinton Declares 'Women's Rights Are Human Rights,'" PBS, October 30, 2017, www.pbs.org/weta/washingtonweek/web-video /hillary-clinton-declares-womens-rights-are-human-rights.

CHAPTER 5: BUILD YOUR TEAM

1. Mattie Kahn, "Campaigns Are Like Marathons—It's Better to Run One with a Friend," *Glamour,* September 18, 2018, www.glamour.com/story /female-candidate-friendships-midterm-campaign-trail.

2. Michael Schneider, "40 Years of Research Proves Women Are Better Managers Than Men Because They Tend to Have This Crucial Skill," *Inc.,* April 19, 2017, www.inc.com/michael-schneider/40-years-of-research -proves-women-are-better-managers-than-men-because-they-tend.html.

3. "Why Diversity and Inclusion Matter: Quick Take," Catalyst, August 1, 2018, www.catalyst.org/research/why-diversity-and-inclusion-matter/.

4. Vivian Hunt et al., "Delivering Through Diversity," McKinsey & Company, January 2018, www.mckinsey.com/business-functions /organization/our-insights/delivering-through-diversity.

5. Jenn Medeiros Charin, "Elaine Luria EMILY's List Interview," February 28, 2019.

6. Kristina Peterson and Natalie Andrews, "Influx of Women in Congress Gives Spouses Club a Makeover," *Wall Street Journal,* June 19, 2019, www.wsj.com/articles/influx-of-women-in-congress-gives-spouses -club-a-makeover-11560945601.

7. Joanna Knight, "Lisa Blunt Rochester EMILY's List Interview," May 31, 2016.

8. Mattie Kahn, "How Rep. Lisa Blunt Rochester Turned Her All-Consuming Grief into Political Motivation," *Elle,* February 2, 2017, www.elle.com/culture/career-politics/a42627/lisa-blunt-rochester-interview-delaware/.

9. Diane Herbst, "These Five Women Were Bridesmaids in Each Other's Weddings—Now They're All State Senators," *People,* November 21, 2018, people.com/politics/five-female-friends-state-senate-colorado-won/.

10. Mattie Kahn, "Campaigns Are Like Marathons—It's Better to Run One with a Friend," *Glamour,* September 18, 2018, www.glamour.com/story/female-candidate-friendships-midterm-campaign-trail.

CHAPTER 6: LEARN HOW TO MAKE THE ASK

1. Amanda Arnold, "Senator Amy Klobuchar Once Raised $17,000 from Ex-Boyfriends," Cut, April 16, 2018, www.thecut.com/2018/04/senator-amy-klobuchar-once-raised-usd17-000-from-ex-boyfriends.html.

2. Kate Tornone, "A Running List of States and Localities That Have Outlawed Pay History Questions," HR Dive, December 20, 2018, accessed March 27, 2020, www.hrdive.com/news/salary-history-ban-states-list/516662/.

3. Eric Zorn, "Democrats Can Take a Few Tips from O'Neill," *Chicago Tribune,* July 25, 2004, www.chicagotribune.com/news/ct-xpm-2004-07-25-0407250364-story.html.

4. Simone Biles, "I'd rather regret the risks that didn't work out than the chances I didn't take at all," Twitter, May 11, 2016, twitter.com/simone_biles/status/730255395554365441.

CHAPTER 7: GROW A THICKER SKIN

1. "You've Got Mail: Quotes," IMDb, accessed March 27, 2020, www.imdb.com/title/tt0128853/quotes/?tab=qt&ref_=tt_trv_qu.

2. "Rosen Offers College Transcript in Response to Heller Ad," Associated Press, July 19, 2018, www.rgj.com/story/news/politics/2018/07/19/rosen-offers-college-transcript-response-heller-ad/804086002/.

3. Peter Galuszka, "Spy vs. Pilot: Democratic Candidates for the 7th District Square Off to Decide Who Will Challenge Congressman Dave Brat," *Style Weekly,* June 5, 2018, www.styleweekly.com/richmond/spy-vs-pilot-democratic-candidates-for-the-7th-district-square-off-to-decide-who-will-challenge-congressman-dave-brat/Content?oid=9412143.

4. Emma Newburger, "Female Candidates Are Calling Out Sexism More Aggressively on the Campaign Trail," CNBC, September 27, 2018, www .cnbc.com/2018/09/27/female-candidates-are-more-aggressive-about -tackling-gender-based-attacks-in-2018-election.html.

5. *Kansas City Star* editorial board, "Rep. Kevin Yoder Says Democratic Rival Sharice Davids Doesn't Have Kansas Values. Huh?" *Kansas City Star,* August 8, 2018, https://www.kansascity.com/opinion/editorials /article216343365.html.

6. Ed Kilgore, "Local GOP Official Wants to Send Native American House Candidate 'Back to the Reservation,'" Intelligencer, October 9, 2018, nymag.com/intelligencer/2018/10/sharice-davids-is-going-to-win-her -election-racism-aside.html.

7. Jasmine C. Lee and Kevin Queley, "The 598 People, Places and Things Donald Trump Has Insulted on Twitter: A Complete List," *New York Times,* May 24, 2019, www.nytimes.com/interactive/2016/01/28/upshot /donald-trump-twitter-insults.html.

8. Paul Kane et al., "Rep. Debbie Dingell Thanks Colleagues for Support After Trump Suggests John Dingell Is in Hell," *Washington Post,* December 19, 2019, www.washingtonpost.com/nation/2019/12/19 /trump-john-dingell-debbie-dingell-hell-backlash/.

9. Representative Debbie Dingell, "Mr. President, let's set politics aside. My husband earned all his accolades after a lifetime of service. I'm preparing for the first holiday season without the man I love. You brought me down in a way you can never imagine and your hurtful words just made my healing much harder," Twitter, December 18, 2019, twitter.com /RepDebDingell/status/1207494427968716801.

10. Stacey Abrams, "Commentary: My $200,000 Debt Should Not Disqualify Me for Governor of Georgia," *Fortune,* April 24, 2018, fortune.com/2018 /04/24/stacey-abrams-debt-georgia-governor/.

11. "Former Gas Station Worker Hala Ayala Is Working to Turn Virginia Blue," NowThis, October 5, 2019, nowthisnews.com/videos/politics /former-gas-station-worker-hala-ayala-is-working-to-turn-virginia -blue.

12. Robert Speel, "Five Key Debate Moments That Altered the Course of a Presidential Race," Conversation, September 22, 2016, theconversation .com/five-key-debate-moments-that-altered-the-course-of-a-presidential -race-65630.

13. Cyndi Schramm, "'Go Cougars!': Sen. Elizabeth Warren's Witty UH Tweet amid Alleged 'Sex Scandal' with Young Marine," *Houston Chronicle,* October 4, 2019, www.chron.com/news/houston-texas

/houston/article/Go-Cougars-Sen-Elizabeth-Warren-s-witty-UH
-14493513.php.

14. Meghan Demaria, "9 Badass Quotes from Female Politicians, Because
You Can Always Use a Little Inspiration," Bustle, September 2, 2015,
www.bustle.com/articles/108113-9-badass-quotes-from-female
-politicians-because-you-can-always-use-a-little-inspiration.

15. Scott Stump, "Monica Lewinsky Unveils Powerful PSA About a 'Silent
Epidemic,'" *Today,* October 16, 2019, www.today.com/news/monica
-lewinsky-unveils-powerful-cyberbullying-psa-epidemic
-t164664.

16. Katie Hill, "Katie Hill: It's Not Over After All," *New York Times,*
December 8, 2019, 2, www.nytimes.com/2019/12/07/opinion/sunday
/katie-hill-resignation.html.

CHAPTER 8: GET BACK UP. A LOSS IS JUST PART OF YOUR JOURNEY.

1. Veronica Villafane, "It's Election Day for Journalist Wendy Carrillo,"
Media Moves, December 5, 2017, www.mediamoves.com/2017/12
/election-day-journalist-wendy-carrillo.html.

2. Javier Panzar et al., "Labor Activist Wendy Carrillo Will Be L.A.'s
Newest Assembly Member," *Los Angeles Times,* December 6, 2017, www
.latimes.com/politics/la-pol-ca-assembly-district-51-special-election
-20171206-story.html.

3. Steve Karnowski, "Craig Sees Path for Success in 2nd Try Against
Lewis," Associated Press, October 29, 2018, apnews.com/5d813eb9d
9dc4bf380aca9d1ffafb350.

4. "Duckworth Tapped for VA Assistant Secretary," United States
Department of Veterans Affairs, February 3, 2009, web.archive.org/web
/20090408194508/www1.va.gov/opa/pressrel/pressrelease.cfm?id
=1650.

5. Charles Johnson, "Montana Dems Name Nancy Keenan as Party's New
Executive Director," *Independent Record*, April 13, 2015.

6. "About Stacey Abrams," Fair Fight, accessed March 27, 2020, fairfight
.com/about-stacey-abrams/.

7. "About Us," Fair Count, accessed March 27, 2020, www.faircount.org
/about-us/#mission.

8. Alex Abad-Santos, "How Did Beyoncé Get Famous?" *Vox*, May 12, 2015,
www.vox.com/2014/8/28/18010406/beyonce-destinys-child-star
-search.

CHAPTER 9: CAMPAIGN JOYFULLY.
SHOW GRATITUDE DELIBERATELY. CELEBRATE LIBERALLY.

1. Andrew Davey, "Kamala Harris Dances with Enthusiastic Drum Line at First in the West Event," McClatchy DC, November 18, 2019, www.mcclatchydc.com/latest-news/article237477244.html.

2. Dory Jackson, "Kamala Harris Dances to Cardi B While Preparing to Give Her Speech," *Newsweek,* January 23, 2019, www.newsweek.com/kamala-harris-dances-cardi-b-giving-speech-1301795.

3. Jennifer Medina, "The Punch Lines Amy Klobuchar Uses to Keep Voters Laughing," *New York Times,* November 6, 2019, www.nytimes.com/2019/11/06/us/amy-klobuchar-comedy.html.

4. Linh Ta, "At Des Moines Pride, Kirsten Gillibrand Slings Drinks, Dances and Talks LGBTQ Policy," *Des Moines Register,* June 7, 2019, www.desmoinesregister.com/story/news/elections/presidential/caucus/2019/06/07/iowa-caucus-2020-democrat-kirsten-gillibrand-campaign-candidate-des-moines-pride-lgbt-policy-rights/1382209001/.

5. Kirsten Gillibrand (@SenGillibrand), "My team and I saw a sledding hill and made a pit stop on the way to Durham, NH yesterday. Highly recommend!" Twitter, February 3, 2019, 11:40 a.m., twitter.com/sengillibrand/status/1092100621069664261?lang=en.

6. "Politics Is Personal: Keys to Likeability and Electability for Women," Barbara Lee Family Foundation, April 2016, www.barbaraleefoundation.org/wp-content/uploads/BLFF-Likeability-Memo-FINAL.pdf.

7. Annie McKee, "Being Happy at Work Matters," *Harvard Business Review,* November 14, 2014, hbr.org/2014/11/being-happy-at-work-matters.

8. Annie McKee, "Being Happy at Work Matters," *Harvard Business Review,* November 14, 2014, hbr.org/2014/11/being-happy-at-work matters.

9. Allison Gee, "Why Women's World Cup Champion Brandi Chastain Bared Her Bra," BBC, July 13, 2014, www.bbc.com/news/world-us-canada-27189681.

10. Des Bieler, "Did USWNT Players Celebrate Their Goals with Too Much Gusto? World Cup Rout Sparks Debate," *Washington Post,* June 12, 2019, www.washingtonpost.com/sports/2019/06/12/did-uswnt-players-celebrate-their-goals-with-too-much-gusto-world-cup-rout-sparks-debate/.

11. Tasneem Nashrulla, "People Were Pissed at This 'Sexist' Tweet About an Olympic Winner," BuzzFeed News, August 8, 2016, www.buzzfeednews.com/article/tasneemnashrulla/she-has-a-name.

12. Allyson Koerner, "Kumail Nanjiani's Response to Emily V. Gordon Being Reduced to Just His Wife in a Headline Is Perfect," Bustle, January 10, 2018, www.bustle.com/p/kumail-nanjianis-response-to-emily-v -gordon-being-reduced-to-just-his-wife-in-a-headline-is-perfect-7848314.

13. Lindsay Gibbs, "Maine's New Governor Moves to Give Health Care to 70,000 People on Her First Day in Office," ThinkProgress, January 5, 2019, thinkprogress.org/maines-new-governor-moves-to-give -health-care-to-70000-people-on-her-first-day-in-office-814ff0af886d/.

14. Susan Montoya Bryan, "NM Gov. Michelle Lujan Grisham Reflects on First 6 Months," Associated Press, July 10, 2019, www.lcsun-news.com /story/news/local/new-mexico/2019/07/10/new-mexico-governor-reflects -first-6-months/1689122001/.

15. Maureen Groppe and Ledyard King, "Virginia Becomes 38th State to Pass ERA for Women, Likely Setting up Issue for Courts," *USA Today*, January 15, 2020, www.usatoday.com/story/news/politics/2020/01/15 /virginia-passes-era-38th-state-amendment-women/4477813002/.

Index

Index

About the Authors

Raised in the copper-mining town of Butte, Montana, **Stephanie Schriock** has been working to get Democrats elected for twenty-five years. Since Schriock became the president of EMILY's List in 2010, she has overseen a decade of phenomenal growth in the organization, raising hundreds of millions of dollars, helping elect record numbers of women to the House and Senate, and recruiting and training hundreds more. EMILY's List is now nearly five million members strong.

Christina Reynolds grew up in and around Marine bases across the country but considers herself a Tar Heel. She has worked for two decades for Democratic officials, from five presidential campaigns to Democratic campaign committees to the Obama White House. She currently serves as the vice president of communications for EMILY's List.